# Spending Advertising Money in the Digital Age

Hamish Pringle
and Jim Marshall

SPENDING
ADVERTISING
MONEY IN THE
DIGITAL AGE
HOW TO NAVIGATE
THE MEDIA FLOW

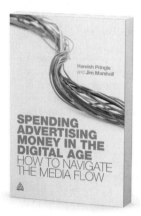

# Spending Advertising Money in the Digital Age

How to navigate
the media flow

Hamish Pringle and
Jim Marshall

**KoganPage**

LONDON  PHILADELPHIA  NEW DELHI

First published in Great Britain and the United States in 2012 by Kogan Page Limited

| | | |
|---|---|---|
| 120 Pentonville Road | 1518 Walnut Street, Suite 1100 | 4737/23 Ansari Road |
| London N1 9JN | Philadelphia PA 19102 | Daryaganj |
| United Kingdom | USA | New Delhi 110002 |
| www.koganpage.com | | India |

© Hamish Pringle and Jim Marshall, 2012

The right of Hamish Pringle and Jim Marshall to be identified as the authors of this work has been asserted by them in accordance with the Copyright, Designs and Patents Act 1988.

ISBN    978 0 7494 6305 2
E-ISBN  978 0 7494 6308 3

**British Library Cataloguing-in-Publication Data**

A CIP record for this book is available from the British Library.

**Library of Congress Cataloging-in-Publication Data**

Pringle, Hamish.
  Spending advertising money in the digital age : how to navigate the media flow / Hamish Pringle, Jim Marshall.
    p. cm.
  Includes bibliographical references and index.
  ISBN 978-0-7494-6305-2 – ISBN 978-0-7494-6308-3   1. Advertising–Management.
2. Marketing–Management.   3. Mass media.   4. Digital media.   I. Marshall, Jim, 1955-
II. Title.
  HF5823.P737 2012
  659.1–dc23
                                                                2011020110

Typeset by Graphicraft Ltd, Hong Kong
Printed and bound in India by Replika Press Pvt Ltd

*To all those who have helped the IPA become*
*what it is today.* **HAMISH PRINGLE**

*To all past media bosses whom I've learnt from, including*
*Mike Townsin and Lionel Becker at Y&R, Adrian Birchall at*
*DMB&B and Media Centre/Mediavest, Mark Cranmer at*
*Starcom, Nigel Sharrocks at Aegis and Ray Kelly who Chaired*
*the IPA Media Policy Group. And of course my late Father.*
**JIM MARSHALL**

*'Life flows on within you and without you.'*
**GEORGE HARRISON**

*'There are three types of media person, those that*
*can count and those that can't.'* **ANON**

# CONTENTS

# FOREWORD

In January 1968 I embarked on my career in advertising as a media assistant at a full service advertising agency where media was a department. No one outside of agencies and ad sales personnel knew what 'media' was. Most major client presentations ended with the words 'and the media schedule is in the document'. A fair reflection of the importance then given to the media plan and execution!

This void created an opportunity for a few agency media people to begin to differentiate their media planning and buying. Concurrent with this came the growth of media research and in 1970 the first media textbook, *Spending Advertising Money* by Simon Broadbent.

By the early 1980s increasing sophistication in strategy development, the growing supply of audience and media outlets, and more effective buying led to those early pioneers creating stand-alone media agencies. This was followed in the 1990s by the unbundling of the media function from creative and account management into the large-scale media agencies of today's scene. It led to a restructuring of the industry and Zenith was in the vanguard of this movement.

This focus on media led to ever-improving performance and the realization that the media strategy was as important as the creative product. More and more advertisers wanted to know how to reach their consumers and follow them through an ever-increasing availability of media and formats.

No one has attempted the task of giving us a new textbook for media in the digital age until now. In this book the authors illustrate eloquently how today's consumers are touched by a constant media flow where they hardly ever disengage from media exposure during their waking hours.

The importance of engaging the target audience and staying with them through the media flow is more important than ever in determining a brand's success or failure.

At heart the media task remains the same – how to set the budget, how to determine the optimum media mix and how to measure effectiveness. It is just a far more difficult task today, and an even more important one, which is why this book, dealing with these issues in the digital age, is long overdue and very welcome.

*John Perriss, CEO Zenith Media 1988–2001*
*and CEO ZenithOptimedia 2001–2004*

# PREFACE

We've titled this book in homage to the celebrated *Spending Advertising Money* by Simon Broadbent – first published in 1970 and updated with co-author Brian Jacobs in 1984. A company's spend on media advertising and marketing communications is one of the largest investments it makes and their work was widely regarded as the best guide to making it wisely. However, things have moved on a great deal since the 1980s, and it seemed timely to attempt a new book which would address both the offline and online media in this new digital era.

The reason that companies keep spending advertising money – some £18 billion annually on media in the UK alone – is that they know the brands they own are amongst their most valuable assets, and brands, like planes, need fuel to keep flying – disinvest and they glide, stall and then crash. These brands require continuing investment in media in order to retain and indeed increase their value in the face of relentless market competition.

Put simply, this book's goal is to help ensure that the spending of these huge sums is carried out using the most effective approach to media planning, and thus lead to more profitable brand-building. We believe that making these investments in media is very far from being the commodity activity that the less well-informed marketing and procurement people often seem to think it is. Obtain best prices by all means, but not at the expense of sophisticated multi-media planning which puts the brand in front of the right person in the right media environment at the right time.

In the opening paragraph of his 1964 book *Understanding Media: The Extensions of Man*, Herbert Marshall McLuhan wrote the following:

> In a culture like ours, long accustomed to splitting and dividing all things as a means of control, it is sometimes a bit of a shock to be reminded that, in operational and practical fact, the medium is the message. This is merely to say that the personal and social consequences of any medium – that is, of any extension of ourselves – result from the new scale that is introduced into our affairs by each extension of ourselves, or by any new technology.

Nearly 50 years later, McLuhan's aphorism 'the medium is the message' has become famous, but we can see also that his notion of media as 'The Extensions of Man' contained a similarly profound and prescient idea. As he suggested, the relationship between human beings and the media they have created has become increasingly intertwined – man is truly a media mammal (or indeed amphibian) stepping in and out of the fast-moving media flow at will.

The landscape has become very complex, comprising not only 'bought' and 'owned', but nowadays increasingly 'earned' media too. Manoeuvring a brand in this media flow requires skilled navigators and we believe that IPA agencies are best placed to carry out this work for clients, delivering very significant added value in the process.

*Hamish Pringle and Jim Marshall*

# ABOUT THE AUTHORS

## Hamish Pringle

 Hamish began his advertising agency career in 1973, having graduated from Trinity College Oxford with a degree in PPE. During a 26-year period he worked on over 50 brands for 30 client companies at 10 agencies: Ogilvy, Benson & Mather, McCormick Richards, Boase Massimi Pollitt, McCormick Intermarco-Farner, Abbott Mead Vickers, Madell Wilmot Pringle, Leagas Delaney, CME.KHBB, K Advertising and Saatchi & Saatchi.

Prior to joining the IPA in 2001 he ran his own consultancy, Brand Beliefs, specializing in brand strategy and cause-related marketing. After that, he was Director General of the IPA, a position he held for 10 years until July 2011.

Hamish has co-authored *Brand Spirit* with Marjorie Thompson, *Brand Manners* with William Gordon and *Brand Immortality* with Peter Field, and written *Celebrity Sells*.

He is also the inventor of the 'Diagonal Thinking' concept, a Fellow of the IPA, a Fellow of the Marketing Society and a member of the Marketing Group of Great Britain.

## Jim Marshall

Jim has worked in media for over 35 years. He started as a tea boy in the media department of Young and Rubicam and rose at a leisurely pace to deputy Media Director and full Board Director. He joined Reeves Robertshaw as Media Director in the mid-1980s before moving on to DMB&B, also as Media Director. At DMB&B, he launched the Media Centre with Adrian Birchall and over subsequent years the organization became Mediavest and eventually Starcom Mediavest. Most recently he has joined Aegis as Chief Client Services Officer.

Jim has had many years' involvement with the IPA and its various committees. He is a member of the IPA Council and spent seven years as Chairman of the IPA Media Futures Group. Outside of work Jim likes sport (particularly football, golf and motorcycling), music (mainly jazz and blues) and does a bit of painting.

# ABOUT THE IPA

The Institute of Practitioners in Advertising (IPA) is the trade body and professional institute for leading UK advertising, media and marketing communications agencies. It was established in 1917 as a servicing body and to negotiate on behalf of its members with client companies, media owners, government departments and unions. The IPA's head office is situated between the Malaysian and Turkish embassies at 44 Belgrave Square in London. Its 250 corporate members handle over 80 per cent of the UK's media advertising, which has an estimated value (excluding press and TV production) of about £18 billion. Amongst many other activities, it is the organizer of the IPA Effectiveness Awards, which are regarded as the pre-eminent competition of its type, and IPA TouchPoints, the world's first consumer-centric media habits research survey.

# ACKNOWLEDGEMENTS

First of all a special thank you to the contributors to the chapters on each individual medium: Tess Alps at Thinkbox, Andrew Harrison and Mark Barber at the RadioCentre, Martin Bowley and Fleur Castell at Digital Cinema Media, Karen Earl at Synergy, Claire Myerscough at News International, Robert Ray at the Newspaper Society, Barry McIlheney at the PPA, Glen Wilson at Posterscope, Amy Kean at the IAB, Martin Kingdon at POPAI, Chris Satterthwaite at Chime Communications, David Payne at the IPA, and of course the author of our Foreword, John Perriss, previously of ZenithOptimedia. We'd also like to thank those who helped these contributors: Lindsey Clay, Thinkbox; Marius Cloete, PPA; Kate Cochrane, Posterscope; Phil Day, POPAI; and Simon Tunstill, Thinkbox.

Secondly, we must acknowledge the many individuals and companies that have contributed generously to our research and the provision of images. There are too many to name them all, but in particular we would like to thank: Louise Ainsworth at Nielsen Online, Mark Howe and Dominic Allon at Google, Mike Baker and Bill Wilson at Outdoor Media Centre, Jennie Beck at Kantar Media/TNS, Guy Black at *The Telegraph*, Louise Brice and Liz Landy at IPSOS, Neel Desor at Haymarket Network, Sue Elms at Millward Brown, Kate Evans at Boomerang Media, Jane Farmery and Jhan Rushton at Hachette Filipacchi UK Ltd, Wendy Gordon at Acacia Avenue, Tim Jones at BBH, Anne Marie Kelly at GfK MRI, Ian Locks at Events Partnership, Professor Peter McOwan at the University of London, Ken New, John O'Donnell and Gideon Spanier at *The Evening Standard*, Dan Photi at Boomerang Media, Simon Redican and Linda Smith at RAB, Sarah Sanderson at Kantar Media, Nick Smith and Adam Swann at Accenture, Anastasia Takis at Digital Cinema Media, Jamie Toward at Redwood Group, Richard Townsend at Circus Street and Brendan Tansey at Wunderman. We're also grateful to Simon Marquis and his agency interviewees who provided valuable background information on key IPA Effectiveness Awards cases: Luke Bozeat at Mediacom, Mike Follett at DDB, Rachel Hatton at BBH, Adrian Hoole at Proximity, Tony Harris at RKCR/Y&R, Nick Walker at Walker Media, Annabelle Watson at AMV BBDO and Faris Yakob at MDC Partners.

We would like to recognize and thank the authors of the IPA Advanced Certificate: Gavin Ailes at The Search Works, Howard Bareham at Mindshare, Kate Cox at MPG Media Contacts, Tom George at Mediaedge:CIA, Andy Jones at Universal, David Peters at Carat, Pete Robins at agenda21, Daren Rubins at PHD, Andy Sloan at ARM, Philip Walker and Steve Williams at OMD.

Our colleagues at the IPA have been most helpful, especially Lynne Robinson and Geoffrey Russell who read and commented on the manuscript, Belinda Beeftink, Flora Malein and Rebecca Watson who provided the TouchPoints charts and insights into the research, and Pamela Perl who has supported the project throughout. Two key consultants to the IPA, Peter Field and Roger Ingham, have provided valuable analysis and guidance relating to the IPA Effectiveness Awards cases. And of course this book would not have been as interesting visually without the tenacity of our picture researcher Louise Dinesen who secured so many images, and Alice Melin who completed the task. Nor would the book have been delivered without the diligence of our manuscript researchers: Caroline Roberts and then Victoria Murray who laid the foundations, followed by Michael Harris, and finally Emma Gibbons who has done an excellent job in bringing this complex project to completion and provided many helpful and intelligent contributions to the text on the way.

Lastly we would like to thank Jon Finch, Sarah Cooke, Shereen Muhyeddeen and the rest of the team at Kogan Page for their patience and encouragement during the long gestation period, for their professionalism in producing the finished article, and for their energy in promoting it.

*Hamish Pringle and Jim Marshall*

# Introduction

At the core of this book is the thesis that people and brands now live lives which are intertwined with the 'media flow'. To explain this idea, picture a dry landscape in the 19th century with infrequent watering holes where people could drink. Then imagine it evolving during the 20th century to become a wetter world with many more lakes and reservoirs where it was possible to take a drink a bit more easily. And now in the 21st century we are living life alongside and increasingly within a media flow with which we can quench our thirst with ease. Media have become all pervasive: Accenture Media Management estimate that the average UK individual's exposure to ads is 1,009 daily (see Appendix). In this world the task of planners is to create a matrix of media channels which puts their brand into the flow in such a way that it has the best possible chance of engaging customers.

**FIGURE 0.1** The evolution of the media flow

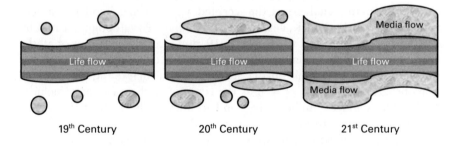

| 19th Century | 20th Century | 21st Century |

The power of the new digital technologies that have created the media flow which now envelopes the life flow is prodigious. For example, whole nations have skipped fixed line telephony and leapt straight to mobile communications. This new environment provides customers and citizens with huge benefits in terms of news, information, entertainment and of course commercial communications, which introduce new products and services and help people make purchasing decisions. The media flow enables multiple 'touch points' at which customers can make contact with brands, and vice versa.

People, too, are in a more or less continuous state of flux within their life flow and they move from non-buying to purchasing mode and back again very frequently. Indeed, leading consultancy dunnhumby, who work for major blue chip clients including Tesco, Macy's, P&G and Kroger, estimate that the average household makes about 150 purchases a week, with the main grocery shopper buying an average of 16 items daily! People are far more mobile now and will travel further and more often, whether for work, socializing or entertainment, using media tools to make the arrangements and sat-navs to get them there. The life flow is becoming inextricably linked to the media flow. For centuries media have touched people's lives but only at certain times; however, nowadays their ubiquity, accessibility and utility have made them an integral part of people's existence. Human beings can now step in and out of the media flow effortlessly and at remarkably low cost. And this media flow is 'on all the time', presenting advertisers and commercial communications with huge challenges and opportunities.

There are seismic changes occurring in the world of media. 'Old' analogue media are being challenged by new digital media, and in the United States there are even worries about the survival of such venerable publications as *The New York Times*, as other leading cities lose their once-powerful print titles. Yet despite so many pundits declaring its death, TV viewing is on the rise in the majority of markets, including the UK and the United States, both in its traditional form and also via new platforms for audio-visual content such as mobiles, PDAs, laptops, games consoles, digital posters and in-car navigators. Hardly a day goes by without news of some innovation – last year everybody was talking about Facebook, then about Twitter too, and now the buzz is around location-based and group-purchasing platforms such as foursquare and Groupon. These new communications channels are having fundamental effects on the way consumers are using and producing media – over half the UK population is now on Facebook – and these behaviour changes are in turn challenging the accepted ways of using media investment to build brands. In the UK, customers of Domino's Pizza bought £1 million worth of pizza in the last quarter of 2010, and already 4 per cent of all the brand's online sales are via the iPhone app launched in October 2009. These sales are driven by a multi-media advertising and marketing communications programme which, as well as the traditional channels, now includes 109,000 fans and 1.5 million 'likes' on Facebook with 21,000 followers on Twitter who benefit from online-only special offers.

Historically, media owners were large corporations with specialist skills, particularly in the production of content. Now brand owners and individuals (in their millions) are becoming media owners in their own right and self-publishing through websites, blogs, and e-newsletters. Additionally, social networking has created a whole new communication infrastructure, giving customers access to a vast range of information and views from other like-minded consumers and adding e-power to word-of-mouth. This is presenting marketers and their agencies with a bewildering array of new opportunities: media are now not only 'bought' and 'owned', they can be 'earned' too. This means that the new art and science of media planning is all about the interweaving of these three media strands within the intermingled life and media flows that customers swim in today.

In the pre-digital era the media planner's skill was all about using a limited number of media to try to intercept customers at various points along their journey from not buying anything particular to purchasing something specific. This process was conceived as a 'purchase funnel' with the different categories of media coming into play at different points along it. Typically, display advertising is deployed when customers are not necessarily in the market, and uses its share of voice to make the brand's presence felt. It can also use creativity of content to reward the reader, listener or viewer for their attention to a message which they're not necessarily in the mood to receive. In a sense, display advertising sugars the pill of commercial information. Then, as the customer begins to research a purchase, information-laden media come into their own, and this includes classified, directory or search advertising which people seek out when they know they need or desire something and want to find out more about it. So the media stretch from the big thematic picture of a TV commercial, all the way down to the small print of the product packaging, with many points in between.

But in the old world the cost of media was relatively high and brands could not afford to be present all the time. This limitation gave rise to copious volumes of analysis and theorizing as to how best to square a brand's circle of need – ideally, a brand would be with actual or potential customers all the time, and present at all points in the purchase funnel, but could never have the funds required to achieve this ideal. However, the new world of the digital media flow is changing all this. Already, individuals can be targeted with 'addressable media', which uses interest-based advertising that relates closely to their needs or desires as indicated by their online behaviour. So a person looking at a review of a new camera can be presented with a display advertisement of the very same model, and that ad can switch immediately into an information-laden one at the click of a mouse. Technology is allowing the brand to be in the same media flow as its potential customers at an increasingly affordable cost, with ever-greater accountability, and thus cost efficiency.

Given the range of media channels and platforms now available, consumers' expertise in accessing and using them from a very young age, and the sheer influence of media in people's lives, the skill of media strategists has never been more important to marketers and their brands. While statistics are at the heart of media planning, there's a soul, too – the unerring ability for the truly great strategists to appreciate the very best place, of the myriad available, to put a particular message for a specific person. When this juxtaposition is done well it adds enormous value to the negotiated price of any media buy.

**FIGURE 0.2**    Great planners know instinctively when the medium is right

Reproduced by permission of Diageo

So this book is designed to help brand owners and their agencies understand and then navigate the media flow, and enable them to spend their advertising money more effectively in the digital age. In so doing we have the great benefit of full access to the IPA TouchPoints research, which provides unrivalled insights into individuals' media habits as they move through their day. We can now see how their activities relate to their media habits as they go about living their lives and planners can understand the times and places at which brands can use media best to establish mutual contact with their customers.

We also have the world-leading resource of the IPA Effectiveness Awards Databank to mine for insights into how media have been used to proven effect in building brands and generating a significant return on marketing investment. Special analyses of the data also enable us for the first time to offer a much more scientific approach to setting the media budget for a brand. We can also give concrete reassurance that the combination of outstanding content and best-in-class channel planning can produce astonishing increases in the return on marketing investment.

Indeed, much of the more recent understanding of how advertising works makes complete sense in the context of the fast-moving, interactive media flow. Is it surprising that emotional communication is more effective than the purely rational when it's so much quicker to feel than deliberate? Is it any wonder that multi-media are more effective than just one when people have need of so many different sorts of touch points with brands? Isn't it obvious that sheer share of voice is such an important factor when our brand is but one amongst many trying to catch the customer in the flow? And isn't it self-evident that the sheer likeability and talkability of a brand's communication would be a key factor in attracting attention, achieving engagement and providing social currency?

In the media flow the boundaries between the various media channels are becoming ever more blurred – if you are watching a short film commercial projected onto the wall of a station, are you a user of the outdoor, cinema, TV or digital medium? The retort is, of course, 'who cares?' as long as the advertising is effective. Even so, it is still very important to understand and appreciate how the individual media operate in order to produce the best mix that will create the optimum communications flow for a brand. Thus, we have invited contributions from leading practitioners as to the merits of the medium they're expert in. These 'elevator pitches' are designed to summarize the characteristics and benefits of each of the main media and help enable practitioners to come to their own view as to how each one might fit into their brand's media mix.

We have also developed a new model or framework for media planning: F.A.I.P.A. This stands for 'Fame', 'Advocacy', 'Information', 'Price' and 'Availability', and we believe these are the five key roles that the ideal media mix should play for a brand.

Overall, we hope this book will be useful to those who either work, or want to work in media, whether within a client company or a specialist agency, but it may also appeal to people who have a general interest in advertising and marketing communications. And, of course, to anyone who lives their life increasingly immersed in the media flow.

# PART ONE
# Media fundamentals

# Introduction

Henry Ford, in an interview in the *Chicago Tribune*, May 25, 1916 said:

> I don't know much about history, and I wouldn't give a nickel for all the history in the world. It means nothing to me. History is more or less bunk. It's tradition. We don't want tradition. We want to live in the present and the only history that is worth a tinker's damn is the history we make today.

Despite his undoubted success we beg to differ! Even though we're putting a strong emphasis on the impact of new digital media we think it's very important to be able to set these new phenomena and the agency structures set up to deal with them in an historical context. This is not a matter of harking back to some 'golden age' of advertising but much more to do with understanding how we got where we are today, and therefore how the industry may develop in future.

So this first section of the book looks briefly at the origins of the first advertising agencies (and there's a lesson to be learned here about intellectual property rights), and at how the modern media planning and buying agency has evolved. Having painted a picture of the agency side of life we then look at the media world from the customer's point of view. Taken together, these two chapters provide the media fundamentals and the context for the subsequent sections.

# The evolution of the media agency

## Introduction

The UK media industry has gone through two major waves of evolution and is in the process of going through a third. The first of these was the era of the dominance of newspapers as a medium, the second wave was typified by the supremacy of television, and now we're in the midst of a third wave where digital media are holding sway. Unsurprisingly, agencies have evolved in the context of these structural developments in the media industry and it's useful to understand this evolution as one of the fundamentals of the business.

With hindsight we can see that the full-service agency, which both bought the space and created the content, was absolutely fit for purpose when the turnaround time was dictated by the short copy dates of newspapers. Separating the media planning and buying from the creation and production of advertisements would simply have been impractical. However, the television medium was not only one that was booked much further in advance; the production processes in producing a commercial were considerably more expensive and time-consuming than a typical press advertisement. This fundamental extension of the timescale made it possible for different agencies to be responsible for media and creative. Now, in the digital third wave, we find ourselves to a degree back where we started. The close integration between content and channel, and the potential for real-time amendments to copy, have led to digital full-service agencies which have reintegrated media planning and buying and content creation. However, the situation is complicated by the fact that 'traditional' media, with longer gestation periods in media and production terms, have continued dominance financially. This means that the separation of media planning and buying and creative agencies is still very much a reality for the lion's share of the business.

It's worth going into more detail about these three waves of agency evolution and thus this chapter is divided into three parts: 'From Fleet Street to the separation', 'From the separation to today' and 'Into the digital age'.

# From Fleet Street to the separation

Unlike the 'chicken or egg' conundrum, the answer to 'What came first, the media or the advertising?' is clear cut: the first advertising agencies grew out of the newspaper owners' need for organizations that could sell their space to clients. It was only later that agencies started to create the advertisements to fill it. The first agencies were created by the media, and thus were the first and main driving force in the development of modern-day advertising. Advertising agents originated in London in the Fleet Street area to the east of the law courts, which was the home of the newspaper publishing industry. According to the History of Advertising Trust, R F White is the oldest UK agency, founded around 1800 by James 'Jem' White.

**FIGURE 1.1**    Fleet Street, London

Reproduced by permission of Diane Elson – www.dianeelson.com

These publishers got their revenues from the cover price of their newspapers and from the sale of advertising space. They exploited the long-established trade-off in which readers got cheap or even free newspapers in exchange for exposure to advertising. As Winston Fletcher points out in *Powers of Persuasion*, this relationship is as old as the hills:

> Advertising is popularly believed to be a modern – or at least a twentieth-century – phenomenon. Not so. [...] Athenians can probably lay claim to the invention of modern commercial advertising as we know it. In Athens there were town criers, chosen for their mellifluous voices and clear diction, who interrupted their proclamations with paid-for advertisements just as advertisements interrupt television newscasts today.

Publishers could either sell their space direct to customers using their own salespeople, or they could appoint agents to do so, paying them a commission for their trouble. Over time, in a Darwinian manner, the level of commission that the newspaper proprietors paid to these independent sales agents settled down at 15 per cent. It's interesting to note that, over two centuries later, Kingston Smith W1, the leading UK accountancy firm specializing in the agency sector, argues that at least 15 per cent is the profit margin required for a sustainable and successful business. Maybe it's just a fact of the agency business?

In another evolutionary process, these third-party space sales agents found themselves being asked by their buyers for advice as to how best to use the space to advertise their products and services. Thus, these advertising agents started to come up with sales strategies and creative ideas to execute them, and then to write the copy, provide the illustrations, and produce the artwork and plates for the advertisements that presented these ideas in newspapers and magazines. The strategic and creative ideas were provided free of charge and all the client had to do was to pay for the media space and the cost of production. Production charging reflected the convention that had already been established in terms of 15 per cent commission on media sales, so that the cost of production was marked up by 17.65 per cent to produce a gross sum equating to the net cost plus 15 per cent agency commission.

Thus originated one of the fundamental dynamics of the advertising business with which the industry continues to grapple. From the early days of Fleet Street, advertising agents gave away their advertising strategies and ideas (intellectual property) for free in return for earning commission on media sales and the production of advertisements. The great benefit for the client was that strategic planning and creative services were provided to them free of charge in exchange for buying media space which they were going to do anyway, and it was the media owner, the newspaper proprietor in those days, who actually paid the advertising agents.

Those advertising agents who were more successful at producing the intellectual property (IP) which increased the sales of the client's product found themselves able to buy more advertising space for their clients, and also to make more money on production. The media owners also benefited from the increase in agency expertise because it demonstrated the effectiveness of their publications as advertising media. Those agents who created very successful and long-running campaigns earned commission with relatively low additional investment in developing IP – so, a win for them. Meanwhile, the client's brand was built by a distinctive and consistent stream of individual but thematically linked, and thus incremental, executions, which embedded the core campaign theme in the public's mind – a big win for the client.

This business model enabled certain agencies to become really very large indeed, with the peak in London being achieved in the 1960s and 70s. The number-one agency at that time was J. Walter Thompson, which employed some 1,300 people in and around its offices at number 40 Berkeley Square, and its full-service facilities included two fully equipped kitchens employed solely for the purpose of developing new recipes for their food clients!

**FIGURE 1.2**   JWT's former home at 40 Berkeley Square, London

Reproduced by permission of JWT and HAT

The engine room of the agency was still the media planning and buying department, but the agency leadership in those days came from account management, and the newly emerging discipline of account planning, working with the jewels in the crown, the creative department. As mass-appeal advertising became ever more prevalent, particularly during the growth of commercial television in the 1960s and 70s, the focus was increasingly on the clever, funny and beautifully crafted 'ads' that generated incremental business – the message rather than the medium. This golden creative era produced iconic UK campaigns such as the Smash Martians, Hamlet and Bach's *Air on a G string*, and Cadbury's Fruit and Nut to name but a few. However, the really smart agencies recognized that having a strong media department was as important (or very nearly as important) as having top-class creative teams. This was all about getting the best possible media exposure for the creative executions, as top agency Collett Dickenson Pearce showed with its use of posters to showcase outstanding campaigns for brands such as Heineken, Benson & Hedges, Wall's and Fiat.

Nevertheless, the media function was not generally held in particularly high regard and media folk were seen as rather 'second-class citizens', though of course the industry was too polite to say it quite as overtly as that! Many 'suits' in account management saw it as something of a commodity activity typified by the media section always coming last in new business presentations to clients, and often given only five minutes of an available hour, or dropped altogether. 'Media on last – it's time to go' became an increasingly irritating joke for media people. There were also class divisions within the full-service agency. Typically, account management, planners and many of the creatives would have middle- or even upper-class backgrounds with public school and Oxbridge educations predominating, whereas the employees of the media department would be more typified by people educated in the state sector and quite often without university degrees. Jerry Hill, then chief executive of Initiative Media and now chief executive officer of RAJAR, encapsulated this with the wry observation that the basic division between creative and media agencies was between 'Oxbridge and Uxbridge' – the former being the dreaming spires of academia and the latter an undistinguished London suburb.

Tim Wootton tells an amusing story which illustrates perfectly the class divide that existed between media and creative departments in full-service agencies. Early in the 1970s, Tim was just 21 and working at Anglia TV as an executive selling television advertising airtime, when a family friend who worked at leading agency Masius Wynne-Williams suggested he apply for the post of account executive, and through this contact an interview was duly arranged. The personnel director interviewed Tim in his office with its antique furniture, wood-panelling, thick pile carpet, and windows overlooking St James's Square, which was also home to the East India Club and Chatham House. These grand offices had given rise to Masius' nickname as the 'Grocers of St James's' owing to the large number of big packaged-goods clients which their charismatic founder, Jack Wynne-Williams, had attracted to the agency, including the famous Babycham account. His interviewer, an ex-Army officer, soon established which public (fee-paying in the UK) school Tim had attended, and which house he'd been in. It wasn't long before the personnel director concluded the interview, saying that Tim was the right sort of chap for the agency and suggesting that he start by working on Allied Breweries, one of their largest clients. Then, just as Tim was leaving, and as an afterthought, the personnel director said he'd forgotten to ask whether it had been Oxford or Cambridge he'd attended. When Tim replied that he hadn't been to university and left school to go straight to work, his interviewer exclaimed, 'I think there's been some kind of mistake – we can't have you here, but you could apply for a job in our media department.' He then directed Tim to a separate department of the agency located in Margram House, a much less attractive modern building on the other side of St James' Square, and much better suited to non-Oxbridge types! An ironic postscript to this story is that the agency's media director, Bert de Voss, was later promoted to the chairmanship of the agency and also elected President of the

IPA. Meanwhile this start didn't do Tim any harm and he is currently chairman of Bristol agency 3Sixty following a distinguished career in commercial broadcasting, including being a founder and chief executive of TSMS Ltd, a director of United Broadcasting, chairman of design agency Lambie-Nairn and non-executive chairman of Zenith Media Europe and Zenith Media UK.

While relationships between the media department and the others were cordial enough, and there was a degree of mixing both in the corridors of the agency and in the pub, there was nevertheless an underlying resentment from most leaders of media departments who were fed up with being treated as second-class citizens à la Tim Wootton. They appreciated the commercial reality of life, which was that the financial power in the full-service agency lay in its media function and its continuing ability to earn 15 per cent commission from media owners. In their view this reality should have resulted in far greater respect for their expertise, higher status within the agency, and of course better personal remuneration.

At this time agencies benefited from a closed shop, in that it was crucial for an agency to have 'recognition' from the media owner trade associations in order to be able to buy space or time, and thus earn 15 per cent commission. In order to be 'recognized', an agency needed to be a member of the IPA (Institute of Practitioners in Advertising), and in order to do that it needed to pass stringent financial criteria and also to sign up to the rules. These included the requirement that a full agency service must be provided where creative and media were under one roof. Agencies were not allowed to rebate the commissions that they had earned from the media owners to their clients and, further, the IPA forbade its member agencies from soliciting each other's clients. However, in the late 1970s the Office of Fair Trading (OFT) investigated the agency recognition system and found that it represented an anti-competitive way of doing business. The results of the OFT investigation were very far-reaching in that they set in train the unbundling of the full-service agency, with many of the departments breaking away to create stand-alone niche businesses. These included artwork studios, TV production companies, market research companies, direct marketing agencies, creative hot shops, new product development specialists, PR companies and design consultancies.

Apart from the changes in the recognition rulings, there was another factor that was fundamental to the creation of the separate media agency sector. Just as newspaper advertising had been the stimulus for advertising agencies, television proved the stimulus for separate media specialist companies. Commercial television launched in 1955, when ITV first went on air. Like the BBC, it was designed to provide public service broadcasting (PSB), including news, information and entertainment programmes. However, unlike the BBC, it was structured on a regional basis, comprising regional franchises across the UK, with the largest being London and the smallest the Channel Islands. Also, unlike the BBC, the entire network was funded by paid-for advertising that appeared in commercial breaks between and during programmes. The launch of commercial television revolutionized the advertising industry. To quote Winston Fletcher again from *The Powers of Persuasion*:

> Within the advertising industry, commercial television changed the relationship with the public, and of the public with advertisers. Its use of sound and motion (and later colour) transformed the nature of advertising creativity and of agency creative departments. This fundamentally altered the power structure in advertising agencies.

By the early 1970s the best creative people wanted to work mainly on TV, where campaigns would not only make their clients famous (eg 'Beanz Meanz Heinz', 'For Mash get Smash', Leonard Rossiter and Joan Collins in Cinzano) but as importantly would also make the creatives famous, with the doorway to Hollywood opening for several of the most talented.

**FIGURE 1.3**   Heinz® Baked Beans

Reproduced by permission of H. J. Heinz Company Limited

At the same time, in agency media departments, TV experts were not only charged with handling campaigns that amounted to millions of pounds per year, but also could demonstrate that their expertise and negotiating prowess could deliver much better schedules and more cost-effective campaigns – sometimes up to 30 per cent or more cheaper. New media 'superstars' were being established: TV buyers who understood the complexities of the audience research system and were able to identify the best programmes for different types of advertiser, and then get those slots at the cheapest rates. And crucially, the TV buy was concluded much further in advance of the copy date than was the case with print media, thus facilitating the separation of the agency responsibility for media from content.

Significantly, after staff, the cost of raw materials and capital expenditure, the media budget was fast becoming many client companies' next biggest item of expenditure. Because media rates, and TV rates especially, were highly negotiable, the combination of clever planning, tough negotiation and astute buying could generate very significant discounts and savings for the client. This in turn increased the volume of the advertising and the potential success of the campaign. In contrast, weak media planning and buying meant that the prices would go the other way, ie up! The difference could be as much as 20 per cent or more either way (20 per cent better than the average or 20 per cent worse) which, as any media person will tell you, is a 50 per cent differential in the cost of the campaign – a huge spread for a client spending millions of pounds on media budgets.

During the 1970s clients also began to recognize the benefits of better-performing TV buying agencies, and both General Foods and Reckitt and Colman placed all their TV negotiations and buying with single agencies Benton and Bowles and Collett Dickenson Pearce respectively, thereby 'centralizing' their TV buying and, more significantly, separating it from the creative agency. Meanwhile, as a result of the OFT ruling, the media owner trade associations accepted that they were no longer allowed to refuse to sell media space and grant media commissions to companies who were not members of the IPA and had no right to disallow the rebating of some or indeed all of the commission to agency clients, irrespective of the amount of fees charged. Nor could they insist on full-service agencies being the only 'recognized' ones since the new criteria needed to be linked to credit worthiness rather than service capability across creative and media. The fledgling media independent sector used these rulings to expand their businesses, arguing that greater resource needed to be given to the media function than the full-service agency management would allow.

The first UK media independent was Paul Green's Media Buying Services (now Initiative), named for its hard-nosed business proposition and focus on negotiating and buying. Other pioneers included David Reich and TMD (now Carat), Chris Ingram and CIA (now Mediaedge:cia), and Alan Rich and The Media Business (now MediaCom). These new agencies competed very aggressively on price and the percentage of the media owner commissions rebated to clients grew progressively larger, with the TV accounts being handled for around 3.5 to 5 per cent in the early 1980s or, in the case of very large accounts, a commission as low as 2.5 per cent. The new wave of independent media agencies were unable to get IPA accreditation since the trade association's rules still restricted membership to full-service agencies, and so they created their own governing body, the Association of Media Independents (AMI) under the chairmanship of John Ayling, to champion the new agency sector.

Bowing to both legislative changes and market developments, and after much soul-searching, the IPA changed its membership criteria in 1987. Instead of an agency having to 'create and buy advertising', the rules were changed to 'create and/or buy'. This enabled the new 'creative only' agencies to join the IPA, and indeed Winston Fletcher, who had been forced to resign from the IPA Council when he started his agency Fletcher Shelton Delaney because it didn't buy media, subsequently rejoined and became President in

**FIGURE 1.4**   Photograph of the Association of Media Independents (AMI), April 1983

Front row (L to R): Mike Yershon, John Billett, David Reich, John Ayling, Martin Lester, Tony Rowse

Back row (L to R): Michael Manton (chairman), Paul Green, Don Beckett, Ian Payne (representing Chris Ingram)

Reproduced by permission of *Marketing Week*

1989. However, the process of re-assimilating the media independents into the IPA was a much slower one, and it wasn't until 2000 that the last of the AMI founder agencies, John Ayling & Associates, joined the IPA following an active recruitment campaign, which included an olive branch (and IPA terms on BARB data) offered over lunch at Le Gavroche!

Though agencies were winning their fair share of media-only business versus the new breed of media agencies, towards the end of the 1980s it became clear that both clients and media agency staff were recognizing the increasing appeal of the independents. And of course the entrepreneurial media practitioners seized the chance to set up their own specialist media agencies. Their entire focus was on media, while it was widely perceived that 'traditional' agencies would always give precedence to creative (in terms of output) and account management (in terms of career development). It also began to be recognized that media could be a profitable business in its own right for advertising agencies, particularly for the bigger agency groups who were already handling sizeable media billings across their various agencies. Official sanction was bestowed on this trend when, in the early 1980s, all government TV advertising through the Central Office of Information (COI) was centralized into a single agency, Young & Rubicam.

In the following years many other significant advertisers followed this example and soon the separation of creative and media started to be applied not just to their TV activity but to their other media as well. This was crystallized by a single event that resulted in a fundamental change to the entire structure of the agency sector in the UK and subsequently in the United States and the rest of the world. In 1988, partly to leverage its overall billings and partly to counter the growing threat of the new buying shops, Saatchi & Saatchi PLC bought Ray Morgan & Partners, a media independent. They then merged it with the existing media departments within their group agencies, Saatchi & Saatchi, BSB Dorland and KHBB, to form Zenith Buying under the leadership of John Perriss. This had a dramatic impact on the UK advertising market and triggered a wholesale restructuring whereby all the big full-service agencies spawned either 'media dependents' – separate media planning and buying agencies, but dedicated to serving the 'creative' agency's clients – or 'media independents', which were open to clients beyond the original agency parent's. When Zenith first launched it was a buying-only operation and the media planning remained in the creative agencies; however, DMB&B's media dependent, The Media Centre, launched in 1992, providing a full media planning and buying service and bucking this trend. Other 'dependents' quickly followed this example and the entire market moved to providing a full set of media services, from strategic planning through to negotiations and buying. The UK model was exported to the United States in February 1995 when Zenith USA began operating under general manager Steve King. Since then, the split between media and creative agencies has become near-universal, only challenged by the advent of a few full-service digital agencies.

As a result of these seismic and often very painful changes there have been some good and not so good results. On the one hand, there is no doubt that the client cost of buying media has fallen significantly as a result of the establishment of separate media planning and buying agencies. By the same token it is also certain that the split resulted in vastly improved thinking about media and much more effective deployment of the considerable sums invested in building brands. On the other hand, the dismembering of the rump of the full-service agency into multiple creative content-providing niches has made the task of developing and delivering integrated advertising and marketing communications much more difficult and expensive. It's also questionable whether the total overall agency remuneration cost has been reduced, given the large number of agencies now employed by the average brand manager...

## From the separation to today

In the period since the separation the industry has faced an increasingly complex and ever-expanding media environment, delivering an almost endless number of opportunities to place advertising messages, but also making the media planning process far more important. To deal with it we now had a separate sector comprising media agencies which met the need for specialist companies to help advise and navigate clients through the complexities of a media flow that is both fragmenting and converging at the same time, and to negotiate the best rates with the media owners. Indeed, the emergence and growth of separate media agencies enabled the craft skills of media people to be better developed, appreciated and rewarded. As we have seen, some of the media agencies were launched as entirely separate businesses, providing media planning and buying services (media independents), but many were previously the media departments of full-service advertising agencies which were separated out and established as specialist businesses in their own right (media dependents). This evolution is pictured schematically as follows:

**FIGURE 1.5** Main creative and media agency evolutions

| Creative Agency | Media Dependent | Media Agency |
| --- | --- | --- |
| O&M and JWT ⟶ | The Network ⟶ | Mindshare |
| Euro RSCG ⟶ | Media Star (then Mediapolis) ⟶ | MPG |
| Publicis ⟶ | Optimedia ⟶ | Zenith Optimedia |
| Grey ⟶ | Mediacom ⟶ | MediaCom (merged with TMB) |
| DMB&B ⟶ | The Media Centre ⟶ | Starcom MediaVest |
| BBH ⟶ | Motive ⟶ | Starcom (merged with Leo Burnett) |
| BMP ⟶ | OMD ⟶ | OMD |
| AMV ⟶ | New PHD ⟶ | PHD |
| Lintas ⟶ | Initiative ⟶ | Initiative |
| McCann Erickson ⟶ | Universal McCann ⟶ | UM |
| Young and Rubicam ⟶ | Mediaedge ⟶ | MEC |
| Saatchi/DSB Dorland/KHBB ⟶ | Zenith ⟶ | Zenith Optimedia |

As these media dependents and independents grew in size and stature, smaller agencies saw the benefit of outsourcing their media planning and buying to them, rather than incurring the cost of media people, media research, systems and resources in-house. And increasingly, creative hot shops breaking away from full-service agencies did not offer media, but partnered with these media agencies, thus consolidating their position.

What we had now was a fully matured media agency sector, comprising an array of media agencies of varying sizes and specialist expertise. But it wasn't just the entrepreneurs who capitalized on the under-valuation of the media function in full-service agencies, or only the smart agency managements who recognized the potential for splitting off their best media expertise into separate companies. A number of clients also saw the value of having greater expertise in this vital area and recruited their own media teams. These in-house experts could advise their brand marketing teams on how to approach investing their advertising budgets with the various media, and could work with the media agencies to secure the best deals from the media owners. This increased focus on media led to the UK client trade association, the Incorporated Society of British Advertisers (ISBA), forming a TV Action Group (TVAG). With Bob Wootton as the current director of media and advertising, the TVAG represents around £2.5 billion of TV advertising spend per annum, equating to almost two-thirds of the UK total, and ISBA now has action groups covering all the other main media. Undoubtedly, the most successful and consistent of all clients was Procter & Gamble, which continues to operate a highly regarded specialist media team today. Apart from its all-round knowledge and planning expertise on behalf of its various brands, the P&G Media Team was and is still well known for securing exceptional deals with all media owners, especially on TV, where it has focused its activity for the past 50 or so years. Over that period of time it must have saved the company literally hundreds of millions of pounds in media value.

**FIGURE 1.6**
John Wanamaker

Negotiation, value and savings have always represented a substantial opportunity in the media process and that is as true today as it ever was – just ask any client chief procurement officer. The early 20th-century retailer, John Wanamaker, said (and Lord Leverhulme repeated): 'Half the money I spend on advertising is wasted, the trouble is I don't know which half.'

Nowadays, the modern media planner, through smart analysis of research and data, can identify where the waste is and, through clever use of targeted channels, editorial environments and new media opportunities, start reducing that waste significantly. The learning from over 30 years of the IPA Effectiveness Awards has also increased the accuracy and accountability of media investment in brands, so that if Wanamaker were to be resurrected and to re-state his position today, he would be regarded as an amateur rather than an authority.

Meanwhile, the many creative or content agencies which were left after the splitting off of the media function lost much of their involvement with media research and withdrew from the interface with media owners. The latter had to gear up significantly to ensure that they could make the case for their medium across the spectrum, often involving the additional challenge of incorporating a cross-media sell. The increased calibre of media owner salespeople, competing hard against each other for budgets, created a virtuous circle in which the professionalism on both the buy and sell sides improved markedly. As a result, media agencies moved into a much more authoritative position vis-à-vis the client, as they were able to demonstrate deeper insights into people's media preferences: it was the media agencies who underwrote the development and launch of IPA TouchPoints, not their creative counterparts.

Another factor in the promotion of the media function to the top table has been the inexorable process of consolidation, which has led to a stark dichotomy. On the one hand, a marketer in charge of a big brand will usually employ one media planning and buying agency, but on the other will roster many specialist content agencies. Thus, there's one media agency voice speaking for 80 per cent or more of the client's advertising and marketing communications budget, and a gaggle of creative ones clamouring for the other 20 per cent. In addition, there is a human factor, which is that many clients are more comfortable discussing concrete numbers as opposed to intangible ideas. So a single relationship with a media agency which is based more on objective and rational issues can be easier to manage than those multiple ones with a plethora of creative agencies whose competing ideas often require subjective and emotional judgements. And of course, if one agency is responsible for the lion's share of the budget, then it's hardly surprising if the client marketer pays it a good deal of attention.

One of the laws of physics is that for every action there is a reaction, and the world of media agencies is not exempt! The dominance of television as a medium and the focus on price led to the emergence of a new agency segment in 1995 offering media planning but not buying. The charge was led by agency Michaelides & Bednash, working closely with Howell Henry Chaldecott Lury, then the hottest of creative shops. They launched on a platform of communications planning alone, with a controversial disdain for quantitative data and a penchant for qualitative research as the basis for strategy development and media channel selection. They were followed in 2000 by Naked, another non-implementation, planning-only media agency, which launched with a mantra of 'media neutrality' and a strong contention that too many media strategies were dictated by agencies with a vested interest in certain media channels, due either to the bulk deals they had negotiated, or the relative operational cost-efficiency of planning and buying one media over another. There were others who joined the 'media neutral' crusade, but these two agencies in particular put the bigger media companies on their mettle and were a key part of the rebalancing of the equation when arguably too much emphasis had been placed for too long on low price as opposed to added value in terms of strategy and planning.

# Into the digital age

Over the latter part of the 20th century and into the new one, most of the original entrepreneurs who built the successful media independents sold their businesses to the emerging communications groups, which in turn consolidated their media operations, so that now over half of all media expenditure is controlled by just five companies. The same sort of process has occurred with creative or content-producing agencies such that six groups now own about 70 per cent by revenues of the creative and media agencies in the UK.

**FIGURE 1.7**   Major groups' media agency brands

| | OMNICOM GROUP | HAVAS | INTERPUBLIC GROUP | WPP | AEGIS GROUP | PUBLICIS GROUP |
|---|---|---|---|---|---|---|
| **Worldwide Staff** | 63,000 | 14,000 | 40,000 | 138,000 | 16,000 | 45,000 |
| **Media Agencies** | Omnicom Media Group | Havas Media | Mediabrands | GroupM | Aegis Media | Vivaki |
| | OMD Worldwide | MPG | UM | Kinetic | Carat | Starcom MediaVest Group |
| | PHD Network | Arena Media | Initiative | Maxus | IProspect | ZenithOptimedia |
| | MGM | Havas Digital | | MEC | Vizeum | Digitas |
| | | Havas Sports and Entertainment | | MediaCom | Isobar | Razorfish |
| | | | | Mindshare | Posterscope Worldwide | |

**DATA SOURCE:** C Squared

This consolidation has inevitably resulted in legacies to be dealt with. In the early days of the full-service advertising agency, by definition virtually all the media planning and buying was concerned with newspapers and magazines, with some activity on posters. When commercial television arrived in the UK in the 1950s, the general tendency was to set up a specialist department to deal with this new medium. The same thing happened when commercial radio and other new media came along. The net result of this was that, by the time the media independents had matured as businesses, it was not uncommon for them to be organized into a number of internal silos dedicated to the management of the main media channels on behalf of their clients. The benefits of this approach were of course those of specialization, with individuals becoming extremely knowledgeable about a single medium and establishing close relationships with all the key people in that particular medium's 'village'.

However, clients became concerned about integrating the communications for their brand effectively, not only across their multiple agencies but within their media agency itself. Thus, over the past few years, many of the leading media agencies in the UK have moved towards client-focused multimedia planning and buying teams, wherein each person is expected to take a holistic view of the advertising and communications task in hand. This process has been a significant challenge to the personnel involved because not only have they had to maintain their knowledge of the medium in which they previously specialized, but they have also had to assimilate a similar mass of information about many other media.

Meanwhile, the number of content-producing agencies with niche specialisms has proliferated and it's not uncommon for a dozen or more to be employed on a big brand. And geography hasn't helped as the agency 'village' has fragmented as it has evolved from its original home in Fleet Street. The second wave, typified by the supremacy of television as a medium, led to Soho in central London being the concentration point for the production houses and agencies involved. And now, in the third wave, the digital media are increasingly holding sway and the new agencies have thrived on the lower rents and big open-plan spaces in old industrial buildings in east London, with Clerkenwell and Shoreditch being the new hot spots. This without mentioning the many good agencies elsewhere in England, Northern Ireland, Wales and Scotland which have places on client rosters.

To add to the complexity facing clients, several media agencies are taking the lead in providing advertising content, either through freelancers or by setting up their own in-house creative resource. In a parallel development some creative agencies have reintroduced media to their offer, either through an implant such as 'Naked Inside' or by joint-venturing, as agency CHI has done with WPP's Group M in forming MCHI, but most are still leaving the buying to the scale operators and their market clout. Meanwhile, some of the big holding companies offer to tailor-make a client-specific agency by cherry-picking a team from within its operating companies to cover all aspects of media planning and buying, plus content creation and production and with quantitative and qualitative research services too. Not quite a return to the one-stop-shop full-service agency, but nevertheless a comprehensive 'group agency' advertising and marketing communications service to manage the brand.

Orchestrating the interaction of all these content-creating agencies with the one responsible for media planning and buying is extremely complex. Whether the client marketer is the 'ring master' or delegates the role to a 'lead' agency within a roster, it's difficult and expensive to achieve a genuinely integrated communications campaign for a brand. There's also the big question of which comes first, the channel strategy or the creative idea for the brand. If the former, then the agencies charged with the production of content are likely to complain that the mandated media mix doesn't suit their creative concept. But if the 'big creative idea' takes precedence, the media agency may despair at the cost of the time lengths or space sizes required. As we have seen, there's a continuous process of agency innovation and experimentation to try to crack the problem. But with the lion's share of the market dominated by five giant communications groups, each of which is fully committed to its separate media agencies, it seems unlikely that it will be solved by a large-scale reintegration of media and creative agencies.

The agency sector continues to evolve and this latest wave of change has been largely stimulated by a 'new entrant' to the media world – namely the internet. As early as 2000, the industry became highly excited by the possibilities of the world wide web, and for a period it enjoyed the dotcom boom, which unfortunately was quickly followed by the dotcom bust, as many fledgling internet companies overstretched themselves financially and disappeared. After this initial hiccup, the internet has grown rapidly as a communication, information and social networking service as well as an ever-expanding advertising network. The IPA Bellwether Report has tracked the growth in expenditure on the internet, and as of 2011 it accounts for about 11 per cent of the total £42bn spend on all advertising and marketing communications, with search engine optimization (SEO) being the most dynamic sector. Apart from a plethora of companies providing specialist expertise, from website building through to SEO, the internet has created its own advertising agency sector, including specialist internet planning and buying agencies of which some provide both creative and media services, such as Profero, some creative-only, such as Glue, and some just digital media services, such as the late lamented i-level. Increasingly, the existing media agencies are developing their own specialist departments or units, providing digital expertise in planning and buying, and even content creation for the internet.

While the power of the traditional media should not be underestimated – commercial television is still watched by just about the entire UK, prime-time programmes will still reach audiences in excess of 10 million adults, and over 70 per cent of all UK adults still read a paid-for newspaper at some point during the week – the internet has changed the way that these media now operate because of course it is a new platform for them as well as a medium in its own right. Newspapers, magazines, television, radio, direct mail (via e-mail) and cinema (via DVDs and now downloads) sponsorship (the broadcast as opposed to the event version) and public relations are all benefiting from extraordinary new leases of life in the online media flow. The challenge for media agencies is to provide their clients with genuinely integrated solutions that reflect the way the modern consumer dips in and out of the various media of their choice, while also having specialists who can execute these strategies across the various media channels and platforms.

Of course, the irony of all this is that as the task of planning and buying media has become more complex and more and more demanding of the agency people involved, there has been a powerful countervailing trend towards marketing and procurement people perceiving media as a quasi-commodity to be bought largely on price. There is a relentless process whereby consolidated media accounts worth many millions of pounds in expenditure are put out to competitive tender, sometimes using a depersonalized online auction system, which almost invariably results in another slice being taken off the remuneration of the successful agency. For example, in early 2009 the Vodafone account was won by Carat from OMD. Then, mid-year, WPP had a tilt at the business, but although unsuccessful put it back in play for OMD to be reappointed in late autumn. No doubt the procurement people are happy with the apparent saving they think they've achieved, but what about the costs involved? The Vodafone brand's media communications planning and buying were disrupted for over a year, which must have had an adverse impact on its competitive position.

Will the media owners who all had to do a mass of unnecessary work still put themselves out for Vodafone or will they do their utmost to retrieve their costs? How will the 'winning' agency achieve the 15 per cent-plus profit margin that its holding company and its shareholders require? And what about the demoralized employees in all the agencies concerned – do they really feel like going the extra mile?

This sort of procurement-driven review has exerted severe downward pressure on personal remuneration, particularly amongst the younger employees of media agencies, whose average starting salary in London in 2010 was about £18,000. At the same time, and exacerbated by the sub-prime financial crisis, agencies have had to make significant numbers of job roles redundant, with the axe falling on many senior people, who are of course the more highly paid. This is perpetuating the cycle which has led to 45.5 per cent of the employees of IPA media agencies being under the age of 30, with only 5.3 per cent of them being over the age of 50. This relentless haemorrhaging of experience creates a downward spiral in itself, with clients not getting the benefit of the advice of senior practitioners who might help them navigate their brands through the increasing complexities of the media flow.

Meanwhile, because of the extreme pressure on agency margins, the groups have consolidated to achieve economies of scale and have become increasingly dependent on their treasury functions in order to make a profit. They have also used their scale and buying clout to negotiate the very best of terms with media owners. While this has benefited many clients, it has also given rise to a steady trickle of allegations of undisclosed volume discounts and over-riders which have accrued to the agencies as opposed to advertisers. These suspicions have encouraged procurement to continue to pursue ever-keener terms of business which may actually exacerbate the propensity to deal in these 'grey areas'.

All this has led these big media agency groups to compete at a strategic level in the early stages of an agency review or pitch, but often to revert ultimately to a price-based dogfight in the final decision-making negotiations. There seems to be no new factor in the market which is likely to reverse this process, so we might expect further consolidation of the media agency market at the group level over the next two years. In the meantime, the challenge to the managements of individual agencies will intensify as they try to balance the need to provide high-value holistic media planning and buying for brands in a fragmented and highly complex media environment, while remaining sufficiently competitive on price to win and retain clients.

One ray of sunshine in an otherwise rather gloomy sky is the latest research by Nielsen Media Analytics on the relationship between share of voice and share of market. This is explored in detail in Chapter 7, but suffice it to say here that we now have concrete evidence of the additional brand performance that can be generated by clients paying for the best-in-class campaigns which outcompete competition through outstanding strategic thinking, channel planning and creative delivery.

So media planning in the third wave of agency evolution has a primacy in the development of a brand's advertising and marketing communications strategy that it hasn't had since the earliest origins of agencies in London's Fleet Street. Whatever the eventual solution in terms of how the brand's media flow is deployed, an understanding of the role and benefits of every platform/channel and its cost-effectiveness in execution is fundamental to successful communications. This is now the territory and skill set of today's media agencies. It is for this reason that managing the media investment has never been more important. As a senior advertising executive, albeit some years ago, said: 'Media is far too important to leave to media people.' Not surprisingly, this statement was not particularly well received by the media fraternity at the time. But the point being made (admittedly with a lack of sensitivity) was not intended to infuriate media practitioners. Rather it was reaffirming that media planning and placement is fundamental to the overall advertising and communication process. Therefore, everyone involved in advertising should have an understanding of media and how it can most effectively be used in navigating a brand into the target customer's life flow.

# People's relationship with media

**W**hat is a medium? Is it a cereal packet with copy and a competition on the back? Is it a telephone line carrying a telephone sales call? Is it the internet and the websites that are served up by it? What about matchboxes, bus tickets, pavements or even an aeroplane writing a brand name in the sky?

**FIGURE 2.1**  Skywriting 'Sage' above Sydney Harbour, Australia

Photograph by Hamish Pringle

It would seem that a medium is any carrier of a message. Peter Souter, former executive creative director of agency AMV BBDO, says he thinks 'about the "surface" his idea will appear on'. So we can define a medium as any communication-carrier and, as Marshall McLuhan pointed out, there is a relationship between the medium and the message, in that the carrier has an effect on the content. A prestigious publication confers some of its high

**FIGURE 2.2**    'Clean it up' pavement poster in Marylebone, London

Photograph by Hamish Pringle

status on its content, and similarly the editorial stance of a newspaper will imbue the news with a particular slant.

In fact, in the context of advertising, the relationships are more complex than McLuhan suggested. There are additional factors: as well as the medium and what it brings to the message, there is the way in which the medium is used by the advertiser, and the relationship that the consumer has with the company, product or service being advertised. Clearly there is an overlap between these three aspects of how a medium works, but they are worth considering separately in order to appreciate fully the potential they offer brands to immerse themselves in the life and media flow.

# 1. The medium

Where advertising is placed will have an impact on how consumers perceive the message and the brand. This is because each medium has brand values in its own right, with its own personality, attributes, imagery and status. And each medium is populated by individual media brands which make specific edits of the available information and content consistent with its own brand positioning, and then present them to their defined audiences on whichever is their preferred 'platform' or point of access. Therefore, the choice of medium cndé the particular title, channel or format within it sets the context for the brand advertising it carries and can send additional signals to the target audience. For example, a luxury goods brand might choose to be amongst its peers in the pages of *Vogue*, or wish to widen its franchise by being seen in *The Sunday Times' Style* magazine.

**FIGURE 2.3**    A natural home for luxury brands

Reproduced by permission of Condé Nast

A media planner considering advertising a brand in a newspaper such as *The Telegraph* may like its editorial context, but worry about the more 'traditional' connotations of appearing in its hard copy version. On the other hand, its online version has more contemporary values, and may be better suited to the target audience. Thus the same advertising, placed in different media and in different titles, channels or formats within each medium, can have different meanings for readers, listeners and viewers. It will also have different response rates, as Drayton Bird sets out so clearly in his seminal book, *Commonsense Direct and Digital Marketing*. He gives the example of an American shoe seller and shows how differently the efficiency rankings turn out for the same advertisement run in five different magazines:

**FIGURE 2.4**    Efficiency ranking for identical advertisements in different magazines

| Publication | Enquiry rank | Conversion rank | Average order | Total sales | Total cost | Cost to revenue | Efficiency rank |
|---|---|---|---|---|---|---|---|
| | | | $ | $ | $ | % | |
| National Enquirer | 1 | 4 | 53 | 19,025 | 5,406 | 28.4 | 1 |
| New Woman | 4 | 1 | 65 | 10,220 | 2,939 | 28.8 | 2 |
| Woman's Day | 2 | 2 | 51 | 44,624 | 12,987 | 29.1 | 3 |
| Redbook | 3 | 5 | 45 | 65,425 | 45,661 | 69.8 | 4 |
| McCall's | 5 | 3 | 51 | 13,633 | 10,429 | 76.5 | 5 |

**SOURCE:** Drayton Bird, *Commonsense Direct and Digital Marketing*, Kogan Page (2007)
Reproduced by permission of Drayton Bird Publications

This precise numerical analysis proves that what the medium brings to the message is a concrete reality, not just a proposition made famous by McLuhan.

# 2. How the media are used

The second aspect of how a medium works is the behaviour of the advertiser in using it. This can and should affect the impact and 'cut through' the advertising as well as affecting the perception of the brand. This works on a number of levels because the choice of medium for its advertising, and its position within it, are part of a brand's 'body language', and consumers are adept at reading these signals as they encounter them in the media flow. Indeed, these brand signals are as crucial in their design as the hand-made flies used to lure a fish.

**FIGURE 2.5**    Think of a medium as a fisherman's fly

Reproduced by permission of Byron Haugh

## Editorial relevance

Perhaps the most powerful way in which media selection can consistently benefit the advertising message is through editorial relevance. This symbiotic relationship between editorial and advertising works especially well in niche areas because, in combination, they create a richer 'marketplace'. This is one of the reasons why consumers buy these specialist publications: cameras advertise in camera magazines, recipe ads appear on cookery pages, automotive advertisers buy into car programmes, new CDs launch in music programmes and on music channels, and so on. As new technologies enable an increasing number of targeted and specialist media products, the opportunities to match the brand's advertising message with relevant content are becoming far more numerous.

## Size and value

Another important parameter to consider is the nature of the space or time available within a given medium and media brand. Take, for example, the use of large sizes in better-quality spaces and positions: colour spreads in the early pages of magazines, longer time-length commercials in prime-time slots on television, and supersize posters on high-traffic outdoor sites such as beside the Cromwell Road in West London. Not only does this approach greatly enhance the visibility of the message but, because people have a tacit understanding that this is more expensive advertising, it gives additional status to the brand, suggesting it is bigger, richer and more successful than its competitors who are using smaller, less prestigious sizes and sites. The Stella Artois 'Reassuringly Expensive' campaign always appeared in reassuringly expensive media spaces! In the same way, 'As seen on TV' is a shorthand for saying, 'this brand is successful enough to be able to afford the most expensive advertising medium, and thus can be relied upon not to go out of business nor let the customer down on product or service quality'.

There's a hierarchy in media and, as a rule of thumb, colour connotes more value than black and white, 'front of book' (for magazines and newspapers) is better than back, prime-time on TV is superior to the afternoon and later evening, morning drive-time on radio is better than the rest of the day, and so on across the various media. *Yellow Pages* research showed conclusively that advertisers who took bigger spaces in their directory were perceived to be more reliable, trustworthy and professional than those who took smaller spaces. As a result of this 'corporate body language' in their use of media, these attributes will be ascribed to the brand, quite apart from the actual content of the advertisement itself.

## Learning the rules – to break them

It's important that media planners and their clients, in marketing and procurement, understand all these conventions and appreciate that their inter-relationships can be harnessed to good effect for a brand. But opportunities also arise simply because these 'rules' exist, and, as we know, rules are made to be broken! Once the conventional thinking has been done it's a useful

**FIGURE 2.6**   Nissan Micra 'small spaces' advertisements

Collage reproduced by permission of TBWA and EuroSpace

**FIGURE 2.7**    Zag when they zig

Reproduced by permission of Volkswagen Group of America, Inc.

exercise to adopt agency BBH's mantra, 'When the world zigs, zag', and re-examine the options from a contrarian point of view. For example, the launch of the Nissan Micra in the early 1990s by agency TBWA brilliantly turned normal car industry practice on its head when it used multiple tiny spaces sprinkled throughout the newspapers, speaking volumes about the nimble agile qualities of this small car. One of the reasons this kind of counter-cultural media strategy worked is that it not only operated as a visual pun of 'small space equals small car', but it also differentiated the Micra in the media-savvy consumer's mind which was used to all other cars taking big spaces. In this way, perhaps Nissan's agency was nodding to agency DDB's great 'Lemon' press advertisement which launched the small car VW so self-deprecatingly and yet successfully in the United States.

There are numerous examples of other ways of using an 'unconventional' approach to gain impact and saliency. Before the loophole was closed, Club 18–30 provoked public outrage by running ads on mass media 48-sheet posters that would have barely raised an eyebrow in their natural niche of 'lad' magazines. Wonderbra projected a poster onto Battersea Power Station and Fosters ran ads upside down for its 'Australia Day' campaign. In each case the 'rules' were broken, and delivered the 'relevant but unexpected', as Barbara Nokes, formerly creative director of BBH, would say.

## Being first

Similarly, 'media firsts' present brands with a rarer, and thus valuable, opportunity to exhibit body language presenting them as early adopters with a sense of innovation and energy, and thus make a bigger splash. Listed below are examples of 'media firsts' and famous uses of media in new and innovative ways, many of which are still remembered and referred to today as role models.

### Media 'firsts'

1899 – First cinema ad: Dewars Whisky (UK)

1955 – First TV commercial: SR Toothpaste (UK), by Young & Rubicam

1973 – First advertisement on British radio: Birds Eye Frozen Food

1979 – First two-minute TV commercial: Fiat 'Hand built by robots', by Collett Dickenson Pearce

1983 – First car glued to a poster: for Araldite on the Cromwell Road, West London, by FCO Univas (UK)

1984 – First TV commercial made to run only once during the third quarter of Super Bowl XVIII: '1984' for Apple, by Chiat/Day (United States)

1992 – First commercial Short Message Service (SMS) text message sent by Neil Papworth, a young engineer at Airwide Solutions, to Richard Jarvis, a Vodafone director, at a staff Christmas party

1993 – First commercial website: Dale Dougherty's Global Network Navigator

1992 – First brand to differentiate itself strategically by placing advertisements on the back covers of magazines: BBH for Boddington's Beer (UK)

1994 – First website banner ad: AT&T's 468 × 60 banner on the HotWired site (United States) by Tangent Design/Communications of Westport, CT

1995 – First time a Rolling Stones song was used in a commercial: *Start Me Up* for the launch of Windows 95, by Wieden+Kennedy (United States)

1995 – First time all the advertising space in *The Times* was taken by a single advertiser: for Microsoft Windows 95, by Wieden+Kennedy

1996 – Pepsi painted Concorde blue: Freud Communications (UK)

1996 – First ever 64-sheet poster: Pretty Polly by TBWA (UK)

1999 – Gail Porter in an *FHM* ad projected onto the Houses of Parliament

2001 – London *Metro* newspaper ran white spaces instead of ads to attract advertisers back in the depth of the recession after the tech-mark crash

2001 – Ford Mondeo poster: the first, and world's largest, to cover the entire 132-metre side of the Fort Dunlop building beside the M6 motorway

2003 – First Gold Spot in cinemas just before the feature film: for Orange by
        Mother (UK)

2007 – First commercial 'widget': 'Coke Bubbles', by Joost (UK)

2008 – First 'live' TV ad for Honda by Wieden+Kennedy London, 4 Creative and
        Starcom

Media planners need to stay close to the marketplace to be alive to these opportunities. But they should take care to match up a 'media first' with the appropriate brand, and not be overly influenced by the discounted rates that media owners often offer to entice brands into their new and untried medium.

# 3. Relationship with the brand

Finally, there is the consumer's relationship with the brand being advertised. This has to be seen in the context of the two main categories of advertising, namely 'display', defined as advertising that goes to people, and 'classified', which is the kind of advertising that people go to. *Display* advertising has a much harder task than classified because it is operating in a situation where the intended recipient is generally not in the market for the product or service being presented. Food mixers and their advertising are simply not that interesting if you're happy with the one you've got, so display advertising for food mixers has to provide its reluctant recipient with some positive reward for paying it any attention at all, let alone achieving a degree of engagement.

On the other hand, if your food mixer breaks down, suddenly you need to dive into the market for a replacement and you find yourself searching for information about possible replacements. This will often include looking at ads for Kenwood, Moulinex, Cuisinart and other brands that may have been screened out previously. Thus the key skill in *classified* advertising placement is being in the flow where *active* shoppers in the market are most likely to be looking – hence the meteoric growth in online search advertising which has powered Google to become the media behemoth it is. By contrast, the core competence in display advertising is to place it where *potential* customers can not only be reached most cost-effectively, but also in the most appropriate editorial or programme context.

The central scenario forecast in the 2007 Future Foundation and IPA report, *The Future of Advertising and Agencies*, predicted that 'classified' advertising (which of course includes paid-for online search) was likely to gain market share at the expense of 'display' over the 10-year forecast period. The report also put forward a new segmentation of the commercial media market, dividing it into 'one-way communication versus two-way', 'anonymous message versus personalized' and 'non-screen advertising versus screen', with the latter category in each segmentation forecast to increase.

**FIGURE 2.8**   Ten year forecast from
*The Future of Advertising and Agencies: 'two-way' increases*

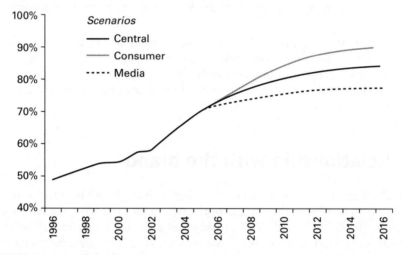

**SOURCE:** Future Foundation/IPA 2007

**FIGURE 2.9**   Ten year forecast from
*The Future of Advertising and Agencies: 'display' declines*

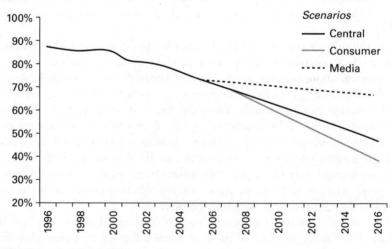

**SOURCE:** Future Foundation/IPA 2007

**FIGURE 2.10**    Ten year forecast from
*The Future of Advertising and Agencies: 'named' increases*

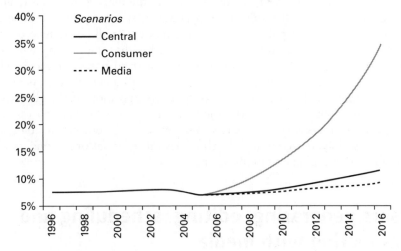

**SOURCE:** Future Foundation/IPA 2007

**FIGURE 2.11**    Ten year forecast from
*The Future of Advertising and Agencies: 'screen' increases*

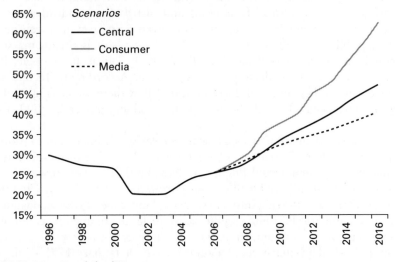

**SOURCE:** Future Foundation/IPA 2007

All of which suggests a progressive increase in the engagement between people and their media. Part of that 'engagement process' includes the advertising that the media carry. It can enhance the consumer's experience because it is providing entertainment and useful information and, as such, improves the consumer's perception and relationship with both the medium and the brand. How all these elements are synthesized by the reader, listener or viewer will relate to their own personality, attitudes, life stage and mindset. These factors, plus whether or not they are 'in the market' for a particular product or service, will result in a media advertising experience unique to that individual at that point in time. This experience will be influenced also by the ability of the customer to interact with either the media owner or the advertiser, or both (and potentially with a third party such as a self-regulatory or regulatory organization in the case of a complaint). As we've seen, timing is of the essence. The accurate juxtaposition of the advertisement in the right medium at the right moment in the buying process can transform the message from one that is screened out by our innate ability to ignore (certainly at a conscious level) irrelevant information, to one that is a useful and engaging communication.

# Users generating, editing, scheduling and interacting with media

Individuals have always had the ability to publish their opinions, whether through letters to the editor, printing leaflets and pamphlets, securing exposure of an article or a book through a commercial publisher, or even by 'vanity self-publishing'. In the online era, the cost of the latter has fallen to virtually zero in terms of materials and distribution, and advances in technology have made it very easy to send a mass e-mail, set up a website or create a public online diary or web log. The 'blogosphere' is already massive, although as Dennis Woodside, Vice President Americas for Google, has opined: 'The average readership of a blog is one.' According to Technorati, estimates at the beginning of 2009 indicated that there were 133,000,000 blogs begun since 2002, with the most popular achieving over 250,000 visits daily.

This mass participation in social media is clearly very important to people. To paraphrase René Descartes, 'I blog, therefore I am.' We media mammals are manifesting and indeed defining ourselves in public in ever-growing numbers despite the steady trickle of warnings from the privacy lobby. What this means is that we're moving into a new media landscape in which consumer-generated content is becoming a potential vehicle for commercial communications. Personal communication via a medium is not a new thing – *The Times* published a letter in its inaugural issue on 1 January 1785 – but the ability to interact with one certainly is.

Obviously people have always been able to choose their newspaper, radio station, music and TV programmes. But hitherto they have not been able to select, segment and schedule in the way they can now using digital technologies:

**FIGURE 2.12** Top 10 Most Popular Blogs of 2010

| Blog | Estimated Unique Monthly Visitors |
|---|---|
| 1. Huffington Post | 28,000,000 |
| 2. TMZ | 17,000,000 |
| 3. Engadget | 11,500,000 |
| 4. PerezHilton | 9,000,000 |
| 5. Gizmodo | 8,900,000 |
| 6. Mashable | 7,000,000 |
| 7. TechCrunch | 6,500,000 |
| 8. Gawker | 4,500,000 |
| 9. Lifehacker | 4,400,000 |
| 10. FanHouse | 4,350,000 |

**SOURCE:** eBizMBA

- The more practised internet users are creating their own news and information feeds using Really Simple Syndication (RSS) to direct content to their own page where the links are displayed for their consumption.
- Others have installed 'ticker-tape' tool bars on their computer screens so they can have a continuous display of breaking news from the likes of the BBC, CNN and *The Times of India*.
- Many mobile phone or PDA (personal digital assistants) owners subscribe to SMS feeds which can provide them with a whole range of useful and timely information such as stock exchange prices, sports scores or weather reports, amongst many others.
- The personal video recorder (PVR), used in conjunction with the electronic programme guide (EPG), enables TV viewers to customize their programme schedules.
- The 'SkyView' research data produced by the combined Sky and TNS panels show that so far only 28% of viewing in homes with a PVR is of recorded material, but this is still substantial.

The new digital radio sets provide the facility to record broadcasts in the same way as PVRs. People are also becoming accustomed to downloading music and video from internet sites for playing back at their convenience. Thus, people appear to be fine-tuning their viewing or listening schedules to their own timetables to take into account meal times, school runs, shopping trips, commuting etc, while still watching at more or less the same time as everyone else, and thus preserving the value of conversations the next day about a shared experience – the 'water cooler' effect. Meanwhile, people are watching more TV over the internet. Nielsen's *Three Screen Report* for Q1 2010 shows that the average American watches approximately 158 hours of TV every month at home, a 1.3 per cent increase year-on-year. In addition, the 134.5 million Americans who watch video on the internet watch on average about 3 hours and 10 minutes of video online each month at home and work. The 20.3 million Americans who watch video on mobile phones watch on average about 3.5 hours of mobile video each month, and while it's still small, there's a growing number of people who watch TV while interacting with related content on their laptop. People's life and media flows are truly blending.

# Push and pull

Meanwhile, the many thriving e-commerce websites on the internet, allied to the ability to follow a customer's online journey, plus the personal data captured at point of purchase and linked back to existing databases, enables increasingly detailed understanding of the role of media in the process. It's our contention that users of media have been guilty of the sin of thinking it's been just about 'push', when all along it's also been about 'pull'. North American smoke signals were 'broadcast' media long before the advent of NBC, but lookouts were posted on high places to see them. It may not have been as obvious as it is now, but people have always filtered out unwanted messages and actively sought out others. 'Search engine optimization' is not new – just try telling that to AA Quick Response Electrics Ltd (their number's in *Yellow Pages*), who figured out a long time ago how to be found first by customers in a hurry. There's also been the sin of thinking media is primarily about 'one-way' communication, when it's always been 'two-way' – it's just that getting a letter to the editor published in *The Times* was so difficult.

Media owners have always tried to personalize their messages to a named individual – after all, the first visiting cards had to be delivered by hand to some-one specific at a particular house and it's postcodes and automation that have made mass anonymous mail possible. Now a medium can be personalized both by its owner and by its receiver. Databases can produce such fine detail on individuals that communication can be tailored very closely to them. 'Behavioural targeting' uses analyses of anonymized journeys on the internet to forecast likely future interests, needs and wants. Users of a medium have always been selective about the content they choose and refuse. Men often start reading their newspaper from back to front because sport is their primary interest. Women are more likely to want to see a romantic comedy than an action movie. But nowadays the facility to be selective has become almost infinite, with video on demand (VOD) and the power of internet search engines.

All this makes the task of investing in media for brands one of the most exciting, demanding and responsible roles in a company, with major implications for shareholders if it's done well, or badly. Great media solutions have always required a strong understanding of the client's consumer and how that consumer is best reached through the various media channels available. However, historically this was seen as a quite simple 'push' approach. Now it increasingly involves the need to achieve effective engagement which, in turn, requires a more active 'push/pull' relationship. Indeed, a 2010 study conducted by the University of Maryland amongst 200 students revealed punitive withdrawal symptoms when they went 'cold turkey' without media for 24 hours. As one participant said: 'I clearly am addicted and the dependency is sickening. I feel like most people these days are in a similar situation, for between having a Blackberry, a laptop, a television, and an iPod, people have become unable to shed their media skin.'

This active thirst for media makes for a very different relationship between advertiser and customer, and emphasizes the importance of appreciating the new 'pull' dynamic as well as the old 'push' approach. Given the plethora of interactive media which people actually reach out for, there is an abundance of opportunities of which advertisers and their agencies can take advantage to get into the media flow. It used to be said that 'you can take a horse to water but you can't make it drink', but nowadays not only does the brand owner not have to do much leading, it can rely on the customer to slake their thirst – it's just a question of making sure the brand trough is full and in position.

# PART TWO
## Overview of the UK media marketplace

# Introduction

In Part One, we provided a brief history of the evolution of the UK advertising and media agency sector from its inception in London's Fleet Street through the traumatic splitting up of full-service agencies into their constituent parts of creative and media. We also gave an overview of people's relationship with media which, as we have seen, is a complex one which needs to be understood fully if advertisers and agencies are to position their brand most effectively in the life and media flows.

In Part Two we turn to the current media landscape and, closely related to it, the media research bodies that provide the vital data on the basis of which billions of pounds are invested in brands. In the latter context we also look at the ground-breaking IPA TouchPoints research, which is the world's first customer-centric media habits survey, enabling planners to gain deep insights into the inter-relationships between people's lives and their media consumption.

Finally, we review the Bellwether Report and show how it can be helpful to planners in anticipating macro trends in the marketplace, which can have a profound impact on media investment strategy.

# The current UK media landscape

**N**ow let's look at the big media river that is such a dominant part of life's landscape today, and consider its overall nature and main constituent streams. Some years ago, the UK advertising market was compared with the US market, and the conclusion was that, while the US market was dominated by a regional retail approach, the UK one was largely about national branded campaigns. Arguably not much has really changed! In the UK, branded advertising continues to be the main order of the day and the media have, if anything, become even more national.

This could be seen as a blinkered view, since 10 years ago the internet hardly existed in media advertising terms, let alone the likes of Google, Facebook and YouTube. And 20 years ago people were only just getting used to Channel 4 – the second national commercial television channel – whereas at the last count there are now over 400. However, in spite of all of the developments that have taken place in digital technology, the growth of the internet, the ever-increasing growth of search and social media and the headlong rush towards convergence, the fact remains that the UK media scene is still largely dominated by the same national media. Furthermore, those media are planned and traded in a frighteningly similar fashion to 25 years ago!

Of course the world has changed and, if anything, that pace of change is speeding up, but at this point the two most fundamental issues that the media industry is wrestling with are the explosion in available media and the need for an integrated approach to planning and trading media. In theory, neither of these in themselves should be a particularly formidable challenge, but the problem is that they represent such a fundamental sea change in the way the industry has operated for... well, just about forever. And, rather surprisingly perhaps, digital technology does not appear on this list. Of course, it has had and continues to have a phenomenal impact on UK media developments but, to date, digital technology has acted more as an 'enabler' for the expansion of existing media, as well as creating a number of brand new ones. It has also blurred the lines between the various media channels – hence the need for a more integrated and holistic approach. However, the full impact of digital technology on the way that media is selected, planned and executed is still some way off – as already stated, national branded advertising on traditional channels is still the dominant approach for most major UK advertisers. Let's consider the implications of today's market situation, where there's more media available than advertising revenues to fund them.

Throughout the second half of the last century, and even into this new millennium, the situation was the reverse – an excess of advertiser demand over media supply. During the second half of the 20th century, the UK scene was dominated by media that delivered mass audiences: TV, newspapers, large-sized posters and general interest magazines. They delivered very high levels of coverage, particularly on a weekly and monthly basis – over 80 per cent coverage of the national adult population weekly and 90 per cent-plus monthly. There were some niche and local media, for example specialist magazines, radio, cinema and local newspapers, but the serious brand advertising monies were spent on the mass audience media, and across most, if not all, of the country.

Those were simpler times and most media planning didn't stretch beyond a couple of media choices (more than that was seen as either highly innovative or unnecessarily complicated, and probably the latter), and it worked. The advertising in the mass media not only reached huge numbers of people but it also made an impact on them – they enjoyed the commercial content, took in the messages, and brands were built on the back of it. For those people who were around then (and even some who weren't), literally hundreds of slogans still resonate, including classics like 'My Goodness, My Guinness', 'Keep Going Well, Keep Going Shell', 'Don't leave home without it', 'Sch... You Know Who', 'Finger-Lickin' Good', 'Go to Work on an Egg', 'Beanz Mean Heinz', '... until I discovered Smirnoff' and 'Plink, plink, fizz, fizz'.

It was also simple because there were so few options available. In the UK, if you wanted to advertise on TV it could only be on ITV, and usually in programmes like *Coronation Street*, *The Sweeney* and *News at Ten*. In peak months, prices soared and there was even 'rationing' of the best slots at these times in some years. Agencies had to work very hard to secure this prime inventory for their clients, and the arrogance of some media owners towards them still rankles today, to their detriment – perhaps a lesson for the new 800 lb gorillas?

Bookings were made and committed well in advance and late cancellations or postponements were not treated sympathetically. If upmarket newspapers were the medium of choice, it was only *The Telegraph*, *The Sunday Times*, and then *The Times* and *The Sunday Telegraph* that could be added to the schedule, but only as additions, not alternatives. In those days, the *Guardian* was seen as being largely only suitable for teachers, social workers and eccentric intellectuals! If you asked for a discount in *The Telegraph*, except for the back half of the paper in the 'graveyard' sites, you would have been met with a stony silence and forgone any potential invitation to a Mad Men-style boardroom lunch at the publication.

The prime positions in magazines – particularly the outside covers, but also facing the 'best matter' – had to be optioned and booked many months in advance, if indeed they were available in the first place. It was also possible to wait years to get the best large-poster sites because many were booked on a long-term basis which was known as 'TC', which meant ' 'til counter-demanded', which in turn meant the advertiser held onto the sites until such time as they chose to release them back. Many of these posters were held by tobacco and brewery advertisers who retained them for many years (and who used to lend them to the Conservative Party during election campaigns until the rules were changed!).

What has all this got to do with the media flow in the modern landscape? A considerable amount, as there is still the same emphasis on many of these same media today. ITV is still the only commercial channel delivering consistently large audiences, though not quite in the same numbers as during the 1970s and 80s. Major national retailers still rely on the Friday and Saturday editions of the large-circulation national newspapers, particularly during key sales periods. *Vogue* remains the 'fashion bible', and the poster supersites on major arterial roads still command a substantial premium price. These core streams continue to flow very strongly, and the habitual behaviour of customers as they dip in and out of them is extremely useful for advertisers.

So what has changed? The difference now is that, while most of the same national media may normally represent the 'core' selection (ITV, *Daily Mail*, *The Sunday Times* etc), they are surrounded and augmented by additional channels and publications. So, in the case of TV, a typical schedule might put up to 50 per cent of the money into ITV, and then allocate the remainder across Channel 4, Five, Sky, Virgin and other various digital channels. What this in turn means is that, where previously ITV represented the entire schedule (and still normally over 80 per cent after Channel 4 launched), it now represents less than half. Additionally, along with an ever-increasing number of digital channels, there is a growing number of iPlayer, VOD and various other online TV opportunities, including of course YouTube. All of this contributes to a highly fragmented but ever-expanding marketplace. The good news is that TV viewing has never been higher and, in spite of all the technology that enables viewers to record programmes and then 'fast forward' through the commercials, overall viewing of TV commercials remains high. The bad news is that the fragmenting TV audience makes the process of planning TV campaigns far more complex and time-consuming, and it may be just a matter of time before ad avoidance starts to have a detrimental impact.

Many of the same issues affect all the other major media. Print has expanded in terms of the number of publications, with more newspapers (national, regional and local), and more sections in the newspapers and more magazines particularly. This has been especially aided by much more sophisticated and economical printing and publishing technology. Clearly this hasn't been at the same rate of growth in TV channels. However, where the print media has expanded most dramatically has been online – now all the major publishers are putting content online, and the launch of the iPad is going to accelerate this trend further. In theory, readership of newspapers is falling; in practice, reading is on the increase – it's just that it now spreads across both offline and online publications and content. Similarly, commercial radio has increased its number of stations significantly – national, regional and local/community – and it too operates across platforms, making it available on radios, TV sets, online, and on mobile phones and many other devices, with the potential to add text and images too.

Posters might seem to be the most stable of media, as there is a policy of not increasing sites, but rather improving the quality with backlighting, better positioning, improved framing, and by culling the poorer-quality ones. However, one of the major developments in outdoor has been the introduction of digital sites, which admittedly has been a costly and relatively slow process, but presents advertisers with 'TV out-of-home'. There's also been the development of other new opportunities – everything from screens in pubs/bars to washroom ads, and from supermarket 'floormats' and trolley ads to messages on hot air balloons, the philosophy being 'If it can carry an ad, why not?' An extreme example is putting them on the packaging of take-away curries!

And of course there is now the internet, with a seemingly infinite number of advertising opportunities covering display, classified, direct response and search. Like the other media channels, the internet has a relatively limited number of preferred advertising sites – Pareto's 80:20 rule seems to obtain online too. Currently the 'stars' of the internet media owners are Google, Facebook, Twitter and YouTube, but portals such as Yahoo, AOL and MSN continue to be major advertising sites, as are the ones produced by publishers such as the Guardian, Telegraph, Mail and Sky. As with the other media, schedules are usually built around a selection of 'core' internet sites. But this is only the tip of the iceberg, because there are an endless number of other possibilities online, from blogs to major manufacturer websites, the vast majority of which offer advertising. And the list grows every day. Consequently there is now more advertising inventory than can ever be sold, and much of it is now dealt with through ad exchanges.

What this all adds up to is a market that offers an infinite amount of advertising inventory, and this has led to strong downward pressure on prices as the supply has exceeded demand. It has also had a fundamental impact on the market in terms of the way that campaigns are now planned, negotiated and bought. For the media, the old premise that they could charge high and pretty inflexible prices for their advertising space and time, and still sell out, is no longer the case. Even the best of the old media (ITV, Associated Newspapers, J C Decaux's supersite posters etc) are finding it tough to secure the same levels of revenue from advertising, and many of the newer and/or smaller channels across all media are finding it impossible to fund their businesses through advertising revenues alone.

Clearly the situation wasn't helped by the worldwide recession of 2008–09, during which time just about every media owner had to reduce their operating costs significantly. But even allowing for the recession, the fact is that the combination of the rapidly expanding media market and an underlying slowdown in the rate of advertising revenue growth has caused an almost 'root and branch' reappraisal of the structure and approach to running and managing media companies. During the period of the recession, it was often asked whether the problems were cyclical or structural, and during 2010 the media and advertising industry generally has seen a rather swifter recovery than most dared to hope for. However, in our view this reversal of the supply and demand equation means that future prosperity for media owners (and even survival in some cases) does require structural changes to the market. There are simply too many individual streams running within the same finite river of life and media for the numbers of buyers and brands that need to swim there.

In the face of this gloomy prognosis, what is most encouraging for the media world is that there appears to be a continuing and, if anything, increasing appetite for high-quality content on the part of consumers. Very importantly, this appetite is for content on the old media channels as well as the new. The success of TV programmes such as *The X Factor* and *Britain's Got Talent* is well documented, with both programmes delivering record audiences on terrestrial TV, earning millions per commercial spot, plus big revenues delivered by huge numbers of votes by viewers over premium-rate phone lines. The additional coverage of these programmes on digital channels and social media sites, as well as via PR, has clearly played an important role in boosting audiences for the live programmes. What was equally impressive was *The Telegraph*'s coverage of the scandal surrounding UK Members of Parliament and their expenses claims, which generated massive coverage across all media channels, created daily updates on a huge number of internet sites (including obviously *The Telegraph*'s), but most importantly resulted in substantial circulation increases for the main newspaper.

Thus the challenge to the media is not in having to compromise the quality of their content, rather it is to structure their businesses in such a way that they can maintain the production of high-quality content and then find as many ways as possible to monetize it. And the fact is that now, unlike for the 20th century, advertising revenues alone are not going to be enough. So how is the media world responding?

Firstly, in order to offset the effects of fragmentation (of both audiences and revenue) and excess capacity, they continue to consolidate in terms of both ownership and advertising sales. Clearly this has been most evident in commercial TV. ITV, having originally comprised 15 different owners of the regional franchises, is now owned by just 3, with ITV the major owner now handling all national advertising sales (the others are the STV Group, which owns the Central Scotland and Grampian franchises, and UTV, which owns Ulster TV). But the overall commercial TV market, consisting of over 400 channels, now has only three other major owners/sales houses: BSkyB, Channel 4 and Channel Five.

We have also seen consolidation across most UK media and advertising sales for radio, outdoor, magazines, regional press, cinema and even the internet – Google now owns YouTube, and Microsoft, though a small shareholder in Facebook (just over 1 per cent), is its exclusive partner in the sale of advertising. Though there hasn't been quite the same degree of consolidation in national newspapers, they are already dominated by a small number of groups and particularly News Corporation (owner of *The Times*, *The Sunday Times*, *The Sun* and *News of the World*), and DMGT (Daily Mail and General Trust), owner of the *Daily Mail*, *Mail on Sunday*, *Metro* and Northcliffe. Very significantly, Rupert Murdoch's News Corp was proposing to take full ownership of BSkyB – currently it owns around 39 per cent. Initially the acquisition was given the go-ahead by both regulators and politicians and it would have been the first major deal involving cross media ownership. However, following the phone hacking scandal at the *News of the World*, News Corp withdrew its proposed take over plans. It is still possible that the deal will be re-established in the future.

Secondly, all media owners are looking to develop new revenue streams beyond advertising. While consolidation has been largely about trying to defend market share and achieve business efficiencies, there is now the widespread recognition that advertising revenue alone is unlikely to sustain the media owners' ability to make, commission and buy the best content. Of course, newspapers and magazines have always secured up to and over 50 per cent of their revenues from cover price sales, cinema still largely relies on admissions, and BSkyB makes over 85 per cent of its revenues from subscriptions and pay per view as opposed to advertising. The real opportunity now for all media owners is to secure revenues from their online channels. In most instances, media owners are providing the same and often more content online, but are able to make only a fraction of the revenue from advertising sales. Increasingly, they are looking to monetize this content through the sale of apps and by setting up 'pay walls', requiring subscriptions for access to the content. It's a tough challenge because most consumers are used to getting their internet content for nothing.

This new over-supplied marketplace is presenting media owners with two significant challenges simultaneously: to increase their operating power and efficiency through consolidation, while restructuring their entire approach to securing revenues for their content. These twin challenges perturbing the media owners are not going to elicit much sympathy from the media agency sector, nor their clients. Meanwhile, the advertising groups and media agencies have been involved in their own process of consolidation. This has been partly to counter the increasing power of the media owners, but also (and more importantly) to put themselves in a better position to carry out their own re-structuring in order to deal with a more complex and integrated world of media planning and buying, increasingly on a global scale.

Like the media owners, media agencies are also at something of a cross-roads. During the latter half of the 20th century, specialization was the approach adopted by agencies. This became especially the case as TV as an advertising medium grew in importance and complexity during the latter part of the century. The growth of the internet further accelerated this trend. By the turn of the century, the market was dominated not only by separate media agencies, with specialist media strategy, planning, research, TV, print and radio departments, but also by separate outdoor and digital specialist businesses and, in the case of the latter, separate specialists in display, direct response and search. The advantage for clients was that they could secure highly expert services for the planning and buying of all media channels, but the disadvantage was that these services became increasingly 'siloed', and as we have seen it has become a problem for clients to unify their approach across all media platforms, let alone tie it in with their below the line, PR and e-commerce strategies.

Digital technology has both enabled the rapid expansion of the available media and fundamentally changed the way that people now access and use them, or more specifically the way consumers find and immerse themselves in content which is of particular interest and appeal to them, whether that content is entertainment, news or information. There is also a blurring of the lines between content and advertising because consumers now expect relevant advertising to provide entertainment, news and information, and they want to be able to follow it across media channels and platforms. For example, they would expect to see a new car launch with a TV ad and/or newspaper ads (and maybe on large posters), followed by more information and reviews in specialist magazines and on the internet, then testimonials and opinions from friends and experts in social media, and finally the ability to secure very detailed technical data and the opportunity for a test drive on the manufacturer's website. And there is also the PR and direct marketing activity targeted at potential purchasers, often compiled from customer lists, using various forms of media from direct mail through to mobile phone alerts. Not forgetting, of course, dealership support and promotions that might use local radio, local posters and/or regional press!

There is no doubt that the most effective campaigns now require a multi-media, multi-platform strategy and execution, from the use of traditional mass appeal media through to search and advocacy activity – a genuinely fully integrated approach to bought, owned and earned media. Much of this is new and underdeveloped territory for the media agencies in terms of both planning and execution. The challenge is to build resource and expertise across the new and changing media, while also creating a structure that is able to pull all the disparate media strands together as a coherent cross-channel/platform strategy, planning and buying service. This is rather easier to say than do, particularly as it represents a very significant departure from the approach and structure of media agencies that have operated for over 20 years or more. Additionally, the remuneration system, still based on commission, and therefore payment for execution as opposed to strategic and planning expertise, is not especially suited to a much more 'upstream' service. Even so, the smarter media agencies are developing these new areas of expertise as well as maintaining their negotiating and buying prowess. Those that do not will be able to provide only a somewhat perfunctory and lower-value execution service, which increasingly will be seen as not much more than a commodity service. Thus, there's the possibility that the market may segment along price/quality lines. Certain agencies and media owners may become bottom-fishers trawling on an ultra-low-cost proposition which exploits the vast amount of low-value media inventory. Others may position themselves at the premium end and use their skills to deliver the high-quality media environment within which many brands prefer to meet their customers.

If both media owners and media agencies are embarking on retooling their business models then the future is going to look very different, and arguably the search business and specifically Google, which represents over 80 per cent of UK search, are providing a number of insights into that future. Too often search is dismissed as being not much more than an electronic directory, and the advertising mainly electronic direct response. It does fulfil these functions, and hugely effectively, but the technologies it uses have far wider applications. Firstly, its trading approach, based on a bidding system and operated on an electronic and interactive basis, has created an entirely different approach to buying. It could well prove to be one of the models for future trading across other media. While it is unlikely to replace the current system of negotiation entirely, alongside a move to ad exchanges it could become a more prevalent system across other platforms, and it's certainly more suited to a world where demand for advertising is far more disparate.

Secondly, Google is tracking online search activity and producing a wealth of data on consumer behaviour – both consumer consideration and actual purchases. These data alone are potentially extremely valuable, but can also be evaluated against other factors, including advertising in other media, thereby showing how search fits into overall advertising and communication activity. Indeed, 'addressable media' are developing fast, enabling planners to put their brand into the media flow with increasing precision. Given that search is now a critical part of the consumer's purchasing journey, the power of these data and how they can help in future behavioural targeting should not be underestimated. Search is clearly a relatively new phenomenon, and the industry is still learning how it fits into the overall communication approach most successfully, but what is indisputable is that Google will be one of the 'powerhouse' media owners of the future. Its impact will stretch way beyond just the search function, and what it is doing now provides real insight into what the industry will look like in the coming years.

# Key points on UK media research

The art and science of media planning and buying have always relied upon the best available 'people' data on target markets and media research metrics, and in the UK we have, arguably, the most sophisticated array in the world. This sophistication is underpinned by a very robust standard industry research approach for all of the main media in the UK, soon to include the internet and mobile too. Additionally, most major media agencies have their own proprietary research surveys and data banks along with specialist teams able to produce both quantitative and qualitative research on top of what they can learn from the industry currencies. Consequently, skilful media agencies are able to plan and execute the most effective campaigns through consumer insight, targeting, optimization, multi-media/channel executions and identification of the most effective editorial environment for the brand to appear in, when, and how.

The industry media research 'currencies' in particular are one of the bedrocks of the UK advertising industry. These currencies are of vital importance to specialist media planners and buyers in agencies because they underpin the trading of some £18bn in space and time annually. They are also used as the basis of key decisions on the programming and editorial content of the media, both commercial and the BBC. In short, the UK media research industry is the world's most sophisticated and the wealth of data it generates enables the navigation of all the eddies and currents within the media flow.

In this context it's essential that practitioners, whether they are media planners, buyers, sellers, or producers of editorial or programming, have confidence in the process whereby the data they depend upon are derived and provided to them. This is where the typically British invention of the joint industry committee or 'JIC' comes in. Comprising the key players on both the buy and sell sides, it provides a forum in which the market research purists and the hard-headed business people can come together and negotiate an acceptable compromise. And compromise it is: the research sample size can always be bigger, the methodology more sophisticated, and the data capture and delivery more frequent, but at a cost which is unaffordable commercially. So it's the role of the JIC to agree the best possible research process within the parameters of the combined industry budget (itself a function of the advertising revenues at stake) and thus arrive at an approximate truth as to people's media consumption. The resulting research data become the basis on which the parties trade – hence the term 'media currency'.

The JICs are always looking to keep pace with developments in the media and to improve upon the quality of their research. Thus they experiment with methodologies and conduct thorough trials of new technologies which sometimes fail. Occasionally, these activities attract the attention of some ill-informed commentators and this can result in adverse press coverage, which is usually damaging for the JIC and potentially disrupting to the market.

As such, if this chapter, which is based on the January 2011 report *The Media Research Landscape in the UK* written by Lynne Robinson, IPA Research Director, achieves nothing more than a better general understanding of the media research sector, it will have been worthwhile. If it increases the respect for the professionalism with which the JICs carry out their complex, difficult and sometimes thankless task, then that would be a bonus. If it succeeds in raising the awareness amongst marketing procurement of the considerable skills required in utilizing complex media research to produce effective communications for brands, then even better.

Industry media research fulfils three key purposes. Firstly, it produces the industry research-based 'currencies' which underpin the efficient operation of the media markets and the trading within them. Secondly, it provides the basic public and commercial accountability measures for each medium. Thirdly, it provides insights into consumer behaviour which are extremely useful for the producers of programming and editorial content. In the UK, virtually all industry media currencies are produced under the auspices of the JIC system, whereby each currency is commissioned by an independent body comprising advertisers, agencies and the relevant media owners. The list is as follows:

Television: Broadcasters' Audience Research          **www.barb.co.uk**
    Board (BARB)
    Chairman, Nigel Walmsley.
    Chief Executive, Bjarne Thelin.

National press (newspapers and magazines):          **www.nrs.co.uk**
    National Readership Surveys (NRS)
    Chairman, Simon Marquis.
    Chief Executive, Mike Ironside.

Regional press: Joint Industry Committee for
Regional Press Research (JICREG)
Chairman, Howard Scott.
Chief Executive, Keith Donaldson.

**www.jicreg.co.uk**

Print/online/exhibitions/broadband TV:
Audit Bureau of Circulation
(ABC & ABCe)
Chairman, Sally Cartwright.
Chief Executive, Jerry Wright.

**www.abc.org.uk**

Radio: Radio Joint Audience Research
(RAJAR)
Chairman, David Mansfield.
Chief Executive, Jerry Hill.

**www.rajar.co.uk**

Out of home: POSTAR
Non-Executive Chairman, Ken New.
Managing Director, James Whitmore.

**www.postar.co.uk**

This joint industry approach has several major advantages. Most obviously the singular JIC produces only one dataset, or 'currency', thus avoiding the confusion amongst buyers and sellers of media space and time that would arise if there were more than one basis for pricing. The research databases produced are robust in that they are industry funded, have the combined industry resources attached to them, are of the highest affordable quality and impartial, since all sides of the industry have agreed to the specifications. JICs are cost-effective since they are run on a 'not-for-profit' basis, and it's the industry's money, so costs are kept to a minimum. Furthermore, in fulfilling their primary role as research procurement experts, contracts are usually put out to tender on a regular basis and this ensures that costs remain competitive and the most-up-to-date research technologies and methodologies are employed. In this way the industry retains control of the media-research-based currency which determines how its medium is traded. This is not the case where a private contractor owns the dataset and, in effect, becomes a monopoly supplier with the potential resultant problems of quality control and cost.

However, there are always trade-offs and JICs do suffer from some disadvantages. By definition, they measure an individual medium and thus tend to reinforce the 'siloed' nature of media planning.

Any major change in an individual medium's research methodology almost always leads to changes in the data produced, and this always means there

**FIGURE 4.1**    A fragmented media research landscape!

Photograph by Hamish Pringle

are both winners and losers amongst the individual titles or channels being measured in a given media sector. As a result, JICs are cautious and tend to be slow moving. All decisions need to be agreed by all parties, which, given the vested interests involved, may take some time and occasionally there's deadlock. This slowness is a particular problem when the media are changing at a fast pace, as is currently the case for virtually all of them. Media currencies are underpinned by large, robust market research surveys which are expensive to undertake. Despite being not-for-profit, and thus the most cost-effective way of providing them, their annual costs are still big in absolute terms. These costs can be increased significantly by new technologies or bigger sample sizes to measure a fragmenting medium and the members of JICs are very mindful of this, especially in recessionary times when their underwriters and subscribers are under huge financial pressure.

Another issue is the definition of an individual's exposure to each medium. This definition varies enormously by channel, particularly in its relationship to potential advertising exposure. It ranges from 'having seen or read a copy of that particular publication within the publication interval' for press, to 'eyes on panel' for outdoor. This lack of comparability is a function of history and technical execution, but is a growing issue in multi-media evaluation. And of course each JIC exists in a silo to serve an individual medium, so their political, financial and technical composition makes it extremely difficult for them to address media other than their own. However, the vast majority of communications campaigns now involve several different media. Although pre-eminent in their measurement of their own medium, their singular focus has led to all the industry currencies losing individual salience within the marketplace in recent years as they each cover a progressively smaller part of it.

In addition to the JIC currency research, other surveys act as quasi-industry currencies in the UK. The first is FAME (Film Audience Measurement and Evaluation), a survey of the audience for cinema and video which is conducted by the two major cinema contractors in the marketplace, with some consultation with their major customers. The second is the long-established TGI (Target Group Index), which is a private, syndicated survey, produced by Kantar and covering product and media usage with an annual sample of 25,000. The third, and most recent, is UKOM (UK Online Measurement), which has been set up by the online media owners to provide an audience-centric planning currency for online. Industry research in the rest of the world is produced by a variety of JIC structures, media owner contracts (MOCs – surveys which are controlled by groups of media owners) and private, syndicated research. The JIC approach tends to be dominant in Europe while the Americas and emerging markets around the world tend to be addressed by private, syndicated studies.

The wealth of media 'currency' research is clearly essential to the media planner, but so is the understanding of how people's media consumption relates to their purchasing habits. This interrelationship is fundamentally important to improving the effectiveness of brand communications. There has also been valuable work done on 'single source' data by the likes of John Philip Jones and published in *When Ads Work*, and by Arbitron via their 'Project Apollo', which was terminated in 2008 owing to lack of funding. These studies use data on media and purchasing habits that are collected by barcode scanners in households that are also panel members for TV research. Thus people's buying behaviour can be correlated with their exposure to media, and the very large number of data points gives a high level of confidence in the findings.

However, there are problems relating to single-source studies, of which media planners should be aware. For example, how does the typical single-source analysis account for how advertising interacts with other variables such as price and promotions in stimulating response, and what synergies exist? The bulk of the existing single-source analysis has been done on TV campaigns, with a few on press, but there has been little done where multimedia have been used and, as we shall see, this is increasingly the norm. There's also a question about timing. John Philip Jones chose to base his calculations for his short-term advertising strength (STAS) on exposure to media within a week before purchase, but others have suggested that the inter-purchase interval could be a critical consideration, thus raising the question of using earlier data points in the buying cycle.

Thus far the learning is, therefore, more applicable to grocery products bought frequently than to durables that are acquired less often, and to TV and press media as opposed to all the other media. But more recently a new power in the land of single-source data has emerged in the shape of the 'SkyView' panel and its links to TNS purchasing data. This huge database enables very detailed analyses of the buying behaviour of different types of homes. Sky's cached hard-drive technology enables the distribution of specific

**FIGURE 4.2**    SkyView is one of the largest panels of its kind in the world

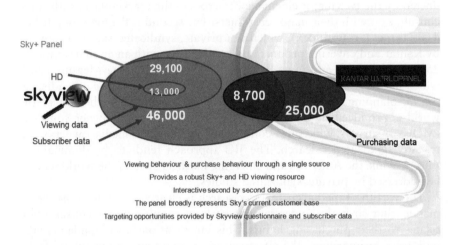

Reproduced by permission of BSkyB

content, including advertising, to specific subscribers and so media planners will be able to observe how life and media flows intermingle on a household-by-household basis.

Currently the industry media research in the UK may well be facing the greatest challenges in its entire history. All the studies are facing the challenges of the migration to digital, the growing reluctance of the population to cooperate with research, and the growth of newer, relatively more expensive interviewing technologies. The growth of digital raises two key challenges: firstly, how to ensure that any audiences delivered through digital means are adequately measured, and secondly, how to provide a robust measurement of the smaller audiences that are the result of media/digital fragmentation. The growing reluctance of the population in general to be interviewed affects all market research. For media research in particular, it impacts on the quality of the data collected if certain target markets, eg the young, ethnic groups etc, are not adequately represented within the system. The availability of comparatively inexpensive research conducted via the internet is no consolation here as the availability/volume of use of the internet has a major impact on what and how traditional media, notably print, are consumed. Therefore, it impacts on the cost of research, as the expense of interviewing escalates as more resource is put behind reaching these hard-to-reach demographic groups.

Another challenge is the whole area of 'brand activation', which covers a vast range of sectors, from field marketing, to product sampling, to exhibitions and live events, with the common denominator of bringing a brand into direct contact with its target market. This very often involves brand 'ambassadors' trained and deployed at set-piece events at carefully chosen locations, so that they can engage and interact with consumers. The problem for the fast-growing brand experience sector, and the clients and agencies operating in it, is to prove the return on marketing investment (ROMI). While basic footfall can be measured relatively easily, assessing the length and nature of an interaction is much more problematic, as are the tracking of the conversion to purchase and the calculation of the ROMI. The IPA has been in consultation with leading brand activation agencies to see if there is any potential for a JIC and a research-based 'currency', and the exploration continues.

The media research industry is also seeing a growth in new interviewing technologies, particularly electronically based ones which monitor passively what respondents are doing. Some of these new methodologies operate more efficiently than others, but all change the basis of the definitions of the measurement of audiences, eg on radio 'listening for at least 5 out of the 15 minutes in a quarter hour' becomes 'within the reception tolerance of the electronic meter'. The combination of the above factors is resulting in an unprecedented amount of testing and experimentation as researchers seek to find new methodologies, or combinations of methodologies, which address their current and future needs within a cost structure the medium can support.

The final issue is one of media convergence, which is increasingly coming to the fore. Each industry currency is trying to measure the growing digital element in its medium's delivery. At the moment, each medium wants to retain sovereignty over its currency measurement. However, the need for comparative measurement and cost efficiencies may change this situation in the future. Cooperation has already begun in that the UKOM Establishment Survey was conducted as part of the NRS. Also, ABC, through its digital arm, ABCe, has developed industry site-centric measures for the web, primarily for print titles, which have been adopted by internet service providers (ISPs) and now by television broadcasters. The website-centric ABCe audit service, underpinned by The Joint Industry Committee for Web Standards (JICWEBS) industry-owned standards, is able to provide a basic count of the majority of digitally delivered content that can be applied by all media owners regardless of the systems (eg Omniture, Google Analytics, Nielsen, comScore etc) used in their businesses. Properly configured, these systems provide a basic accountability for each media vehicle in terms of the number of times content was served.

Meanwhile, the quest to provide an industry audience-centric measure of the internet continues, and these measures will obviously overlap to a greater or lesser extent. The Joint Industry Committee for Internet Measurement Systems (JICIMS) was set up in January 2007 by the Association of Online Publishers (AOP), the Internet Advertising Bureau (IAB), the Incorporated Society of British Advertisers (ISBA) and the IPA to try to create an audience-centric measure of online usage. It was hoped that the development of JICIMS' audience-centric measurement of online could lead to further convergence; however, despite gaining industry consensus on why and what should be measured at a summit meeting on 16 October 2008 under the chairmanship of Mark Cranmer, the project ultimately failed owing to a lack of funding commitment from the major media owners (as did JICIMS' predecessor, JICNET, under Roger Holland and Bob Hulks). Subsequently the AOP and IAB have committed to a 'third way' of providing this much-needed planning data to the marketplace but this will be in the form of a Media Owner Contract (MOC) approach under the name of UKOM, with Douglas McArthur as its inaugural chairman. The online media owners continue to develop their own research under the UKOM banner working with Nielsen Online, but the picture has been made more complex by comScore's announcement that it too intends to upgrade its research methodology. Clearly neither approach can achieve the status of the basis of a media research 'currency' without the support of ISBA, representing clients, and the IPA, representing agencies within a JIC. In the meantime, the major mobile operators have come together under the auspices of the GSM Association (GSMA) to provide usage data for their telephone services.

The only certainty for the future is change, the pace of which will inevitably be driven by the scale of the money at risk, and the challenges of new technologies and multiple media platforms. Thus the never-ending task of improving the veracity of the research-based 'approximate truth' of people's behaviour in the media flow, on which 'currency' the industry agrees to trade billions annually.

# New insights from IPA TouchPoints

It's not often that an off-site 'awayday' results in such a significant out-come as the one that was held on 20 May 2002 and which ultimately resulted in the launch of IPA TouchPoints in 2006. There were some core issues which sparked this ground-breaking initiative and it's worth reprising them since the industry is still grappling with them today. But before we do so, let's have a brief review of some of the broad findings from TouchPoints which are so useful to planners in gaining insight into the intertwining of people's life and media flows.

## Some top-line findings

Let's start with some interesting 'big picture' Q&As:

Q: How much waking time do we really have?

A: Less than you'd think – only 15 hours 14 minutes per 24-hour day.

Q: Does this differ by demographic?

A: Not really except for 15–24-year-olds who tend to sleep longer: around 9.75 hours a night compared to 8.77 hours for all adults.

Q: How much time do we spend working?

A: Of the full-time or part-time working population's waking time, only 29% is spent actually working.

Q: How does that compare with time spent consuming media?

A: For the working population 45% of time awake is spent consuming any media, ie considerably more than is spent working.

Q: Has this media consumption changed over time?

A:    Comparing TouchPoints1 (2005) with TouchPoints2 (2008) and TouchPoints3 (2010), there is very little change, despite the continuing proliferation of and increased access to media.

Q:    How much media consumption is shared with/in the presence of other people?

A:    Sixty-two per cent of time spent with media is with other people compared to 39% in isolation.

Q:    If working accounts for less than a third of our time, what else are we doing?

A:    Ranking activities by pure time spent shows that 'relaxing' accounts for 26.5% of our time when we are awake while 'eating and drinking' accounts for 12.9%. However, people can be relaxing and doing other things in the same half hour, or eating and drinking and doing something else in the same half hour – our life and media flows do intertwine.

Now let's look in more detail at some other things people do on a daily basis:

- 54% of adults use a computer;
- 51% of adults drive a car;
- 50% of adults use the internet at home;
- but only 30% use the internet at work;
- 22% use social networking sites.

And what about the main things people do weekly?

- 65% of us visit or shop at large supermarkets with their own car parks;
- 47% of us visit or shop at a local corner shop or newsagent;
- 36% of us shop in a local high street;
- 34% of us watch pre-recorded DVDs/Blu Ray;
- 29% of us go to the pub;
- but only 25% of us play sports.

Seeing the relative importance of these habitual behaviours is extremely useful in plotting a brand's media strategy, so now let's turn to the main overview question of how much time people spend with which media:

**FIGURE 5.1**    All adults: weekly reach vs. time spent with media

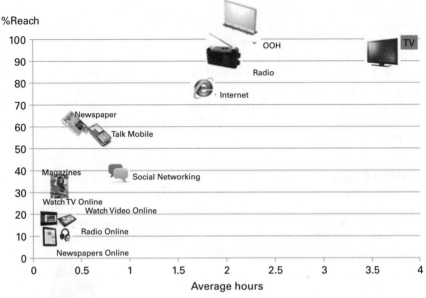

**SOURCE:** IPA TouchPoints3

So TV is the dominant medium for adults, but, we hear you cry, 'What about young people?!' Thankfully TouchPoints can teach us a thing or two about the new generation's media habits:

**FIGURE 5.2**    Adults aged 15–24: weekly reach vs. time spent with media

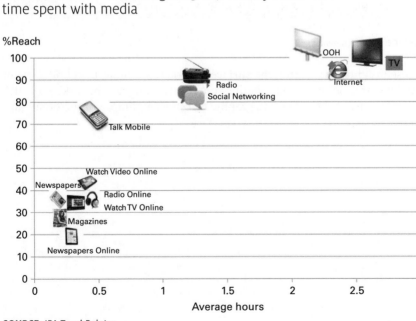

**SOURCE:** IPA TouchPoints3

Remarkably similar to adults, though the internet is closing in on TV, but isn't the increasing bandwidth leading to TV online? And isn't a small but very significant proportion of the out-of-home (OOH) real estate being turned into screens? Audiovisual content is still going to be the dominant media form because it's the closest proxy to human perception. The beauty of IPA TouchPoints is the juxtaposition of life and media flows which can be seen in a multiplicity of situations of which the following is just one of thousands. This chart illustrates the media day of 'school-run mums' and leads us to the conclusion that it is more effective to target these women while online than on daytime TV. Clearly this kind of insight can have huge value to media planners.

**FIGURE 5.3**    School run mums in London (driving with kids between 8.00 and 9.30 or 3.30 and 5.00 Mon-Fri)

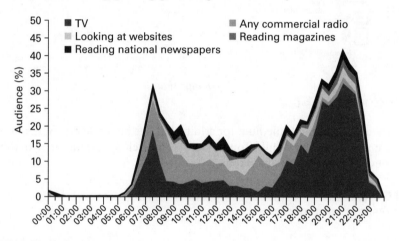

SOURCE: IPA TouchPoints3

These insights just scratch the surface and there's a mind-boggling amount of data and so many fascinating questions that can be asked of IPA TouchPoints, so the following graphic gives just a glimpse of the potential:

**FIGURE 5.4**    The TouchPoints 360° view of social media users

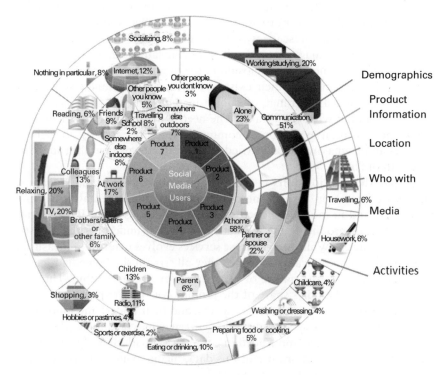

**SOURCE:** IPA TouchPoints3

IPA TouchPoints has been a game-changer for UK media strategists and planners and it looks likely that this is another innovation, like the separation of media from creative, that will have global ramifications.

# Origins of IPA TouchPoints

So how did TouchPoints come about and what was it in the early part of this century that spawned it? At that time the government and all the other stakeholders in the UK media industry were starting to come to terms with the reality of the convergence brought about by the digitization of media. This was one of the central drivers of the UK's 2002 Communications Act, whose very title was significant in its departure from that of previous legislation enacted under the banner of Broadcasting Acts. The December 2003 launch of Ofcom replaced five separate entities: The Independent Television Commission (ITC), The Broadcasting Standards Commission (BSC), The Office of Telecommunications (Oftel), The Radio Communications Agency and The Radio Authority. Consolidating the old siloed regulators was a legislative answer to the challenges presented by convergence, but the members of the IPA Media Policy Group were only too aware that they too needed to develop more industry tools to address the new media landscape.

The global media landscape was evolving at an unprecedented rate. New communications media were (and still are) being launched, while traditional media were experiencing an explosion in the number of channels, titles and formats, thus fragmenting their existing audiences. Consumers were faced with an ever-increasing range of choice in which media they use, where they use it and in what time frame. The need to understand this new landscape had led to an explosion in communications research as advertisers, agencies and media owners alike tried to chart an effective path through this labyrinth of choice.

Despite these major shifts in the tectonic plates of the media landscape, and as we have seen earlier, one thing remained fundamentally the same in the UK, and in most developed advertising markets – the JIC structure responsible for producing the market research that underpins the industry media 'currencies'. While each of these services evolves in terms of measuring its respective communication channel, they all remain single-media focused, despite the multi-media nature of the world they operate within. This isn't surprising since the lion's share of the funding for these expensive research contracts is provided by the media owners, and their underlying motivation is to provide an industry-agreed trading currency in which their advertising inventory can be priced and traded in competition with that of other media channels. Given the importance of this data, media owners are reluctant to cede any control to rival media groups.

From the late 1990s onwards there had been a rising concern amongst leading advertisers that their media agencies were not adjusting quickly enough to the new multi-media digital era. Despite these worries it was not until September 2005 that the World Federation of Advertisers' Media Committee published their *Blueprint for Holistic Research*, calling for 'the development of additional audience measurement that was both "consumer-centric" and "holistic" (i.e. multi-media and beyond just exposure to media)'.

One obvious way in which media agencies were still locked into the analogue media landscape was in their internal structures. While the smaller companies might have employed people who would plan and buy all sorts of media on behalf of their clients, nearly all the big players deployed specialist teams operating within individual media categories such as television, press, radio, outdoor and latterly online. These siloed agencies found themselves open to attack by critics who believed that their choice of media channel, and in particular television, was driven more by overall buying deals and low transaction costs than by target marketing considerations. As we have seen, this led to a new breed of media agency, typified by Michaelides & Bednash and Naked Communications, which launched on a platform of 'media neutrality' to capitalize on this concern by providing media planning only and leaving the buying and implementation to other agencies.

At the awayday in May 2002, the IPA Media Policy Group under the chairmanship of Jim Marshall decided to re-launch itself as the 'IPA Media Futures Group' to signify the adoption of a more proactive approach. A range of forward-looking topics would be investigated, including creating efficiencies within media agencies, for example in the use of market research for planning and buying purposes. Morag Blazey, then CEO of agency PHD Media, chaired a sub-group with a remit to develop proposals for reshaping media/communication research in the UK and to explore the possibility of a consumer-led approach spanning all media.

Clearly this was an extremely ambitious project and one that would have very significant implications for the nature of media planning and buying in the UK. There was also a risk that the IPA initiative might be seen as threatening to the established media research JICs and perhaps even as an attempt to supersede them. This quite natural concern was heightened by BSkyB's proposed SkyView audience measurement panel which would have over 20,000 homes on its panel, dwarfing the 5,100 sampled by BARB. The more far-sighted within agencies also realized that a new piece of consumer-centric research which captured people's media habits across the board would likely require a much broader skill set to match. In order to allay these fears, to elicit the 'shopping list' of requirements for the research and to get 'buy in', the IPA commissioned Rosemary Taylor Associates to carry out a wide-ranging consultation with all the key stakeholders in the marketplace. Given the circumstances, the results were remarkably positive. The JICs were persuaded that the proposed research might actually be complementary to, and supportive of, their own measurement systems. Agencies could envisage that a more holistic study might enable more sophisticated multi-media planning and buying. Those already investing in their own proprietary research in this area could see the benefit in syndicating a foundation study of media habits data via a shared IPA survey and adding their individual value by focusing on research in involvement and engagement. The client community was, of course, enthused by the idea of a research solution that could deliver greater media neutrality and a more sensitive means of engaging with their target audiences. The initiative elicited a mixed response from media owners; however, there were those amongst them, particularly newer media lacking industry currencies, who saw the potential of multi-media research to support their arguments for a share of the client budget.

By the autumn of 2003, and as a result of industry consultation, Lynne Robinson, IPA Research Director, was able to outline the potential role of electronic measurement in cross-media/consumer-centric research, and to confirm that outline briefs had been sent out to a range of major research companies to gain their views on the best route forward. At the 'Future of Media Research Conference' on 18 November, it was announced that the IPA was committed to launching a major new piece of consumer-centric market research into media habits. In March 2004 it was revealed that the new survey would be called 'TouchPoints'.

**FIGURE 5.5**    IPA TouchPoints logo

The ambitious project was underwritten by the 11 agencies represented on the IPA Media Futures Group at that time and 10 like-minded media owner founding partners who helped both with funding and technical input:

**FIGURE 5.6**    TouchPoints founders

| Media Owners | Agencies |
| --- | --- |
| AOL (UK) Ltd | Initiative |
| BBC | MediaCom |
| Chrysalis Radio | Mediaedge: CIA |
| ITV | Media Planning Group |
| J C Decaux | MindShare |
| News International | OMD UK |
| SMG Access | PHD Media |
| The Guardian | Starcom |
| Tesco Media | Universal McCann |
| Wancedoo | Vizeum |
| | Zenith Optimedia |

The IPA TouchPoints initiative was designed to deliver new and fresh insights in its own right, to act as a gateway across data sources and to provide a mechanism whereby different data sources can be integrated, not to act as an alternative to current industry media research. Indeed, it was conceived as a multi-media 'hub' sitting in the middle of the current industry currencies to bring them together through a process of data fusion to provide a fully integrated multi-media planning currency. This hub survey produces, for the first time on a commercial basis, a wealth of information linking an individual's media exposure, now including word-of-mouth, to time of day and various activities, especially shopping. Again, in a global media industry first, the TouchPoints hub data were 'fused' with the data from all the other UK media research surveys from the media 'currencies' listed earlier. In the absence of properly established 'currencies', simulated ones have been created using agreed industry data from various sources. This produced an integrated database which can be used to compare one medium properly with another, and thus make sophisticated multi-media planning an operational reality. Further, the hub survey has been designed not only to provide the 'hooks' for the media currency data to be attached to, but also other key data sources. As well as extracting significant extra value from their client's existing research assets such as quantitative usage and attitude surveys, these include TGI which enables brand purchasing to be linked in through data fusion.

**FIGURE 5.7**   Schematic of the TouchPoints Initiative

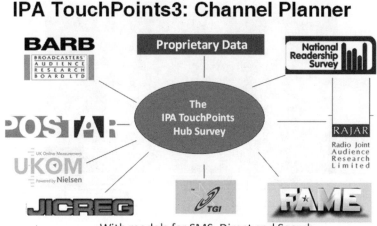

SOURCE: IPA

Thus TouchPoints has two distinct phases: 1) the production and publication of the hub survey; and 2) connecting the industry currencies to the hub survey to create the channel planner. When planning the hub survey, a key requirement of the research design was the inclusion of 'hooks' to be used for integration with industry currencies, and these hooks needed to mirror the currency measures. In order to provide these and also provide new insights into people's daily lives and how their media usage fitted into this, it was decided that the TouchPoints hub survey needed to involve each respondent in two separate tasks: the first was the self-completion of a substantial questionnaire covering detailed usage and attitudes to television, radio, press, outdoor, cinema, online, SMS, event sponsorship and direct marketing. A wide range of lifestyle, attitudinal and detailed shopping questions were also included.

**FIGURE 5.8**   Original TouchPoints hub survey

**SOURCE:** IPA

The second task used an e-diary to collect data on what the respondents were doing, who they were with and what media they were using on a half-hourly basis. Following the success in 2002–03 of a major time-allocation study for the BBC (The BBC Daily Life project), which had pioneered PDAs to collect data, a similar methodology was used for TouchPoints.

**FIGURE 5.9 & 5.10**   TouchPoints PDAs

**SOURCE:** IPA

The methodology enabled the capture of a huge range of media activity half-hour by half-hour, including:

- communicating – talking, e-mailing, texting, writing;
- listening to radio – stations;
- watching TV – channels, video/DVD, games console, programme genre;
- reading – newspaper title, magazine genre, book;
- internet – site genre, buying/seeking info, e-mail, work.

On a half-hourly basis respondents were also asked what mood they were in, and on a daily basis, their claimed exposure to cinema, directories, direct mail, telemarketing calls and commercial text messages was collected.

Stage 2 of the IPA TouchPoints initiative was the integration of industry currencies into the hub survey to produce a probability-based, multi-media planning system. This was one of the most ambitious data integration programmes ever undertaken and was carried out by RSMB Research Ltd. The process is too complex to go into here in any detail, but an excellent account of it can be read in the ESOMAR paper, 'The TouchPoints Initiative: Creating the missing link', by Lynne Robinson, Jennie Beck of TNS Media and Steve Wilcox of RSMB. Suffice it to say that the approach used a mixture of demographic and media links, with the relevant commercial contacts attached to each respondent, which, when completed, represented a single-source media contact survey comprising the following:

Television – fusion from BARB

Magazines and national newspapers – fusion from NRS

Radio – fusion from RAJAR

Regional press – profile-matching from JICREG

Posters – calibration from POSTAR

Cinema – calibration from CAA admissions

Internet – fusion with UKOM

Search – inference from TouchPoints

Direct mail – inference from TouchPoints

SMS – inference from TouchPoints

Product usage – fusion from TGI

At the end of the data fusion process, the integrated database is a large, representative sample of the population. The information available for each respondent is:

- demographic, geographic and geo-demographic classifications;
- all classifications from the TouchPoints hub survey;
- a full TGI product usage record;
- a media usage record from each of the integrated media currencies.

A great deal of the data available in TouchPoints can be found in other surveys. However, this was the first time that all these metrics had been brought together in one survey, which allowed them to be cross-referenced. Furthermore, it allows the analysis of consumer behaviour by time, media, channel usage, behaviour and lifestyle. The primary application of the channel planner is multi-media schedule reach and frequency analysis, incorporating the construction of sophisticated market definitions, target markets and consumer relationships. In summary, IPA TouchPoints enables the following:

- allows all media channels to be evaluated on an equal basis at the start of the planning process;
- gives new insights into how communication channels are used, singly, together, and on a time of day basis;
- allows post-evaluation of mixed media campaigns;
- acts as a hub to marry disparate media data sources together;
- gives the industry a better understanding of the communication process.

IPA TouchPoints presented agencies with several key challenges. The database was, by its very nature, both large and complex. Therefore, users needed to familiarize themselves with its content and get a clear idea of how they could use it most effectively. Clearly, if used to its full potential, it would revolutionize the way that media are planned and therefore facilitate fundamental changes in the current working practices of the media industry.

However, changing long-established work practices takes time. This process is still ongoing some five years later and has required a massive investment in training and further convergence in the communications marketplace so that multi-media planning is starting to become a reality in the leading IPA agencies. Whether TouchPoints was the cause or a symptom doesn't really matter now, but what we have witnessed is a deep-seated change to the structure of media agencies.

With members of the IPA Media Futures Group leading the way, multi-disciplinary teams are becoming the established means by which the most sophisticated media planning and buying solutions are delivered to clients. More and more people have the ability to use IPA TouchPoints as a day-to-day part of their working process and thus can have a genuinely media-neutral approach to client briefs. If they take advantage of the opportunity to integrate proprietary research into the hub survey they can, for example, combine a brand's consumer usage and attitude data with their media habits, which can result in some truly insightful communications planning.

There's a great interest in TouchPoints and a number of countries have begun to experiment with 'me-too' versions, while the IPA has linked up with Ball State University and Sequent Partners under their joint venture: the Media Behavior Institute (MBI), formed in 2008 to develop TouchPoints in the United States. At the 4As 'Transformation 2010' conference held in San Francisco, MBI announced their strategic partnership with research company Mediamark Research & Intelligence (MRI). MBI has licensed exclusively the TouchPoints name and methodology for use in the United States with the goal of launching a syndicated, consumer-centric, multi-media database that could transform the way media are planned, bought and sold in the United States. The first trial research was conducted successfully in the autumn of 2010.

There is an increasing body of case history material which documents how sophisticated media planners have used IPA TouchPoints to gain valuable insights into customers' daily lives and how their various activities are juxtaposed with their media consumption. This is the first time that media research has been able to do this, and thus TouchPoints is one of the key underpinnings of the concept of the 'media flow', and the primary tool that planners can use to understand how best to position their brand within it.

## 06

# How the Bellwether Report can help

Having reviewed the UK's media research landscape it's clear that there is a massive amount of data to assist the sophisticated media planner in developing strategies and plans with which to put the brand into the media flow. But what is the best way to develop a longer-term strategic perspective when, by definition, media research is a well-documented version of the past? Later we will examine the various ways in which the brand's media budget can be calculated, based on the latest research into the relationship between share of voice and share of market. But again, how should we anticipate the likely level of expenditure by the brand's competitors so that we can plan accordingly in order to achieve our business objectives?

Some pretty authoritative assistance in crystal-ball gazing is provided by the Bellwether Report, which was commissioned first by the IPA from Mike Waterson at NTC Research (now part of Markit) in 2000, and this unique research has been conducted and reported on quarterly ever since. The reason for embarking on this ambitious project was to validate the IPA's hypothesis that there was a close link between advertising expenditure and the wider UK economy as expressed by gross domestic product (GDP) and other measures. If this could be shown to be true, then not only would agencies be better placed to advise their clients, but government, the City, journalists and other opinion formers might begin to take the advertising industry more seriously and to appreciate better its role as the lubricant in the engine of the economy. Given that the Bellwether would be published in advance of other government statistics, if the link were true then it would be a de facto forecaster of the economy and thus provide IPA member agencies and other subscribers with up to six weeks' advance warning of any major movements that might affect their businesses.

Waterson warned the IPA from the outset that the information derived from simple questions such as: 'Has your budget increased, decreased, or stayed roughly the same since we last spoke to you?' might seem superficial, but he predicted that over time the trends and relationships with other data

**FIGURE 6.1**    Pamela Pringle as Madame Arcati in the Nassau Players production of Noel Coward's 'Blythe Spirit' in 1984

Photograph by Tony Betts

sources would become increasingly revealing. This has proved to be the case. The Bellwether sample is drawn from a panel of about 300 decision-makers on marketing expenditure in companies, representing the broad sweep of industries and geographies in the UK. The methodology, which continues today, is based upon Waterson's mantra that such questionnaires should be able to be answered 'without opening a filing cabinet'. The key benefits of this approach in market research terms are that the panel of respondents is relatively stable and the compliance is higher than average, thus leading to a greater consistency in the data.

We now have 10 years' research which has validated the original hypothesis and provided those who use the information with an actionable tool. For example, the market top in 2007 was indicated clearly in the October Bellwether, as was the market bottom in April 2009, and any investor who acted on the latter would have made +50 per cent on the FTSE since then. And its role as a forecaster has been reinforced by the closeness of its correlation with another survey run by the same company that produces Bellwether. This is the 'Purchasing Managers' Index', or PMI, which shares a very similar

**FIGURE 6.2**   Bellwether 10<sup>th</sup> Anniversary Report

12 July 2010                                                              mark**it**

# Bellwether Report

10th anniversary edition (supplement enclosed)

IPA
44 Belgrave Square
London SW1X 8QS

Tel: 020 7235 7020
Fax: 020 7245 9904
Email: info@ipa.co.uk
Web: www.ipa.co.uk

**BDO**

BDO LLP
55 Baker Street
London W1U 7EU

Tel: 020 7486 5888
Web: www.bdo.co.uk

Markit Economics

Henley on Thames
Oxon RG9 1EL, UK

Tel: +44 1491 461 000
Fax: +44 1491 461 001
Email: **economics@markit.com**

The Bellwether Report is researched
and published by Markit Economics on
behalf of the Institute of Practitioners in
Advertising and its sponsor BDO LLP.

The report features original data
drawn from a panel of around 300 UK
marketing professionals and provides
a key indicator of the health of the
economy.

The survey panel has been carefully
selected to represent all key business
sectors, drawn primarily from the nation's
top 1000 companies.

The Bellwether Report is available
via annual subscription.
For all enquiries please contact
economics@markit.com.

**The next Bellwether Report will be
released on:**

**18 October 2010**

The intellectual property rights to the Bellwether
Report provided herein are owned by Markit Group
Limited. Any unauthorised use, including but not
limited to copying, distributing, transmitting or
otherwise of any data appearing is not permitted
without Markit's prior consent.

Markit shall not have any liability, duty or obligation
for or relating to the content or information ("data")
contained herein, any errors, inaccuracies, omissions
or delays in the data, or for any actions taken in
reliance thereon. In no event shall Markit be liable for
any special, incidental, or consequential damages,
arising out of the use of the data.

## Total marketing budgets revised down in Q2, highlighting fragile nature of recovery.

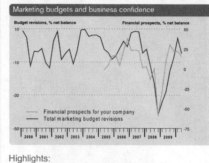

Both series shown on the left
are derived from the *Bellwether*
survey panel of 300 marketing
executives:

**Financial prospects:**
"Taking all things into
consideration, do you feel more or
less optimistic about the financial
prospects for your company than
you did three months ago?"

**Marketing budgets:**
"In the last three months, has
your total marketing budget for
the current financial year been
revised up or down, or is it
unchanged?"

Highlights:

■ Total marketing spend revised down in Q2 2010.
   The *Bellwether* signalled that total marketing budgets were revised down in Q2 amid uncertainty
   regarding the economic outlook. Almost 20% of respondents to the *Bellwether* survey reported
   a downward revision to their 2010 annual budgets, against 15% that reported an increase.
   As a result, the net balance fell to -4.6 in Q2 from +4.5 in Q1. Furthermore, the Q2 downward
   revision to spend suggests that actual spend for 2010 is unlikely to rise at the pace expected
   at the start of the year.

■ Business confidence dipped further in Q2.
   The downward adjustment to spend was linked to a smaller improvement in business confidence,
   with companies upbeat about prospects for their industries as a whole to the lowest degree
   for a year. Similarly, marketing executives were less optimistic about financial prospects for
   their own companies. Nevertheless, around 41% of respondents felt more confident than three
   months previously, against 25% that grew more pessimistic.

■ Third-fastest downgrade to sales promotion budgets in the survey history.
   Main media spend was revised down in Q2, following a modest upgrade in the previous
   quarter. Meanwhile, current year 'all other' and sales promotion budgets were also revised
   down, with the decrease in the latter the fastest since Q1 2009. On a more positive note, direct
   marketing budgets were revised up in Q2, while the internet category also saw a further upward
   adjustment to spend. Nonetheless, the rate of growth was the slowest for three quarters, with
   'paid search' also rising at a slower rate than in Q1.

■ Actual spend in 2009 down for second successive year.
   According to the latest data, actual total marketing spend fell in 2009. Although considerable
   by the historical standards of the *Bellwether*, the annual decline was much slower than in 2008,
   and slightly less pronounced than implied by initial budget setting.

■ UK adspend returns to growth in Q1 2010.
   The rebound in economic activity seen since the peak of the downturn was signalled by the
   *Bellwether* survey in advance of official estimates, and was reflected in the latest data from the
   Advertising Association (AA), which signalled that UK adspend rose for the first time in seven
   quarters during Q1. The Q2 *Bellwether* survey, coupled with PMI data, now suggest that the
   initial strong rebound in economic activity is waning and that the UK economy is now entering
   a phase of slower growth.

                                                                   compiled by markit

**SOURCE:** IPA/BDO Bellwether Q2 2010

methodology (it too was started by Waterson and is now owned by Markit)
and whose sample is drawn from amongst those people responsible for
procurement within companies, which, like investment in advertising and

**FIGURE 6.3**    Bellwether 10th Anniversary Report supplement

12 July 2010

# Bellwether Report 2000 2010
## 10 year summary.

Sir Martin Sorrell, Chief Executive of WPP on who the major players will be on the world's economic stage, how the marketing industry must adapt to the changing nature of communications, and where the unrealised areas of growth are...

THE WORLD has been reset, as Jeff Immelt of GE famously said. The way we consume, the geography of economic growth, the way our industry works, have all changed. Anyone who thinks things will return to where they were before 2008 is deluded. For some, there may be no comeback.

We are pulling out of recession. Although there will be bumps along the way (currently the threats of contagion in western Europe), the global economy – and with it marketing spend – will grow, but not as we have known it. The spotlight has moved to the East and also to the South and the South East.

One can consider the world economy as a series of soccer teams, modelled on the English league system and scored by growth potential. In the Premiership are the BRICs economies as identified by Goldman Sachs – Brazil, Russia, India and China. Also, Goldman's Next 11 – Bangladesh, Egypt, Indonesia, Iran, Mexico, Nigeria, Pakistan, the Philippines, South Korea, Turkey and Vietnam. These represent the powerhouses of growth over the coming decade. WPP, incidentally, has leadership or near-leadership positions in nearly all these countries. In China we have a market-leading 15% market share, for example.

In Division I is the US, recovering from the sub-prime crisis at a faster rate than expected, still the most consistent consumer market in the world, its energy, entrepreneurial spirit and innovation undimmed. In Division II are the laggard nations of Western Europe, in danger of a double-dip recession and permanently diminished status if their Governments do not deal with their debt vigorously.

The new markets, the Premiership stars, already account for 27% of WPP's business. That will soon rise to a third. The tide is running in one direction only – WPP will be more Asian, more Latin American, more African, more Middle Eastern, and more Central and Eastern European.

It will also be more technology-based. New media also currently accounts for 27% of our business. That will rise. Back in 2001, according to the *Bellwether Report*, the internet accounted for 2% of total marketing spend in the UK, rising to 11% by 2009, a figure still considerably behind the percentage of time Britons now spend online. So, fewer newspapers and magazines, new models of television and entertainment, more iPads, iPhones, personal

> "We are pulling out of recession...the global economy – and with it marketing spend – will grow, but not as we have known it."

video recorders and social networking. Mobile advertising, in particular, has huge unrealised potential, especially in China, with 700 million plus subscribers (one operating network alone, China Mobile accounting for 550 million of these) and India with 425 million, a figure that will soon double.

These changes will be ruinous for some media owners. Others – like Rupert Murdoch – understand instinctively that they are in the communications business, and not the newspaper or the television business. Fortunately for us, we need only apply the relevant technology to meet clients' requirements. We are not obliged to place bets on which devices will succeed.

> "The way we consume, the geography of economic growth, the way our industry works, have all changed. Anyone who thinks things will return to where they were before 2008 is deluded. For some, there may be no comeback."

The overall share of traditional areas such as television, radio, newspapers, magazines, outdoor and cinema has declined – in favour of Consumer Insight, Public Relations & Public Affairs, Branding & Identity, Healthcare, and Specialist Communications (which embraces direct, interactive and internet).

Non-traditional marketing services now provide more than 60% of our business. It will eventually reach two-thirds. That means ever more accurate and personal profiling of the tastes of consumers and quantitative analysis of creative ideas. Such measurability is not necessarily welcomed by agencies, but clients demand evaluation, as they must to justify increased marketing spends to their boards. The recession has made that more so.

Clients want more for the same money and that often means integrated solutions. Different specialities must be brought to bear coherently on a campaign. More and more clients are asking us to put together bespoke teams from across WPP, drawing the best talent from the group's many renowned company brands. Thus you have Team Ford, Team Unilever and Team Vodafone.

Egos must be reined in if we are to put clients' interests first. So must traditional ideas about functional pecking orders. Parent or holding companies are increasingly important for clients, even if the trade magazines scoff. It also remains crucial that we consistently recruit the best people from the greatest universities and business schools. Not nick them, when we need them. Talent is king. Paradoxically, human capital is one of the few commodities in short and diminishing supply in a world of overcapacity.

Through all this, innovation and branding remain crucial. You can only do so much cost-cutting, as the American car industry knows. In a world of industrial overcapacity and profitless discounting, differentiation of goods and services through tangible and intangible qualities is crucial. That is what we do and will continue to do.

At the same time, we must encourage people in the US and Western Europe to consume more responsibly. Some companies still treat corporate responsibility as an optional extra, a bit of icing on the capitalist cake. It is not. Doing good is good business. We in the West borrowed too much and overspent. We have to learn to save; the Chinese and Brazilians need to learn to spend.

compiled by markit

**SOURCE:** IPA/BDO Bellwether Q2 2010

marketing communications, is a forward-looking activity. While the fit is not perfect it can be seen that there is a close long-term correlation between PMI, the UK's GDP and expenditure on advertising and marketing communications. A similar relationship has been observed in other economies, albeit with differing ratios.

**FIGURE 6.4**    Bellwether and UK Gross Domestic Product

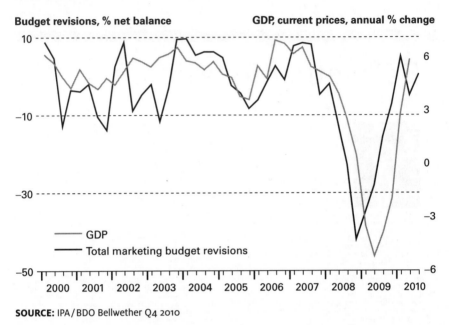

SOURCE: IPA / BDO Bellwether Q4 2010

**FIGURE 6.5**    Bellwether and PMI

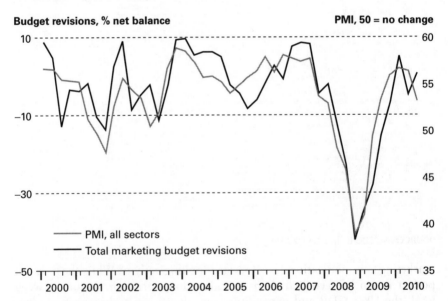

SOURCE: IPA / BDO Bellwether Q4 2010

It's important for media planners to appreciate this correlation for three main reasons:

1 History shows that when there is an economic downturn or recession most marketers and their finance directors have a Pavlovian response: they slash the advertising and marketing communications budget. Bellwether gives planners a pretty good idea in advance that this is going to happen. And of course, those who understand the significance of the relationship between share of voice (SOV) and share of market (SOM) see a recession as a great opportunity to build a brand.

2 At any given point in time there is a finite amount of money in the marketplace and history shows that new media will always struggle to establish a foothold in what is a relatively conservative marketplace. Therefore there is great value to be had for early adopters, not just in terms of price, but also position.

3 In this context another important thing that the Bellwether Report provides is a perspective on the changing shape of the advertising and marketing communications landscape.

**FIGURE 6.6**   Media market share 2010

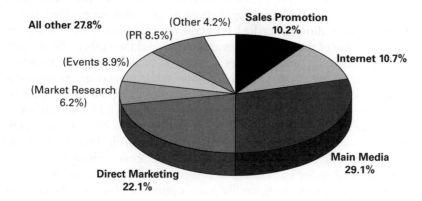

All other 27.8%
(Other 4.2%)
(PR 8.5%)
**Sales Promotion 10.2%**
(Events 8.9%)
**Internet 10.7%**
(Market Research 6.2%)
**Main Media 29.1%**
**Direct Marketing 22.1%**

**SOURCE:** IPA/BDO Bellwether Q4 2010

**FIGURE 6.7**   Media market share 2001

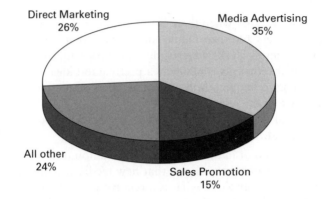

SOURCE: IPA/BDO Bellwether Q4 2001

From the Bellwether's beginning in 2000, internet expenditure has been monitored and observers have been able to see that this sector has gained share steadily every single quarter since. More recently, questions about internet search advertising have been added and again the growth in that key area has been evident, despite the recession of 2009. Taking a long-term overview, there does seem to have been a trend towards more accountable media. This has been evidenced by the increasing share of direct marketing and the internet, while the more traditional media have come under pressure. We can also see that certain types of media seem to be more favoured than others during hard times – for example, price-led sales promotion benefits during a recession when brands have to resort to buying sales while marketing communications activities categorized under 'other', such as exhibitions, tend to suffer.

The Bellwether Report continues to evolve and in 2005 additional questions were included to gauge the confidence levels of marketers, in terms both of their own company and of the market sector in which it operates. Again, we have been able to observe a fairly close correlation with other datasets, but with the Bellwether's advantage of earlier publication. It's also interesting to note that marketers are generally more optimistic about the fortunes of their own company in comparison with their sector, ie their competition!

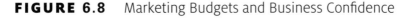

**FIGURE 6.8**  Marketing Budgets and Business Confidence

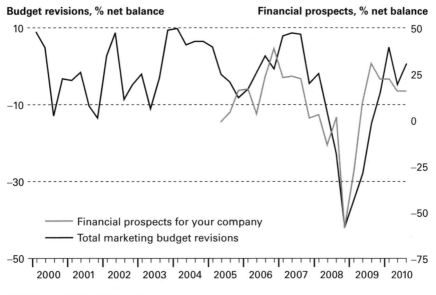

**SOURCE:** IPA/BDO Bellwether Q4 2010

These data are useful for media planners and their clients because they help them to anticipate trends in the marketplace and to take these into account when optimizing the schedule for a brand. The benefit for agency managers has been the ability to look ahead to the likely skill sets that will be needed to serve clients best as the media flow evolves. For financial analysts in the media sector the Bellwether provides them with primary data as a key input to company valuations, while the City at large can use it as an early gauge of sentiment.

Chris Williamson, the chief economist at Markit who has been in charge of producing and writing the Bellwether Report on behalf of the IPA since its inception, has the last word on its value:

> The Bellwether has become one of the most closely watched indicators of marketing and advertising, providing a simple but very timely snapshot of whether spend is rising or falling, and which activities are growing in popularity. In doing so it also gives us an idea of how businesses are coping more generally, for example whether they are in cost-cutting mode or stepping up their investment. The report therefore adds to our knowledge of the economy and, we hope, helps businesses and policymakers to plan more effectively.

# PART THREE
# How to make media work more effectively

# Introduction

In this section of the book, we get down to the practicalities of developing an effective communications strategy for a brand, which will lead to it being interpolated into the media flow in such a way that it intertwines with its target customers' life flows.

Clearly, a fundamental starting point is to ensure that there is an effective budget and we're taking the opportunity to put forward a single-minded recommendation as to how best to set this based on the latest research into the relationship between share of voice and share of market. For the first time, media budgets can be set on the basis of sophisticated data analysis rather than using any number of 'fingers in the air'.

Another crucial building block is a good brief, and here we can rely on the best-practice work that the IPA, ISBA and others have done. We emphasize how important it is for media planners to take the time and trouble to interrogate their client's brief and to make absolutely sure that its cornerstone is a clear statement of hard business objectives as opposed to softer intermediate goals, valuable though they may seem to be. We dwell on the crucial issue of target audience, as a lack of clarity on this key point is so often the undoing of a media strategy.

Nowadays, most people accept that multi-media strategies are more effective than those which rely on a single medium, and we have important confirmation of this from analyses of the IPA Effectiveness Awards. However, less has been written about the reasons why this is the case, and we've set out some explanatory theories which should help media planners in thinking about their strategies and plans. We have also provided guidance in choosing a multi-channel mix and made some suggestions as to how this skill will develop in future as our understanding of the media flow evolves.

# How to set an effective media budget

## 07

The foundation of any successful advertising and marketing communications campaign has to be the budget on which it is based. This is because the brand's strength of presence within the media flow as perceived by customers is in competition with all its direct (and indirect) market competitors. This begs the crucial question of how that budget should be set. Over the past few decades there have been many books, publications and articles which have put forward various ways in which a media budget can be established. One of the notable things about this period in marketing history is the sheer diversity of methodologies proposed, and the lack of rigour of many of them. This can't have done marketers any favours when making their case to their finance directors, chief executives or other senior colleagues. Nor has it been helpful to agencies who have struggled to rationalize their spending recommendations.

For example, Roderick White, in his *Admap* article of December 1999, noted a total of no fewer than 15 ways in which the budget can be set:

1 Intuitive/rule of thumb: 'enough to do the job', based on experience
2 Maintaining previous spend, sometimes inflation adjusted: advertising as fixed cost
3 Percentage of previous sales: backward-looking, compounds failure (or rewards success)
4 'Affordable': what's left after cost and profit requirements are met
5 Residue of last year's profits: focuses on source of funds, not their use
6 Percentage of gross margin: begs questions of cost-efficiency
7 Percentage of forecast sales: most common method
8 Fixed cost per unit of sales: like percentage of turnover
9 Cost per customer/capita: mostly business to business
10 Match competitors: assumes they are right

11  Match share of voice to brand share: like the above

12  Marginal return: direct response approach

13  Task approach: define objectives, and cost out how to reach them. Best in theory, but may require modelling

14  Modelling: the most sophisticated approach, and not easy

15  Media weight tests: looks empirical, but usually difficult to evaluate or replicate.

However, ever since the pioneering work of Simon Broadbent in 1989, John Philip Jones in 1990 and Stephan Buck in 2001, there has been a growing confidence in using the relationship between SOV and SOM as the most important determinant of the budget level required. This relationship has also been explored in detail by the IPA through the torture test of three UK recessions with original analyses by Malik PIMS, and latterly Millward Brown and Data2Decisions. These have shown conclusively that the companies that increase their relative share of voice perform better during recessions and recover more quickly afterwards. Indeed there's a growing realization that economic recessions provide ambitious brand owners with a much better opportunity to build market share than bull markets do.

More recently, there has been a flurry of analytical activity and subsequent publications which have elucidated the relationship between SOV and SOM and made it absolutely central to the process of setting a brand's media budget. First of all there was the seminal *Marketing in the Era of Accountability* by Les Binet of DDB Matrix and Peter Field, marketing consultant, published in 2007 as the second in the IPA Datamine series of monographs. In their key third chapter, on 'Budget setting', they put forward the concept of 'equilibrium SOV', as shown in the figure below:

**FIGURE 7.1**    The concept of equilibrium SOV

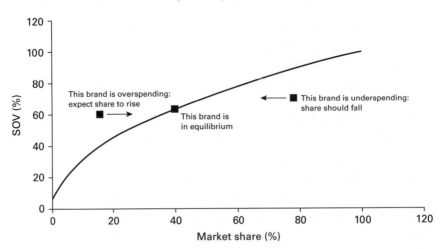

**SOURCE:** *Marketing in the Era of Accountability* (IPA report, 2007)

Binet and Field then went on to provide compelling evidence to show that the relationship between SOV and SOM varies according to the nature of the brand and of the market it's operating in, and thus provides the fundamental parameters for setting the brand's media budget. This was followed up two years later with the publication in July 2009 of the IPA report by Peter Field called *How Share of Voice Wins Market Share*. This presented the findings from a major piece of work by Nielsen Analytic Consulting on fast-moving consumer goods (FMCG) brands, which proved that the key relationship between SOV and SOM not only obtains for the elite IPA Effectiveness Awards campaigns, but also for 'average' brands with 'average' campaigns. Moreover, the comparative analyses of the IPA Effectiveness Awards and Nielsen databases provide benchmarks not only for media budgets, but also for the extra impact that high-quality strategy, media planning and creative content can deliver. The report's key finding was that the critical metric that determines the level of a brand's value market share growth is its extra share of voice (ESOV), defined as SOV minus SOM. Furthermore, the relationship between ESOV and growth still holds for typical brands in the digital era. The report also set out some key guidelines for setting budgets and targets:

1 Share of voice over and above market share delivers growth.
   For an 'average' campaign for an 'average' FMCG brand, expect
   value market share growth of 0.5% per year for each 10 points
   of extra share of voice (ESOV).

2 Significant differences do exist across categories and brands.
   Therefore, it is important that a brand measures its specific
   relationship between SOV and SOM to provide a more accurate
   benchmark.

3 There are certain factors which drive the level of market share
   growth year-on-year. Accelerated growth can be expected by bigger
   brands. Based on a 10 percentage point differential between SOV
   and SOM, on average, FMCG brand leaders can expect 1.4 points of
   growth. Challenger FMCG brands can expect a more modest growth
   of 0.4 points per year. Brands in younger categories also drive greater
   market share gains.

4 Brands benefit from investing in quality (ie more effective)
   campaigns: IPA Effectiveness Awards-grade campaigns respond
   at a significantly higher level (60% more effective) than typical
   ones. Brands benefiting from 'new news' derived from launching or
   re-launching also respond at a higher level (15–25%). For smaller
   brands ESOV alone may not be enough – they will also need to invest
   in quality.

5 During economic downturns, short-term investment cuts damage
   the brand in the long term. Brands that choose to invest in effective
   campaigns and at correct SOV levels during this downturn will
   emerge in a stronger market share position.

**FIGURE 7.2**   Key findings from the IPA Databank and Nielsen

| IPA Databank findings | % growth in share of market (SOM) per 10% points of extra share of voice (ESOV) |
|---|---|
| Services brands | +2.7% |
| Durables brands | +2.4% |
| FMCG brands | +0.8% |
| IPA average across all sectors | +2.2% |
| IPA non-winner average | +1.8% |
| IPA award winner average | +2.4% |

| Nielsen findings | % growth in share of market (SOM) per 10% points of extra share of voice (ESOV) |
|---|---|
| FMCG brand leaders | +1.4% |
| Challenger FMCG brands | +0.4% |
| An 'average' campaign for an 'average' FMCG brand | +0.5% |

**SOURCE:** *How Share of Voice Wins Market Share*, a report of key Nielsen and IPA Databank findings from an IPA seminar, IPA, 2009

From Peter Field's further analyses of the IPA Effectiveness Awards cases for *Brand Immortality*, we now also know that as market categories age the return on extra SOV flattens progressively as they move from new, to growth, maturity and decline. Brands in new categories generate seven per cent more value share growth (in proportional terms) per point of extra share of voice (SOV – SOM) than in the average category. Successful brands in growth markets achieved around one percentage point of market share growth for every seven percentage points that their share of voice exceeded their share of market, whereas in mature categories the ratio is 1:8. In declining markets it falls to 1:12.

From these findings it can be seen that setting the brand's budget is not simply a question of sticking a finger in the air and saying, 'Let's do what we did last year plus a bit for inflation', or asking, 'What's the average advertising to sales ratio?' and matching that. On the contrary, it's a sophisticated analytical process which requires accurate information on the brand's competitive set, its status within it, and the history of advertising and media expenditure in its category. For example, is there a challenger brand which uses innovative media and creative strategies to punch well above its weight?

And what's the previous behaviour of competitor brands during periods of economic recession – do they exhibit the Pavlovian reaction of so many and cut their budgets? Or does the brand leader seize the opportunity to pile on the pressure on the weaker players?

In a downturn there's the knee-jerk reaction by the majority of competitors either to reduce their media budgets or to stop investing altogether, so a brand's share of voice can be increased automatically just by maintaining its expenditure or not reducing it as much as its rivals. Secondly, because there is less demand, the price of all media falls, and thus buying share of voice becomes much cheaper. During the recent recession, TV airtime in the UK was trading at 1980s prices and thus presented an absolute bargain for ambitious brands. The companies that pursue this extra SOV strategy tend not to talk about it for obvious reasons – they know it's giving them massive competitive advantage – but there is anecdotal evidence that the owners of big powerful brands in FMCG markets, such as Procter & Gamble and Reckitt Benckiser, have taken the opportunity to capitalize. We also know that the returns on extra SOV are even greater in markets where the distribution chain is less dominated by a handful of multiple retailers, and thus recessions present brands in durables and services markets with even more potential upside – if they hold their nerve!

And of course it's not just a question of the sheer weight of media money; it's all about the content of the brand's message, and whether or not it is based on a compelling consumer insight resulting in an engaging communication, delivered accurately to its target market. The latest analysis has proven, for the first time, the concrete link between creativity and effectiveness. In 2010, research conducted by Peter Field and commissioned by Thinkbox and the IPA proved, for the first time, the concrete link between creativity and effectiveness.

Field analysed the correlation between a campaign's performance across the creative awards as recognized by The Gunn Report, and its business performance in the IPA Effectiveness Awards (2000–08). The research showed a direct correlation between strong advertising creativity and business success, with creatively awarded campaigns being, on average, 11 times more efficient – indeed, the more awarded the creative work, the more effective it was. An update to this report, extending the time period analysed (1996–2010), was published in June 2011. Not only did this larger sample confirm a strong correlation between creativity and effectiveness, but Field was also able to look at the time trend to creativity, and discovered that creatively-awarded campaigns are becoming more effective over time.

The analysis also revealed that many of these highly awarded campaigns were starved of budget, thus reducing their brand's SOV. In relying largely on creative stand-out, the advertiser was missing a major trick, as increasing the competitive pressure with extra SOV would have achieved far bigger gains in market share. Since these outstanding campaigns are a rarity, if a client has got one it really is a golden opportunity to build their business.

Brand managers and agencies alike need to be aware of these key factors and develop their budget proposals and campaign plans in full recognition of the strength of their authority. Finance directors, marketing directors and agency directors now have the market-based metrics and benchmarks they need to budget and plan advertising and marketing communications expenditure professionally. They also have a proper basis on which to assess agency performance. No agency or marketing client can guarantee to continue to deliver the same level of business performance for a brand if ESOV is falling as a result of under-investment in media and marketing communications. Brand strategy and creative content that are exceptional in effectiveness terms can mitigate the effects of declining ESOV for a time, but sooner or later 'gravity' will assert itself and the brand will suffer. Clearly, it would now be ludicrous to expect a campaign to increase a challenger brand's market share in an FMCG category without acknowledging the budget level required to do so. Or, if the brand lacks the necessary financial firepower, it must be determined to have the degree of strategic insight, channel management skill and creative inspiration to compensate.

So ESOV is a key metric for any payment by results (PBR) model which has a business results component – the setting of objectives without a counterbalancing measure of scale of investment (eg ESOV) is not a sound basis for the contract between agency and client. In future we would expect that any sensible and fair agency incentive agreements would be agreed in the context of these parameters. Indeed, it would be prudent if brand marketers' and marketing procurement professionals' own bonus schemes were framed in the same way, especially as this would reinforce the importance of the underlying brand metrics to their boards.

Using the model of the media flow makes eminent sense of the importance of SOV in relationship to SOM and its variations according to brand size, market category, market life stage and the nature of the message. Hundreds of thousands of brands are swimming in the media flow which customers are dipping in and out of for nearly half their waking hours. So the competition is incredibly intense. Bigger brands have an inherent advantage, as Ehrenberg first showed with his 'double jeopardy' analyses, largely because they are relatively dominant in the distribution system. FMCG markets are incredibly tough because they are dominated by very powerful distribution and retail chains whereas brands operating in less constricted sectors such as services have much more freedom to manoeuvre in the flow. New brands in new markets, and brands with 'new news' to impart, have an advantage, because human beings are like magpies with silver objects when it comes to novelty. Brands that produce truly outstanding creative content and achieve true fame not only stand out in the flow, they generate valuable word-of-mouth and third-party recommendation. Brands that spend enough money and marshal all their media resources to provide more prominent and multiple touch points for their customers do better than those who under-invest.

# The importance of a good brief

## 08

The client brief is an early hurdle at which the agency media strategist can fall. Too often it will not supply sufficient, clear, or even accurate information. There is a technical term for this problem and the strategy that will result: 'crap in, crap out'. But the responsibility for this is not solely the client's – it also rests with the agency strategist, whose first responsibility is to interrogate the client's brief to ensure that it provides all the necessary information and data, including a specified hard business objective. If it doesn't (and you can generally assume that it won't all be entirely clear), additional discussions must take place. Gratifyingly, the recent research by ISBA to update the joint industry best-practice guide on briefing revealed that a significant number of UK advertisers are now using the questions proposed in the original guide published in 2003 as the basis for their briefs to their agencies:

- Where are we now?
- Where do we want to be?
- What are we doing to get there?
- Who do we need to talk to?
- How will we know when we have arrived?

Thus one simple way of envisaging the client's brief (and the strategist's interrogation of it) is to treat the business challenge as a bridge and then answer two questions relating to first one end of it, and then the other: 'Where are we now?' and 'Where do we want to be?'

It is the job of the agency to build the bridge between these two points, and to put in place the measurement systems to make sure that the brand actually arrives at the other end. Most media agencies will operate their own internal briefing process and adapt their client's brief to it. However, the key areas of information are usually as follows.

**FIGURE 8.1**   Where are we now, and where do we want to be?

Photograph by Max Gibbons

## 1. Where are we now?

Analysis of the IPA Effectiveness Awards database for *Brand Immortality* has shown conclusively that certain strategies are more effective than others, depending on the life stage of the market category that the brand is operating in. Thus, the first thing for the media strategist to do is to establish whether the brand's sector is new, growing, mature or in decline, and accept that this is the fundamental operational context. Having done so, a more detailed inspection of the competitive position needs to be undertaken, and this should include pricing, distribution, market share by value and volume, consumer usage of and attitudes towards the brand and its opposition, and their respective positionings, as expressed by packaging, advertising and marketing communications campaigns. This strengths, weaknesses, opportunities and threats (SWOT) analysis provides the essential definition of the starting point at one end of the bridge from which the brand must embark on its journey to the other side.

## 2. Where do we want to be?

As we shall discuss in more detail in the chapter on media strategy, it's vital to nail down in the brief the hard business objective such as increasing market share, reducing price sensitivity or improving profitability. It's also important to specify any behavioural objectives such as increasing penetration through trial or retrieving lapsed users, and intermediate objectives such as building brand awareness or enhancing brand image. And it's essential to understand the distribution system the client operates within, what aspirations they have for improving their position and how the media strategy can help.

As analyses by David Cowan of Forensics have demonstrated, even at high levels of distribution relatively small improvements in the availability of the brand can make an enormous difference in terms of its market performance. It's likely that there are several distribution channels wherein the brand has differential levels of presence and thus valuable room for improvement. For example, are sales mainly through wholesalers supplying high-street retailers, or is a dealer or intermediary network involved? Is the brand market sector dominated by powerful multiple retailers who make relentless demands on the brand for promotional, advertising and marketing communications support? Is there a direct interface between the end user via the company's outbound telesales operation, or via its online search advertising linking to its website and e-commerce platform? Does the brand have its own retail outlets or a direct response vehicle such as a catalogue? Or perhaps the brand employs a sales force or has party planners?

The media strategy can have an influence on all these distribution systems, and both client and agency need to agree on realistic targets for each of them. For example, if it's direct response, what capacity will the call centre, stock control and despatch teams have? If it's a campaign which needs to support the client's sales force's attempt to improve the brand position within national grocery multiples, what media channels are going to have the most influence? And if the goal is to increase the proportion of sales taking place via e-commerce, does the website have the necessary scalability? How competitive is the market for the relevant search terms?

## 3. What are we doing to get there?

What is the client doing in marketing terms to get there? Are they renaming, repackaging and relaunching their brand? Introducing a new flavour?

Increasing the price? Opening new stores? Launching an application for mobile? Clearly the media strategy needs to be developed in full coordination with the marketing activities to deliver them. For example, for a motor manufacturer, these might be any one of: launch a new model, introduce a new used-car guarantee, promote a special offer on after-sales service or build strong brand equity for the marque as a whole. Hold on, you could argue, it could be all four of these. Yes, it could be, and they certainly aren't mutually exclusive, but there has to be a clear understanding of what the most important marketing activity is – there is no point in building long-term brand equity if the company goes out of business because it's not shifting enough metal!

# 4. Who do we need to talk to?

It's crucially important to developing an effective advertising and marketing communications strategy for a brand to identify the precise target audience. Despite the fact that a vast market research industry has grown up to help advertisers and their agencies achieve clarity on target audience, it still requires the very practical ability to empathize with customers and really understand the role that the brand plays in their lives to come to the right conclusion about whom to talk to and in which media. Too often (and this is exacerbated by the overly rapid turnover of employees and the cult of youth at the expense of experience), the target audience for a brand is based either on a false premise or on a received view which has not been challenged for many years.

Take, for example, the seemingly indestructible myth that it's possible to increase a brand's frequency of purchase by its main users by using advertising, which is reinforced on a weekly basis by misleading trade press reports and articles. This false premise, based on a misunderstanding of the nature of 'loyalty', results in millions of pounds being invested in campaigns which are directed at the wrong people using a model of advertising that has been proven fallacious for decades. The only way for our brand to increase its market share is by stealing customers from other brands. And from all the statistical analysis by the likes of Andrew Ehrenberg, Gerald Goodhardt, Chris Chatfield and latterly Byron Sharp, we know that this opportunity lies amongst light or infrequent users of our brand, not its regular or heavy ones. It is in the nature of mass media that in communicating to these prospects it's more than likely that our brand's messages will also be seen by our existing users and thus help retain them.

The $O_2$ campaign of 2005, which has often been described incorrectly as designed to increase loyalty, was in fact hugely successful not for that reason but because it recruited so many new users who liked the way the brand was treating its existing customers. Hence the name of its Gold Award-winning IPA Effectiveness Awards case in 2006: '$O_2$ – The best way to win new customers? Talk to the ones you already have: the story of $O_2$, Chapter 2'. So, talking to existing customers, with the right messages and in the right tone of voice, turned out to be a more effective acquisition strategy than the previous 'acquisition-driven' approach.

Within the overall question of 'Who do we need to talk to?' the supplementary ones are: exactly who are you trying to reach and influence, how often, where (locality), when (key times, days or periods) and how/in what environment? In theory, these shouldn't be difficult questions to answer, but in practice they can prove to be so and all too often are not resolved with the degree of precision necessary to generate the most effective strategy. Let's take each of them in turn.

## 'Who?'

Probably the most consistently 'fudged' part of the brief is the question of whom the advertising is targeting. Too many briefs still state that the target is everybody or mostly everybody. In our experience it rarely is, or should be. This will invariably come back to the business objectives – for example, whether a brand is looking to increase its market share either through increased penetration or by reducing its price sensitivity. 'Yes, but I want to achieve both' is a nice goal to have but is probably unrealistic and certainly won't allow for a clear targeting strategy. Famously, the 'Guinnless' campaign, run for the Irish dark beer in the 1980s, set out with the objective to get infrequent Guinness drinkers to drink just the very occasional extra pint, which made it easy to target and, more importantly, it worked. Additionally, there is the issue of 'influencers', which is particularly relevant to certain product sectors and audiences, eg baby food products where mothers will often rely on advice from their peer groups, friends, families and professional bodies. In these instances it's vital to target both the purchaser and their key influencers.

**FIGURE 8.2**    Mothers are hungry for baby advice

Photograph by Christophe Beauvais

It's very important to be clear with whom the brand needs a dialogue, and both qualitative and quantitative research are key to understanding the target audience. As we have seen from our overview of the UK media research landscape, the industry is now armed with an abundance of data – from joint industry media research such as BARB to the IPA's own TouchPoints survey – which enables the identification of the media habits of not only standard classified audiences (age, sex and social demographic) but also most other consumer classifications. But all this has no value unless the strategist determines exactly whom the communications should be targeting.

The following are some of the more common ways of defining target audiences. This is not a definitive set, merely examples designed to provoke thought and a thorough examination of the company's or the brand's true audience. As we saw above, intermediaries might be an important audience for the brand, and these include wholesalers, retailers and their employees, agents, re-sellers, representatives, brokers, franchisees, professional advisors and opinion formers. Customers might be defined as potential or new, existing or lapsed, with a range of user profiles described in various ways, including light, medium, heavy, infrequent, occasional, frequent, promiscuous, loyal or non-user. Plus a whole range of demographics such as gender, age, social class, educational attainment, employment status, marital or partner status, with or without children, and ethnicity.

Research sources such as TGI offer segmentations according to degrees of agreement with a whole range of lifestyle statements, such as people who are keen on value for money, who like to try new products, who tend to buy branded goods, who tend to prefer own brand or private label, and those who support brands associated with charities or good causes. IPA TouchPoints offers a plethora of ways to look at people, including their moods by time of day and in relation to their media usage and other activities. It's also easy to identify people via geo-demographics, such as those who live in upmarket residential neighbourhoods, in areas with large numbers of people of non-British origin or in parts of the country with relatively high crime rates. Techno-demographics can also be a useful segmentation tool that allows the media strategist to go after people who live in homes with multi-channel TV or who are early adopters of new technologies such as iPads or Kindles.

For decades, data mining has been a powerful tool, and there are myriad ways in which a database can be sliced and diced into non-responders, responders, buyers, recent buyers and buyers on promotion. And with the advent of online behavioural targeting, the media strategist can use the data-mining approach to target ever more tightly defined clusters and to see in real time if their approach is working. The algorithms being employed enable the placing of interest-based advertising, which relates to the topics being searched for or looked at on websites. This increases the utility of the brand communication for the web surfer, especially if they are in purchasing mode. There's much more on this key area in the full Client Brief and the Communication Strategy best-practice guides, both of which can be found on the IPA website.

## 'How often?'

This is a complex and, to some extent, a judgemental question. Clearly the empirical IPA studies on the relationship between share of voice and share of market, the link between creativity and effectiveness in relation to SOV, and adstock data (based on the client's historical advertising weights) can help. However, there are a number of other considerations, which include competitive activity, whether the product is in a high- or a low-interest sector (a top of the range car versus a paper towel), the purchase cycle (insurance is normally purchased once a year, while tea is drunk most days) and how impactful the message is, both the creative content (original and dramatic versus conventional) and the format (big versus small spaces or long versus short spot length). While it is often difficult to be precise, it's critically important to make a judgement on the required frequency for the campaign, both within a specific period and over time, because it will have a significant impact on the media choice or combination of media – TV and national press tend to be relatively low-frequency media, while posters and radio tend to be much higher.

## 'Where?'

If the product is distributed and sold nationally, then you will probably want to do something country-wide, but if it's only available in Des Moines, it's probably best to advertise only in Des Moines! However, there can be additional considerations and opportunities outside of this approach. In the case of national products, there may well be 'hot spots' in certain regions or areas which could justify an up-weight or even concentration of the activity into just those most lucrative locations. If the product is available only in Des Moines, it may well be that people will travel from further afield to buy the product or that 'spreading its fame' will generate demand and eventual distribution and sales elsewhere. Some years ago, when Sainsbury's was largely concentrated in southern England and was running its 'Where good food costs less' campaign, it purposefully used national magazines covering people in areas of Britain who had never even seen a Sainsbury's store. Interestingly, they found that the advertising was successful in establishing a strong reputation for the brand amongst shoppers who had never used their supermarket, which in turn helped Sainsbury's launch new stores successfully in the north of England some years later, despite strong local competitors.

In a similar vein, when luxury toiletries brand Molton Brown was in the early stages of developing its reputation, it carried out a long-term sampling programme on cruise ships. Small bottles of its body wash product were provided in all the bathrooms and holidaymakers were able to enhance their sense of relaxation and pampering by using these high-quality products while in a calming, positive environment. And of course, when they returned to dry land and discovered that the brand was sold only from a shop in London's exclusive Molton Street, this added to the brand's cachet.

**FIGURE 8.3**    Sampling on holiday can heighten the experience

Reproduced by permission of Molton Brown

## 'When?'

Timing will often seem to be self-determining. If a product is only or predominantly available on a certain day or at certain times of year (eg *The Sunday Times* on a Sunday, Easter eggs at Easter or sun tan lotion in the summer), it makes sense to coincide the advertising with those times. The same can apply to purchasing behaviour, both by day of week and seasonally – weekday versus weekend, Christmas gift shopping, booking holidays etc.

There is also the further consideration as to when the desired audience is likely to be most open to the message. So a busy mother is likely to be more receptive later in the evening after the family has been settled, or a businessman is more likely to be relaxed on a Sunday evening having had the weekend to recover from work. Thus, timing can be planned carefully, but it doesn't always have to be exactly in line with purchasing peaks. This is because the advertising may have a longer-term role to play in building the brand, and may be about more than a purchase now, tomorrow or the next week.

We would argue that while the value of short-term responses and sales should never be underestimated, the power of longer-term branding and reputation building has potentially greater value. In this context, the variable pricing of the various media by day of week or time of year becomes a key consideration. So, in the cases of 'where' and 'when', the superficial answer is 'fish where the fish are', but the better answer is 'certainly fish where the fish are, as well as where they are likely to be in future'.

## 'How?'

This final question is an environmental and creative one. If a medium or media have been mandated in the brief by the client or another agency without proper consideration or consultation, good media strategists should challenge this immediately, otherwise they will be effectively operating with one hand tied behind their back. The mantra now is 'don't start with an ad', because there are an increasing number of communication vehicles (the owned and the earned) that do not necessarily involve a conventional advertisement. Any brief that prescribes a predetermined choice of media to be used (or more specifically, what media can't be used), runs the risk of being less effective than when the options are kept open.

The strategist should have the freedom to consider all the possible 'bought' media opportunities like TV, cinema, radio, out-of-home, newspapers, magazines, direct mail, online mobile, point-of-purchase and sponsorship. All the brand's 'owned' media must also be taken into account, such as their employees, customer magazines, catalogues, websites, customer mailings, e-mails, call centres, packaging, sales promotions, 'branded content' – the engaging material (eg a book, film or TV channel) made by a brand that appears in the culture (eg a bookstore, online, on TV) in non-paid-for media – and brand experiences such as promotional events, exhibitions, field force sampling, product demonstrations, vending machines, kiosks, dedicated retail outlets or shops-within-a-shop and even their head office building. Public relations activity to generate 'earned' media has become increasingly important, as have the social media channels such as blogs, Facebook, Twitter and LinkedIn. And, of course, the media strategist must establish how all these channels will link back to the client's website and e-commerce business.

Why would a communications strategist discard these potential opportunities and the exciting combinations of 'bought', 'owned' and 'earned' media to create the optimal strategy for the brand? So 'how' should be about ways the message can be most effectively communicated, meaning which channels and formats can best reach the audience and deliver the message. 'How' should also be answered in the context of the creative brief: what is the message that is going to be communicated, and how can the media strategy both inform and influence the creative approach in terms of how it might be executed across the various media channels and platforms?

# 5. How will we know when we have arrived?

Having travelled this far, the media strategist might be forgiven for wanting to lie down and rest! However, the work is not complete until a clearly defined set of correct criteria have been established by which the direction of travel and indeed arrival at the destination can be measured. Media strategy is an iterative process whereby the solution is proposed, accepted by the client and translated into a plan which is then tested in the marketplace, evaluated, revised and re-proposed to the client for another cycle of implementation.

Experience has shown that over and over again one of the simplest ways to establish whether or not a campaign is working is by setting up test and control areas or regions, ie where the brand campaign is either not in the flow at all, or is, but to a much lesser degree than elsewhere. Ingeniously, the famous BMW case by Tim Broadbent at agency WCRS which won the IPA Effectiveness Awards Grand Prix in 1994, used Germany, France and Italy as the 'control' vis-à-vis the UK market! A similar effect can be achieved by utilizing staggered starting points for a campaign, differential media weights or ideally no advertising and marketing communications at all versus a full campaign. So whenever possible it's extremely useful to establish test and control regions in order to be able to determine the return on marketing investment more easily.

In the absence of a test and control opportunity, it is possible to use econometric modelling to try to tease out all the different factors that contributed to a brand's success or otherwise, but it's not easy and quite expensive – one problem is a phenomenon called 'multi-colinearity', which makes it impossible to tease apart the effect of individual channels when they run together consistently across time. More on this topic can be found in the IPA guide *Econometrics Explained*, co-authored by Les Binet, Louise Cook and Mike Holmes.

## Going the extra mile

All of the above is important basic information, but the great media strategist's due diligence should go far beyond this. Good ones will take pride in trying to get under the skin of a client's business. This may be achieved through data analysis, possibly some econometric modelling and even detailed analysis of the client's historical ROMI performance. But it also needs personal involvement as well.

Creative people will tell you that inspiration often stems from understanding a brand's 'essence', and this can be achieved by visiting the factory and the R&D department to understand the ingredients or components of the product. Insights can also be gained by sitting in on the call centre, talking to the sales force, attending focus groups, working in the store or becoming a customer of the product or service as well as those of its competitors. Doing as many things as possible to 'live' the brand experience from both inside and outside the company can so often lead to creative inspiration rooted in how the brand fits into people's lives.

Exactly the same is true for media strategists. One of the best worked on the Alfa Romeo account. Neel Desor was a pretty good media planner, but his real strength was that he loved Alfa Romeos. In fact, he knew more about Alfas than just about anybody else in the world, which impressed everyone he worked with, but most of all the client. Being amongst the marque's true aficionados enabled him to empathize deeply with the Alfa owner or prospect and to come up with media strategies that were a level above the norm. For Alfa Romeo part of the challenge was to ensure that Alfas were seen alongside the likes of BMW and Audi as well-built, prestige cars with a sporting heritage. However, it was also recognized that Alfas would never compete effectively with German cars on their own territory – engineering precision and perfection. The overall Alfa proposition of 'Cuore Sportivo' (Sporting heart) was translated into a media strategy that identified that those likely to be more responsive were people who displayed a passion for how they lived – what they ate, what they wore, their hobbies and of course what they drove. Crucially, it was also about their media consumption, so the strategy was as much about where the advertising appeared as about the content and Alfa Romeo adopted a single-minded focus on moments of intense involvement across all media. For example, the only Alfa advertising that appeared on ITV was in the F1 Grand Prix coverage. Neel was not only the strategist on the business but also part of the target audience as evidenced by his ownership of a beautiful silver Alfa GTV.

**FIGURE 8.4**   The best planners empathize with the brand

Reproduced by permission of Alfa Romeo

In summary, we would urge all media strategists to ensure they have a good brief from their client which includes a clear and focused hard business objective for the brand to achieve. If not, he or she must be prepared to challenge the brief and badger the client in order to secure the necessary clarity of direction and adequacy of information. The strategist must also have a clear picture of the persuasion model they are working with, and be very specific as to what business, behavioural and intermediate measures need to be taken in order to establish progress and to include these in their recommendations to their client. After all, the lion's share of the brand's advertising and marketing communications budget is spent on putting the brand into the media as opposed to paying for production. So the financial responsibility that sits on the shoulders of the media strategist, and their client, should be taken very seriously indeed.

# Developing a successful media strategy

## 09

For the media planner, strategy development is a potentially intimidating concept. This is because, in the modern digital world, there are so many media channels and platforms available that the environment has become much more challenging and the thought processes are rather demanding. That's why we've chosen some Dilbert cartoons to lighten things up!

## FIGURE 9.1

Reproduced by permission of United Media

Here are the main factors that the media strategist needs to contend with nowadays:

- Media has fragmented, making it harder to find mass audiences in traditional advertising channels.

- Consumers are under increasing time pressure in their lives, making their attention harder to attract and leaving their patience in shorter supply.

- The internet has provided an unprecedented source of information to consumers about brands that would have been previously the subject of offline advertising.

- The digitization of media has armed consumers with tools (eg personal video recorders, anti-banner and anti-spam software) to edit out the ads.
- New channels (eg live brand experiences) have emerged, and existing ones, such as couponing via mobiles, are providing many more advertising options.

This new environment demands a holistic approach to planning how a brand engages its audience, and communication strategy has moved centre stage. It means that, whereas once the creative content of messages was the priority, nowadays we must consider the creative content *and* the media channel equally. And where individual channel activity was often treated separately, we must now plan it together. The old distinction between 'above and below the line' has become meaningless, and we must conceive a media strategy in the context of the entirety of touch points between brand and consumer. While in the past brands placed their advertising only in the time and space bought between programmes and editorial, now they can also develop their dialogue with customers in their owned and earned media channels. Media planners still argue about the merits of 'drip' versus 'burst' in the flighting of campaigns, or the importance of 'recency' as opposed to 'frequency'. But nowadays the increasing power of owned and earned media are rendering these debates less meaningful as brands can be present in the flow on a continuous basis (while not forgetting the importance of share of voice as we have demonstrated in the chapter on budget setting). In the face of this complexity it can be difficult to know where to start, so in order to make sense of this wealth of choice it is worth using these broad guidelines:

1 Strategy is simply the basis of a plan to achieve an objective. Therefore, the starting point must be to understand the objectives and then develop the best strategy to deliver them.

2 The best strategies require sacrifice: it's not just a question of what the strategy sets out to achieve – it's as important to set out what it isn't going to do.

3 Much in media is scientific and quantifiable, but good strategy also requires judgement and intuition, so it shouldn't just emerge from research and data.

4 The strategy is not a media plan – it is the basis upon which the media plan is created and thus it has to be executable, ie translatable, into a viable media laydown, which includes being affordable. Integration is no longer an innovation, it's an imperative.

# 1. Objectives

So how do you begin the process of developing the media strategy? If it's all about delivering against the objectives, then defining and understanding them has to be the starting point. And sometimes there's a confusion right here at the outset between an objective and a strategy.

## FIGURE 9.2

Reproduced by permission of United Media

A simple way to clarify this is that the statement of an objective should begin with the word 'to', as in 'to increase brand share by 5 per cent'. On the other hand a strategy should begin with the word 'by', as in 'by introducing a new low-fat variety'.

The meta-analysis of the cases in the IPA Effectiveness Awards Databank by Les Binet and Peter Field has proven beyond reasonable doubt that those campaigns which are based upon a concrete business objective, like recruiting new users or decreasing price sensitivity, as opposed to intermediary effects such as increasing brand awareness or changing attitudes, are far more likely to deliver a significant return on marketing investment. Hard business objectives include brand goals like increasing its market share (ideally value as opposed to volume) by creating consumer desire for the brand through emotional affinity and improved perceptions of quality. Other objectives might be reducing its price sensitivity by building the perceived relative quality of the brand, or improving profitability by increasing price and/or by reducing the reliance on price-promoted sales. But having an agreed hard business objective will make a fundamental difference to the communications strategy. For example, if the goal is to make it possible for the brand to increase its prices without leading to a damaging decline in sales by reducing the price sensitivity of the brand, then the resulting communications will be somewhat different from those arising from an objective of building volume through encouraging trial.

Peter Field's analyses for *Brand Immortality* shed further light on the importance of having the right objectives and an appreciation of their hierarchy:

> Objectives can be broadly divided into three types: business objectives (such as have already been discussed), behavioural objectives (such as penetration and loyalty) and intermediate objectives (such as brand awareness, brand image and so on). A clear priority is shown by the Databank: business objectives should

dominate behavioural objectives, which should dominate intermediate objectives. Campaigns which observe this hierarchy with appropriately prioritized objectives are twice as effective as those that don't. It is of course perfectly sensible to set and monitor secondary intermediate objectives, especially if one can be confident that they are directionally consistent with the desired business outcomes. For example, creating awareness of a new or little known brand is likely to help drive trial and hence share. But the important primary objectives in this case are firstly share and then trial whilst there will be many other secondary intermediate factors that will contribute to success (such as emotional affinity with the brand and perceptions of differentiation and quality). One of the most important general findings of the Databank is that the pursuit of single intermediate objectives generally reduces effectiveness – marketing needs to target broad shifts across many intermediate factors to improve its chances of success.

# 2. Sacrifice

If you set out to do too much, and in the wrong order of importance, you will be in serious danger of doing nothing effectively. Great strategies, like great creative ideas, require sacrifice: sacrifice of secondary objectives; sacrifice of non-core audiences; and sacrifice of 'nice to have' but non-essential commercial and financial targets.

## FIGURE 9.3

Reproduced by permission of United Media

Great strategies have to be single-minded and have the confidence to exclude everything that isn't essential to delivering the agreed objective. They shouldn't be encumbered with provisos which require that the strategy will only be accepted if it also covers all of the client's business/marketing challenges or all the other theoretical stakeholders in the process, eg the sales force has got to like it, as have the overseas investors, and the PLC board. (Incidentally, if it's successful we promise you all the stakeholders will not just like the strategy, they will love it!)

# 3. Judgement and intuition

We are fortunate as media practitioners in that we have a lot of research and data available to us and we should use it unstintingly. But though research, data and analysis can help the process a lot, it cannot alone come up with the overall answer – that's down to interpretation, along with human judgement and even intuition. Furthermore, there is a potential risk in an over-reliance on research and analysis: it looks at the past, and even when it tries to identify future behaviour, that will always be framed by existing views and experiences. As a media researcher once described research and econometric modelling: 'It's a bit like rowing a boat – you have a perfect panoramic view of where you have been and how you have got there but you can't see the rapids in front of you.' As an example, for all of the forecasting by the telecommunications business, not a single mobile phone producer was able to predict the staggering use of text messaging, let alone the use of that facility as a central part of the strategic proposition to potential cell phone consumers.

**FIGURE 9.4**   The best media planners combine linear and lateral thinking

SOURCE: IPA

The importance of these complementary analytical and intuitive skills has been validated by a five-year IPA research project through John Gage and Sarah MacPherson at specialist consultancy AgencyPeople. Their research showed that the combination of top-level ability in 'linear' or inductive logic and 'lateral' or creative thinking was highly correlated with success in all the key job roles in an agency, including media. This combination of thinking abilities has been christened 'Diagonal Thinking', and those who possess it are able to switch seamlessly from linear to lateral mode.

Thus, top media planners can not only scrutinize a mass of data and appreciate the relative weighting of key factors, but they can also see patterns and have creative insights into the process. And when presented with a creative idea they can see immediately how data can be used to support the arguments in its favour. Two years' data gleaned from the Diagonal Thinking

Self-Assessment tool (**http://www.diagonalthinking.co.uk/**) shows that only 10 per cent of the UK population have this special thinking skill. So, thank heavens that in the highly sophisticated and increasingly scientific process of setting a media strategy, human interpretation, intuition and ideas are as important now as they have ever been.

# 4. Executability

Strategy is not execution, which is why a media plan is not a media strategy. A media plan is the translation of the strategy into its execution, across the various media channels and platforms, to best effect. However, the strategy has to be executable, because there is no point in creating a strategy that is impossible to implement. For example, a client once suggested that the strategy should be advertising on the BBC – admittedly he was American and he hadn't been in the UK long, but it was still a difficult moment for the agency!

**FIGURE 9.5**

Reproduced by permission of United Media

Obviously the strategy has to be affordable, but the budget constraint that may or not be put on the strategy is, like the plan, generally an issue of execution. In purist terms, the budget should be the last consideration in the development of the strategy. And even then it should generally have little or no effect on how the strategy is set. Why? Because the budget should not dictate what the strategy should be. The same strategy should be developed, irrespective of whether the budget is £10 or £10 million. Going back to our client who wanted to advertise on the BBC, which of course was not possible, the strategy probably should have been something like: 'The advertising should reach BBC One viewers in media and environments they have specially chosen.' What this allows for is an execution that will deliver BBC One viewers in a media environment they have a particular affinity with, even though it won't be on a BBC channel, which is probably what the client was really trying to say. The budget should not dictate the strategy. However, it will clearly have an impact, particularly with regard to the frequency of communications and the length of time the campaign runs. So if the strategy calls for continuous advertising at a high frequency over an extended period of time, but the budget is only £11.50, there will be a problem. Therefore, you cannot entirely divorce the budget from the development of the strategy and that's why setting the budget has a chapter all to itself.

Execution of the strategy, which is effectively the media plan, is a very different part of the process. A smart strategy should give the media planner a lot of freedom to select the media channels and determine how they should be used, both individually and in combination. What does this mean in practice? The best strategies are simple but precise statements that reflect and encapsulate the business, marketing and advertising objectives of the brief and provide clarity, understanding and inspiration for the purpose of producing and executing the media plan. But of course, the strategy has to reflect the opportunity to use and leverage the multitude of media platforms and channels now available – the world of bought, owned and earned media which comprise the media flow, which consumers now dip in and out of at will.

## 5. Integration

In the old days it was not unusual to build a plan around a single medium – say television – and maintain the same or a similar campaign structure as for previous years – say two or three periods of advertising during peak sales periods, maybe spring and autumn. There was nothing wrong with this at the time, particularly if there was a proven history of success. However, it would now be deemed correctly to be lazy and inadequate thinking.

**FIGURE 9.6**

Reproduced by permission of United Media

In the modern world of digital media, where there are both many more options and a much greater degree of complexity, far more precision is required in translating the communication (and business) requirements into the media strategy and then turning that into a media plan. Media strategies can support the core business and advertising requirement, which will still normally require a sales response, but may also include communications designed to leverage a brand's wider consumer proposition and assets. And media strategies now need to be clear on how they want consumers to respond to the brand's advertising and wider communication activity. Clearly a sales response of some kind is usually going to feature, but this can be augmented with a strategy designed to create advocacy, particularly amongst key consumer groups. For example, through:

- its promotional activity, either through the paid media, online or in store;
- its links with other 'consumer-facing activities' in sport, music etc;
- its corporate social responsibility (CSR) aspirations;
- its website or links/sponsorship of other websites;
- its e-commerce programme.

## FIGURE 9.7

Reproduced by permission of United Media

As in the past, activity in a core medium (say television) may still be part of the answer, and a large part of the answer at that; however, it would be not just surprising but also highly unlikely for this to be the only answer. Consumers continue to have a healthy appetite for traditional media – broadcast, print, out-of-home, in fact all of them. But consumers are also increasingly adept at multi-tasking in their increasingly immersive media behaviour, for example being online and texting at the same time as they are watching TV or listening to the radio. They also expect their favourite media, whether feature films, TV or radio programmes, newspaper or magazine articles etc, to provide additional information, activities and interactivity. Nowadays, a consumer's experience doesn't begin and end with just the programme or article. They want to know more, they want to comment on and discuss it, and often they want to do or buy something associated with it. The modern digital media world is designed to deliver this to consumers, whether it's providing catch-up TV, YouTube, a mobile application or additional information online; whether it's texting, blogging, tweeting, joining an online forum or Facebooking; and whether it's a coupon, direct mail, telephone number or a purchase online.

## FIGURE 9.8

Reproduced by permission of United Media

Consumers regard brands and their advertising in exactly the same way – if they like them they want more information about them, they want to talk about them and (ideally) they want to buy them. In fairness, this has always been the case, but what is now different is that there are many more media channels and platforms in the flow that can help and enable consumers to do this. Effective communications leverage all these opportunities, and normally most successfully when they are used in combination, ie the combination of bought, owned and earned media. The strategy, therefore, has to recognize this and provide the direction to generate a campaign that takes advantage of the world of new digital opportunities along with, of course, the more traditional media.

# 10  Why using multi-media works

The IPA Effectiveness Awards were founded in 1980 so we now have a wealth of data over a period of over 30 years based on case histories entered into the most rigorous competition of its kind in the world. Clearly this data does not represent the mass market of advertising, media and marketing communications campaigns. Rather it represents best practice and therefore provides important lessons for marketers and their agencies seeking to improve performance in driving their businesses forward. As well as over 1,200 cases, the additional assets generated by the IPA Effectiveness Awards programme are the author questionnaires which have to be completed as part of the entry process. The questionnaire has over 200 data fields covering more than 30 topics, so it generates a mass of information which can be analysed to produce insights into best practice at the very highest levels of strategic thinking, channel planning and content development.

One of many useful things that we can look at is the number of media or channels of commercial communication that have been deployed by the campaigns documented in these excellent case histories. As can be seen from the table, there has been a slow but steady increase in the number of media used by the winners of the competitions which are open to campaigns with budgets of any size. In the 1980s when the author questionnaire offered just nine media options, about two were being used, whereas in recent years, as the number available has increased steadily, so too has the average number employed, reaching nine in the 2010 competition.

There's a slightly different, but not unexpected pattern in the relatively new IPA Effectiveness Awards competition limited to brands with budgets under £2.5 million where the average used has risen to about six channels, with just over a third of those possible being utilized.

**FIGURE 10.1**   Increasing number of media options and usage

| Year of competition | No. media options listed in author questionnaire | Average no. media used by winners | % of media options utilized by winners |
|---|---|---|---|
| 1980 | 9 | 2.40 | 26.67% |
| 1982 | 9 | 2.16 | 24.00% |
| 1984 | 9 | 1.76 | 19.56% |
| 1986 | 9 | 2.00 | 22.22% |
| 1988 | 9 | 1.63 | 18.11% |
| 1990 | 9 | 1.91 | 21.22% |
| 1992 | 9 | 1.70 | 18.89% |
| 1994 | 9 | 1.77 | 19.67% |
| 1996 | 10 | 1.72 | 17.20% |
| 1998 | 11 | 3.83 | 34.82% |
| 2000 | 11 | 4.09 | 37.18% |
| 2002 | 12 | 4.37 | 36.42% |
| 2004 | 12 | 6.25 | 52.08% |
| 2006 | 13 | 6.03 | 46.38% |
| 2008 | 17 | 7.48 | 44.00% |
| 2010 | 20 | 9.18 | 45.90% |

SOURCE: Roger Ingham, Data Alive/IPA Effectiveness Awards

**FIGURE 10.2**   Average number of media used by brands with limited budgets

| Year of competition for budgets < £2.5 m | No. media options listed in author questionnaire | Average no. media used by winners | % of media options utilized by winners |
|---|---|---|---|
| 2005 | 12 | 4.13 | 34.42% |
| 2007 | 15 | 5.56 | 37.07% |
| 2009 | 17 | 6.33 | 37.24% |

SOURCE: Roger Ingham, Data Alive/IPA Effectiveness Awards

We can also look at best practice in terms of the combinations of channels that were used in the 157 winning cases in the five 'open' IPA Effectiveness Awards between 2002 and 2010. While this is not a huge sample, it represents the latest state of the art and thus gives valuable guidance for media planners. Here, Roger Ingham of Data Alive has analysed the relationship between a given medium and the additional media used with it. As can be seen, TV is the dominant medium and was used in 145 ie 92 per cent of the winning cases, and is partnered with the fewest additional channels – just five compared to sponsorship at the other end of the spectrum which was in a mix with over seven other media.

**FIGURE 10.3**   Average number of additional media used by a medium 2002–2010

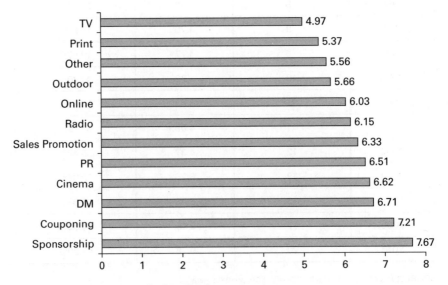

**SOURCE:** Roger Ingham, Data Alive/IPA Effectiveness Awards 2002–2010

Interestingly, in the latest competition in 2010 where there were 38 winners, SMS was used alongside an average of just over 11 other media, but in very few campaigns. Because SMS seems to come so low down the hierarchy of importance of channels it gets used by only the most prolific of multi-channel campaigns. TV is the top priority, so it gets used by nearly every campaign – including a number of single-channel ones – hence the lower number of other channels used.

But is this increased use of multiple media channels a result of media planners employing them just because they're there and because they can, or is there concrete evidence to prove that it works? In their seminal work for Datamine 2, *Marketing in the Era of Accountability*, Les Binet and Peter Field examined the IPA Effectiveness Awards cases from many points of view, including whether or not multi-media cases were likely to be more effective per se. Their conclusion was unequivocal in stating that effectiveness has been aided by the wider choice of channels available and that campaigns which use a combination of advertising and other communications channels generate significantly faster growth for the same share of voice. Further, they showed that there is no limit to the number of non-traditional advertising channels in terms of diminishing return on investment. By using SOV analysis Binet and Field showed that this was not simply the result of bigger budgets, as multi-channel campaigns actually make the same budget work harder, delivering 2.4 per cent increase in £ SOM per 10 percentage points extra SOV versus 1.2 per cent for single-channel ones. Thus integrated multi-channel campaigns are twice as efficient as traditional advertising-only campaigns.

With campaigns that use 'bought' advertising alone it seems that about three different media is the optimum number, rising to four for campaigns with bigger budgets, and thereafter there are diminishing returns. A possible explanation for this is that non-advertising 'owned' or 'earned' channels are able to perform different tasks in putting the brand in front of people in various modes within the media flow, whereas extra 'bought' advertising media tend to compete with each other to perform the same roles. So social media, spreading views about a brand via 'word-of-mouth', fulfil a different function from display advertising's overall emotional umbrella, or from its search advertising which enables users to obtain useful information vis-à-vis an impending purchase.

To shed some additional light on this we have the benefit of some interesting new analysis of the approaches to integration used in IPA cases published in Datamine 3, *New Models of Marketing Effectiveness*, and co-authored by Kate Cox, John Crowther, Tracy Hubbard and Denise Turner. There's a wealth of detail to be explored therein, but it is possible to cite some broad conclusions they arrived at:

- Campaigns with no obvious integration, or which use only one channel, are just as effective as the whole database on a number of important measures but they are less likely to have a major impact on market share gain or defence and can be better at reducing price sensitivity.

- Advertising-led campaigns (ie ones with a powerful unifying creative idea such as 118 118 with its moustachioed twin runners) are more effective at share gain and customer acquisition.

- Brand idea-led campaigns (ie ones with a powerful unifying brand attitude such as Johnnie Walker's 'Keep Walking') are very good all-rounders in that they deliver effective results across a range of hard business measures. In particular, they are highly effective in customer retention and share defence when compared to the whole database.

- Participation-led campaigns (ie ones which require a degree of customer interaction, via digital media for example) perform above average on market share defence because they excel mainly at rewarding existing users who are prepared to commit time to exploring the riches offered by a brand with which they already have a relationship. They tend to underperform on other hard measures. However, more detailed analysis shows that they can be effective on a wider range of measures over a longer term for more mature brands.

The authors' interpretation of their analysis is that the more a campaign demands of its audience, the more effective it is at engaging with its existing users, and the less effective it is at acquisition; whereas conversely, the less a campaign demands of its consumers the more likely it is to reach out to new users. This conclusion chimes in with what we know about selective perception where brand users are much more attuned to and interested in their brand's messaging than non-users. It also seems to fit with our picture of a fast-moving life and media flow, and with recent learning from behavioural economics, which suggests that any effort, no matter how small, can militate strongly against people taking an action. In the final section of the book we look at some new ideas such as transmedia planning, but if the Datamine 3 analysis is anything to go by, it looks more likely that a multi-media campaign with self-contained strands within it is likely to be the dominant approach for some time to come.

So, in summary it looks pretty certain that a combination of: three or four different 'bought' advertising media in combination with other activities such as direct mail, sales promotion and sampling, in coordination with the brand's 'owned' media including its website, customer magazine, packaging and point-of-purchase material, plus other 'earned' channels of communication such as public relations and social media, makes for a greater increase in market share for a given share of voice. It's extremely helpful to have a proven rule of thumb which says that between three and four paid-for media is the optimum number, but why should this be the case? There are a number of possible explanations and these include the following, each of which we'll examine in some detail:

1  the simple mathematical consequences for reach and frequency of extra channels added to a schedule;

2  the modulation or enhancement of the brand message by different media;

3  the brand body language of self-confidence through multiple display;

4  the consumer utility of different media at different stages in a purchase process;

5  the cognitive utility of several sources of information.

## Reach and frequency

From the point of view of paid-for advertising media we know that additional channels will increase the coverage of a given target audience towards

100 per cent and the frequency of its exposure to the message. The question for the media planner is how many people of what type need to be exposed to the brand message, and on how many occasions, before they comprehend and engage with it? Clearly, if the offer is free £10 notes, then whispering it to one person in a crowded pub will probably do the trick! On the other hand, if the communication is to do with a complex financial services product, or a message which challenges a deeply ingrained social behaviour, then it's very likely that repetition will be required.

In this context the IPA's work on share of market versus share of voice is crucial. As people live in the media flow they are swimming in the streams of communication for a myriad number of market and product categories and it's the job of each brand to strive to maintain the highest possible 'bought' media presence, and thus salience in the river. However, there are diminishing returns in terms of coverage – after a certain point, adding more media does not give you much more reach – and each additional channel that is added will incur additional agency fees and production costs.

# Modulation or enhancement of the brand message

Clearly the use of multiple advertising media isn't just a dry mathematical construct because each medium has its particular and characteristic effect on the message that it carries as a result of the special relationship with its readers and listeners or viewers, as is discussed in detail in the chapters on each individual medium. For example, newspapers by their very nature are 'of the moment' and thus an advertising message appearing in a news environment can have a sense of freshness and urgency. On the other hand, a brand appearing in the pages of a magazine which is being browsed during leisure time can capitalize on the reader's relaxed mood and interest in gathering information.

Radio is both a background and a foreground medium, and a commercial in that context, which capitalizes on the particular benefits of audio, can enhance the intimacy of the brand. Television clearly has enormous impact through sound, vision and motion, which is a powerful combination in creating emotional engagement, either in the commercial break or via pro-gramme sponsorship. Outdoor advertising can offer massive coverage very quickly and create a sense of scale and sheer impact through the use of the larger formats, or alternatively influence brand choice by close proximity to the point of sale.

Direct mail and e-mail can deliver timely messages to carefully targeted segments of the population, providing useful information and motivating offers when people are in the market for them. Public relations can enhance the reputation of the brand through influencing the editorial content of all these media channels, as can the media that the brand itself owns such as its customer magazines, websites and direct marketing communications with customers. Point-of-purchase material can direct the eye and make an offer just when people are making up their mind. And of course a brand's packaging is absolutely fundamental to attracting attention and making the sale. The surging power of the internet as a medium is that it can operate on all of these levels and actually take the customers' money too.

And it's not just the editorial context which has a modulating effect on the brand's advertising: re-executing the core idea for each individual medium does so too. People who are fans of a particular kind of computer game will enjoy it in its many manifestations whether playing it on their console, reading about it in its magazine, watching its movie or listening to the soundtrack. Perhaps this relates to an innate human ability to spot small differences in the environment which can signify threats or danger. On a more prosaic level, this might also explain the perennial popularity of the 'spot the difference' item which appears in many newspapers and magazines both online and offline – people are intrigued by small differences.

**FIGURE 10.4**    Spot the differences

Reproduced with permission of PSC Photography

The same is true of a good advertising idea – if we like it, we like it in all its varieties, as each execution, tailored to the attributes of the medium that carries it, shows off the concept in a slightly different way, giving us a variety of perspectives on the idea we are interested in.

# Brand body language

We pointed out earlier, in Chapter 2, that there's an understanding that different media and the variety of spaces and times available to advertisers within them have differential costs – the majority have bought a classified ad at one time or another. As a result of this knowledge, viewers, readers and listeners make inferences from a brand's media behaviour as to the brand's standing. Big successful brands use big expensive spaces and more often in more different media than lesser brands because they can afford to, and the reason they can is because they're popular and have lots of customers buying their products or services. As Mark Earls has pointed out in his book *Herd: How to Change Mass Behaviour by Harnessing Our True Nature*, a great deal of what we do is done because other people do it. So a brand's sheer popularity and sense of 'everybody's buying it', which can be exhibited by the scale and variety of use of different media, is an important sales tool for a brand. In addition, a brand's advertising style can reflect very well on it, as Rory Sutherland former IPA President and Creative Director & Vice-Chairman of OgilvyOne, has pointed out:

> Good advertising is usually taken to signify a good product. After all, someone putting in the effort and expense required to conceive and execute a good advertising idea is only likely to do this if they have long term faith in the efficacy and value of what they are selling. Moreover, if a campaign is expressed skilfully through various media in a way which brings out the best in it, then the inferred quality is even higher – since the effort and expense of doing this is greater still. We tend – logically if subconsciously – to infer good products from good advertising. You might call this the advertising heuristic, whereby quality advertising signifies quality merchandise.

Thus it's essential that the media planner is sensitive to these nuances of meaning conferred by the media context and can put together a channel matrix that flatters and enhances the brand's conversation with people at the right point in their journey. In addition to 'bought' media the brand needs to deploy its 'owned' media in all its forms to synchronize with this paid-for exposure and to make sure that the messages being communicated are fully integrated and reinforcing each other. Meanwhile, the other 'earned' media, which are accepted as potentially much more influential because they give the brand third-party endorsement, are very important contributors to the reputation and fame of a brand.

Brand fame is crucial, as Binet and Field have shown, but other leading thinkers believe it too. Inspired by Victoria Beckham's statement that: 'Right from the beginning, I said I wanted to be more famous than Persil Automatic', advertising's sage Jeremy Bullmore titled his speech to the British Brands Group 'Posh Spice & Persil'. He is in no doubt that fame is the key to brand success:

It has been suggested that brands are the real celebrities. For most human beings, fame not only holds a powerful fascination, but bestows an incalculable value on anything that enjoys it. We value the famous far more highly than the little known. It is not enough for BMW to be known only to that 5 per cent of the population wealthy enough even to contemplate buying one. For BMW to enjoy real fame, it needs to be known almost indiscriminately. For manufacturers and for brand marketers, I don't think the question of why matters very much. It only matters that it is. Fame is the fundamental value that strong brands own. The image of a brand is no more and no less than the result of its fame: its reputation. And like a reputation, it can be found in only one place: in the minds of people.

# Consumer utility of different media

As we have discussed, every individual is moving constantly from the position of 'not buying' to 'buying', and points in between. As they get into buying mode and start to seek out information (advertising and offers included), the brand needs to put as much 'bait' in their way as possible in the form of direct incentives to purchase and easy opportunities to do so. In this context it's always so tempting for marketers, especially ones under pressure from their colleagues in sales, to throw too much money at the problem and just bribe their customers into purchasing.

Sadly, so often this is a complete waste of money and undermines the good reputation of the brand that has been so hard fought for. As we have seen, Andrew Ehrenberg and others have shown beyond doubt that frequency of purchase in a given market category is more or less constant and thus trying to persuade your main existing customers to buy your brand more often is a doomed enterprise. What this means is that the immediate or so-called 'below the line' activities designed to trigger purchase must wherever possible avoid the risk of discounting a sale that the brand was going to get anyway, either from its current users who may be going to buy that week in any event, or who buy forward and stockpile because a silly price has been offered. Experienced fishermen know the dangers, as pointed out by Burnt Store Anglers, a voluntary club of recreational anglers, in their dictionary of terms:

> Chumming. To attract fish or get them biting again, you can throw 'chum' into the water where you're fishing. Be sure not to over-chum. You want to get them interested in feeding, you do not want to stuff them before they get a chance to go after your hook.

Even more insidious than the short-term sacrifice of margin is the long-term damage that is being done to the reputation of the brand – all those hundreds of thousands of pounds spent putting it up on a pedestal while similar sums of money are spent knocking it down. But worse than that, the consumer sees the brand doing this damage to itself and that sets out a fundamental contradiction: if this brand owner thinks their product or service is so great and telling me that in wonderful glossy advertising, why is it having to give away so much money persuading people to buy it? Maybe it's not so great after all. Stella Artois fell into this trap by undermining its 'reassuringly expensive' positioning in its celebrated advertising campaign by agency Lowe with too many aggressive price promotions.

So this is why strategies and tactics designed to attract new users are so much more profitable. Richard Dorset, who founded one of the first wholly owned sales promotion subsidiaries of a mainstream advertising agency, Boase Massimi Pollitt, called the new venture 'Print Promotions and Publicity' because he knew that, with inventiveness, spending £1 creating a competition, sourcing a plastic toy or producing a recipe booklet could produce an item with a perceived value of £2 or more. This is the basis of added value sales promotion, which relies on creativity rather than discounting.

## Cognitive utility

It may also be the case that multiple sources of information about a brand have a cognitive utility for customers. Wendy Gordon of qualitative research consultancy Acacia Avenue, who has been conducting focus groups for over 20 years across a vast range of products and services, has an interesting insight into the decision-making process. From thousands of hours spent listening to people Gordon has drawn the following conclusion:

> We use the 'Theory of Three' to describe a consumer response that we have noticed. Often people in the course of explaining why they did what they did, chose what they did, or explaining any sort of behaviour can re-trace three touch points, eg Saw the book advertised, saw someone reading it on the train, saw a poster – so I decided to read it. Substitute any three touch points that you like, eg Why do I use premium fuel – my garage recommended it, my friend mentioned that his car goes further, saw an ad... It is a kind of triangulation that seems to add up to more weight than individual touch points.

It's interesting that Gordon has derived her 'Theory of Three' on an a priori basis as it seems to coincide with a wealth of other examples showing that human beings seem to like sequences of three in so many other aspects of life. Satisfying stories have a beginning, middle and end. Great speech makers use the rhetorical 'rule of three' to make their points powerfully and almost tell us when to applaud them. Presentation skills coaches encourage their students to 'tell them what you're going to tell them, tell them, and then tell them what you've told them'. Many jokes have a three-part structure – the Scotsman, the Irishman and the Englishman – and in folktales, fairytales and mythology it usually takes three attempts before success is achieved. And of course the notion of the Trinity is deeply embedded in Christian religion.

So if we relate this back to Binet and Field's findings it's interesting to note the 'rule of three' being observed there too (although as they point out, depending on budget size, four is the optimal number of paid-for media to be used in getting a brand's message across). Thus from a number of points of view the media planner and their client can be reasonably confident in this rule of thumb in developing an advertising and marketing communications plan. However, this still leaves some very big questions to be answered, namely amongst the plethora of 'bought', 'owned' and 'earned' media channels that are available to the brand, which particular combination is most fit for its particular stream within the media flow?

# Choosing the multi-media mix

11

In 2002, Sally Ford-Hutchinson and Annie Rothwell of The Thinking Shop produced *The Public's Perception of Advertising in Today's Society*, a report on a major piece of qualitative research conducted on behalf of the UK's Advertising Standards Authority. In it they said:

> The first interesting finding was the extent to which the term advertising encompassed for consumers every piece of brand, product or service communication. It obviously included the key media of television, posters (surprisingly high in a strong second place), press, cinema and radio. It also included other aspects of 'selling' such as Direct Mail, door drops, the Internet, branding in store, branded clothing, sponsorship, commercial text messages and even telephone sales. Advertising is simply everything that has a name on it.

This basic realization, that as far as the public is concerned literally anything can be an advertising medium, means that the media planner has an extraordinarily broad canvas on which to paint. And this of course presents a major challenge: how to select from such a rich choice which particular channels are used to deploy the brand's message. The crux of the matter in choosing the right multi-media mix for a brand depends on five main factors:

1 being clear on the underlying model of communications;
2 understanding the customer journey, which media fit in, and when;
3 the budget and its constraints;
4 discerning the relevance of media to the brand's product category;
5 realizing which of these media can enable the creative idea to flower.

Let's examine each of these in turn.

# 1. Being clear on the underlying model of communications

The first step in choosing a media mix is to have a communications model in mind. Despite the complexity of customer journeys and an increasing body of market research which suggests that the decision-making process is far from rational and often circuitous, there is still a very strong tendency for people to believe in a linear or hierarchy of effects (HOE) persuasion model, such as the classic Attention Interest Desire Action, or 'AIDA', whereby messages are pushed out to the target audience, received and acted upon.

The attraction of a HOE model is that it is sequential and rational. It fits neatly with the notion of advertising as a persuasive force. It can be broken down into measurable steps and is amenable to research techniques such as persuasion-shift ad-testing and day-after recall tracking to see how consumers are progressing along the model's path. But many successful ads seek to engage, not to persuade, and there is increasing evidence that ads can work without people recalling them, as Robert Heath and others have shown. The IPA's exploration of behavioural economics, inspired by 2009–11 IPA President Rory Sutherland, has also revealed the significant extent to which attitudes follow behaviour, not the other way around.

In order to deconstruct and analyse AIDA, Spike Cramphorn of Add+Impact International tested a HOE model using a dataset of 4,000 ads collected in over 40 countries. He defined four variables to replicate the AIDA model:

Ad Attention

Brand Ideas (News or Interest)

Brand Feelings (Attitudes or Desire)

Purchase Intent (Action)

Cramphorn found that 'Ad Attention' does not lead to better assimilation of 'Brand News', conveying 'Brand News' successfully does not increase 'Brand Feelings', but increasing 'Brand Feelings' does increase 'Purchase Intent'. He did find that 'Purchase Intent' is affected to a degree by both 'Ad Attention' and 'Brand News', but he showed there was no hierarchy of effect.

In a paper entitled *Cognitive Neuroscience, Marketing and Research* given at the 2006 ESOMAR conference, co-authors Graham Page and Jane E Raymond set out a practical rationale of the application of recent thinking and research into the way consumers process advertising. They described a 'mental workspace' model of the way the brain processes incoming information to form memories that are stored for later use, such as when we make purchasing decisions. This mental workspace model is based on three 'megamodules' of brain processing capability: knowledge, emotion and action.

**FIGURE 11.1**   An illustration of the mental workspace and the creation of representations

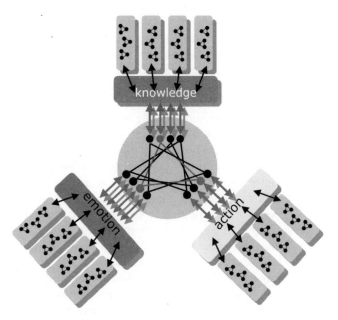

Reproduced with permission of Millward Brown and Jane Raymond

These three mega-modules work together to form 'representations' about things, events, concepts etc, and of course brands. The speed with which the brain can build these representations depends upon the accessibility of the basic information. Thus, Page and Raymond explained that familiarity (which includes components such as 'suits my personality', 'felt right for me' and 'want to try it') is an important facilitator in the brain's construction of representations. Marketing's communication task, therefore, is to get consumers to assemble representations of brands repeatedly, so they can be evoked easily when the consumer faces a purchasing decision.

The brain's workspace has very limited capacity; therefore it is difficult for a brand to get access to 'processing time'. Page and Raymond's paper supports strongly the principle of 'communication by engagement' and sets out two important implications. Firstly, marketing communication must take into account, and be sensitive to, the mindset or task-orientation of consumers at the time they encounter a message. Secondly, only the aspects of a particular communication that are relevant to the consumer's mindset or task-orientation at the time will enter the workspace.

The doubt that's been cast on the linear AIDA type of communications model by the likes of Cramphorn, Page and Raymond, and others has also undermined the selection of the media mix on a purely sequential basis predicated on a simplistic picture of a customer's journey. Not only is the brand's target audience simultaneously at different stages in the decision-making process, but the speed with which they move from 'not buying' to 'buying' also varies enormously. A purchase can be expensive for one person and thus needs consideration and saving up for over time. For people like this the brand must provide detailed information, reviews and reassurance. On the other hand, a wealthier individual buying the same thing might do so almost on impulse, so in this case the brand just needs to be sufficiently famous and to hand. Thus, the brand needs to be in the flow in a number of different modes for as much of the time as the budget and its skill in managing both 'owned' and 'earned' media will allow.

Using a single medium can undoubtedly reach the target audience effectively, in large numbers and in a potentially sympathetic environment; for example, a car commercial on TV during a major football game or a retailer in the Saturday edition of a national newspaper. However, if we now know our targeted consumer also listens to the radio, is a regular cinema visitor, checks for information online, is a consistent user of social networks and passes poster sites on work or shopping journeys, there is clearly the opportunity to achieve increased resonance for the message by using a mix of media. This will have the effect of extending the message into other parts of the consumer's 'media life' and, in harness with the creative content, will amplify the impact of the campaign. And nowadays many customer purchase journeys take place almost entirely through the media they use, from finding out about the product, learning about it, discussing it with friends, taking advice from peers and experts, and finally making a purchase online.

So we've moved on from the linear approach and the simple duality of 'theme' and 'scheme' in campaign planning, and in this new context we propose five key customer considerations that can be translated into 'communication streams' for a brand. These are 'Fame', 'Advocacy', 'Information', 'Price' and 'Availability' (or FAIPA at the risk of adding another acronym to the industry's alphabet soup!):

Fame is about product awareness and salience, and that 'buzz' which is so influential to brand perceptions.

Advocacy is about testimonials, reviews and other third-party word-of-mouth, plus being able to discuss a brand with peers and make personal endorsements.

Information is about how the brand performs in functional terms, ideally presented to meet the customer's personal requirements.

Price is about the cost of the product, with special offers or tailored payment terms, and what value these represent to the customer.

Availability is not only about where you can buy the brand offline, but also via the media itself acting as an online purchasing channel.

These five considerations cover the main customer product and purchasing needs and each of them translates into a potential stream within the media flow – for example:

**Fame:** TV, outdoor, sponsorship...

**Advocacy:** social media, ad-funded programming, PR...

**Information:** print media, the internet, brochures...

**Price:** sales promotions, direct mail, point-of-purchase (P-O-P), reader offers...

**Availability:** the internet, inserts in local papers, in-store TV, radio...

The media planner has to decide which of these streams are necessary to the brand, and this mix will vary over time and depend on circumstances. If fame is the key consideration then that will comprise the main media stream and some or all of the others will flow alongside it. For example, in the case of a car brand, its fame could be built by a thematic TV campaign and sponsorship; its information through car magazine ads and the marque's website; its advocacy via PR and social media; its distribution from the internet (book a test drive) and local dealership ads; and price/value from a number of these, including an interest-free credit bumper as a 'top and tail' ad on TV, bracketing its thematic commercial.

These various media create the overall media flow for the brand – a matrix of streams of various strengths, depths and types, as tributaries to the main stream, running alongside each other and together. And all the time consumers in their life flow are able to 'dip in and out' of the media flow dependent on its relevance to them.

# 2. Understanding which media fit in, and when

As long ago as 1986 in their paper to the MRS conference, *A great ad – pity they can't remember the brand – true or false?*, Roy Langmaid and Wendy Gordon said the following: 'Branding may be thought of as the process of creating the totality of meaning which consumers attribute to a brand – the unique and relevant bundle of values that are internalized and combined with past experience and/or current perceptions of the brand itself.' So understanding the way in which a brand fits into the user's life and giving it meaning has long been a skill of agencies. It's been built upon several decades of sophisticated qualitative and quantitative market research used to map in great detail consumer behaviour in the marketplace, and in particular the decision-making processes which vary enormously from one product category to another.

Having understood fully the sociology of the brand in a world where consumers are constantly bombarded with commercial messages, and where their 'mental workspace' is hard to penetrate, the media planner has two broad options. Firstly, it's still possible to use big-budget clout and cut-through creative to 'interrupt' the audience with advertising, while remembering

Martin Boase's warning that 'we should never forget we're the uninvited guest in the living room'. So when interrupting, it's always better for the brand to bring with it a rewarding piece of entertainment, a funny joke or some interesting news. Secondly, the planner can put themselves in the shoes of the customer and walk their journey every step of the way, appreciating all the points at which there's the potential for the brand's media to be engaging and useful.

A good example of the latter skill is the 2008 IPA Effectiveness Awards case by agency RKCR/Y&R on their campaign for the Home Office: 'Cutting the cost of crime'. This is a master class in selecting media that the target

**FIGURE 11.2**    "A moment of careless stupidity"

Reproduced by permission of RKCR/Y&R

Photograph by Jonathan Winstone

audience engages with at the right place and time. The media strand to build awareness was broadcast TV bought in the four regions of the UK which experienced the majority of acquisitive crime. Meanwhile, the 'moments of careless stupidity' strand was designed to reach people at the precise moment when they, as potential crime victims, were most at risk.

Given that nights out are key times of vulnerability, when students going home are often a bit the worse for wear, ads were placed in pub washrooms, near fast food outlets and on kebab wrappers and pizza boxes. Hurrying commuters who are the prey of muggers and pickpockets were targeted using tube panels in the London Underground and posters near ATMs and bus stops. Careless motorists who might leave possessions visible inside their vehicle were warned by posters at petrol and car park barriers. And there were door drops in postcode areas with a high risk of burglary, and door hangers placed in student accommodation where walk-in theft is prevalent. The campaign was a big success, reducing the cost of crime to the UK taxpayer by £189 million and generating payback of £14 for every £1 spent.

Being able to see how media fit into people's lives is fundamental to successful engagement and, as we have seen, the UK media industry has always been able to operate with the benefit of high-quality media research data. This comprises both industry research into the audiences of the individual media and increasingly proprietary research which identifies consumers' media behaviour. These include BMRB's TGI survey, NRS data and TNS research, along with a number of media agency surveys, such as Aegis' CCS survey. The launch of the IPA TouchPoints survey in 2006 was something of a breakthrough for media planners. In IPA TouchPoints we now have an incredibly powerful tool to aid us in discerning which media people engage with and when. Because the respondents are required to keep a diary for a week and to account for where they are, who they are with, what they're doing and what mood they're in for every half-hour of the day, we can get a very good understanding of the media habits of a very wide variety of demographics. To take just one example from amongst hundreds of possible ones, the chart overleaf shows what activities young men are engaged with on Saturdays.

With that understanding we can now look at exactly the same target audience in terms of their media habits throughout Saturday and we can see how these young men can be reached in the context of their other activities.

As this one example demonstrates, TouchPoints is an incredibly powerful tool in the media planner's hands, especially as the hub survey can be fused to all the media research occurrences to produce the integrated planning database and also other data such as TGI and brand-tracking studies. This enables the agency planner to get an unparalleled understanding of how the flows of media and life intertwine, and thus where and when the brand can best make its presence felt by interrupting or, even better, by making itself useful.

**FIGURE 11.3**    Activities of young men on Saturday

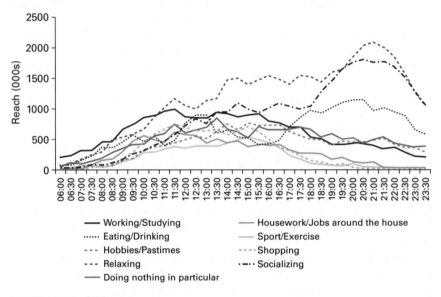

**SOURCE:** IPA TouchPoints3

**FIGURE 11.4**    Media habits of young men on Saturday

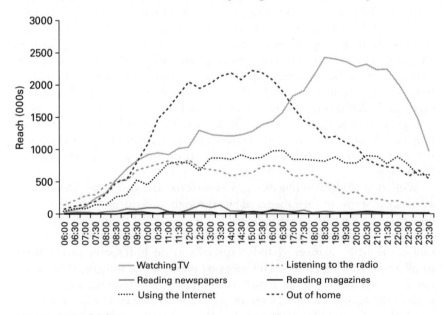

**SOURCE:** IPA TouchPoints3

# 3. The budget and its constraints

As the Rolling Stones once said, 'You can't always get what you want', and the same is true of advertising. The budget will generally dictate both which media can be considered and in what combination. As most media planners will agree, there's never enough money to use all the media they would ideally recommend, or in the way that they would aspire to. On the basis that the best media strategies are focused and involve 'sacrifice', it is far better to do an effective job in fewer media than dilute the activity in each medium (particularly those judged to be the most effective) by utilizing too many – it's a case of paring away those that are not essential and making the most of the synergies.

Firstly, there's the opportunity afforded by the positive effect of combining the different media. For some years the radio industry has promoted radio advertising in support of television (and latterly online) to extend the campaign period and add extra frequency to the communications. The argument being that, once a campaign has been established on television, the same audience can be reached through commercial radio but at a far cheaper cost, and the audience will 'conjure up the visuals' from the commercial through the audio association. There is no cast-iron evidence to prove this effect, but common sense and the RAB research suggest that there is a good case for it. More recently, the Newspaper Marketing Agency (NMA) has produced similar research that shows that newspaper advertising, in combination with another medium, is more effective than just using a single one. There is therefore a strong argument to use media for their synergistic effect, and as we have seen, the analyses of the IPA Effectiveness Awards cases confirm the benefits of using a multi-media approach.

Secondly, there's the opportunity to use different formats, which can secure a presence across different media and platforms – for example sponsorships, advertorials, promotions and competitions.

These, either individually or linked to other activity, will also have the benefit of providing synergies. Thirdly, there are the cross-platform opportunities provided by the new world of digital media. All major media now have their own online sites and many have links to other content providers and extend into other platforms, such as mobile phone applications. And all of these carry advertising. Therefore it is not only possible but also increasingly recommended that a campaign running on the media owner's main channel or publication should also move into these other online areas as well, as they are not currently particularly costly.

Finally, there are the opportunities afforded by non-paid-for communications. As we have already discussed, the media world now comprises 'owned' and 'earned' media along with the traditional 'bought' media. Clearly, leveraging the client's owned media – its websites and web pages, its properties and delivery vehicles, its packaging and even its workforce if possible – should be an essential ingredient of a modern communications and media plan. In the case of 'earned' media, the opportunities through PR, social media and content aggregator websites are increasing at a staggering rate. In

**FIGURE 11.5** The power of editorial endorsement via an 'advertorial'

*ELLEpromotion*

Cotton shirt £60
Denim waistcoat
£75 Demi Curve
Skinny Piecinsin
Worn Or £105

*ELLEpromotion*

## the future of denim

*Too long? Too tight? Too saggy? Buying jeans has always been a complicated affair, but Levi's CURVE ID is set to change everything*

**CURVE ID**

WE ALL KNOW HOW HARD IT CAN BE TO FIND THE ONE. Is it a long-term commitment or just a brief love affair? Is it really right for you? Are you sure that it's what you really, really want? Yup, finding the perfect pair of jeans isn't easy. The most startling statistic from a recent survey by Levi's is that 87 per cent of women wish they could find jeans that fit better than the ones they own. Out of these women, only 28 per cent actually believe that jeans are designed to fit their bodies. No wonder we find shopping for denim so difficult.

In the biggest piece of global 'fit' research in recent history, Levi's talked to thousands of women about their size, shape and, most importantly, their curves. The findings are astonishing. Two thirds of those surveyed believe that jeans are designed for women with 'ideal' figures. And as we all know, in reality the 'ideal' figure just doesn't exist. Whether it's a trend that fails to flatter, a style that doesn't quite work or a size that just won't fit, buying jeans is a complicated affair. In fact, more than half of women admit to trying on at least ten pairs to find just one they would actually buy, and only a third of women believe that most jeans are made to fit their curves.

This is where Levi's revolutionary Curve ID jeans come in.

After studying the shapes of over 60,000 women through 3D body scans, Levi's has created Custom Fits For Women as a unique solution. The pioneering research identifies three distinct body shapes that account for 80 per cent of women across the world and Levi's new collection is based on this fact, celebrating shape rather than size. The global design team, plus 'fit' technicians and pattern cutters, have crafted a range of fits that finally deliver on the promise of perfect jeans.

In stores, Levi's Curve Consultants are trained to share the way to identify your own personal Curve ID. This bespoke way of fitting is key to finding your custom jeans: Slight Curve, Demi Curve or Bold Curve. All work with the curves of a woman's body, based on her individual proportions. Within these three shapes are an array of fits and finishes to ensure that your denim is just as unique as you. After this, shopping for jeans will never, ever be the same again. ▶

*Of the thousands of women surveyed, more than half try on at least 10 pairs of jeans in order to find just one pair they would buy*

*87% of women wish they could find jeans that fit better than the ones they currently own*

fact, a modern-day advertising and media planning challenge is to create campaigns that generate more coverage in 'earned' media than is paid for in 'bought' media – the new generation of viral advertising!

However, all these media choices need to be weighed up against the need to achieve an effective weight in the primary medium, the creative treatment and production costs. And production costs are an important issue, as increasing the number of media used inevitably adds cost in both time and materials. This is an important reason why the 'matching luggage' approach to integrated communications has so many followers, especially amongst multinational brands: one core set of creative origination and production can be iterated out into the different channels and markets much more cost-efficiently than a myriad of different approaches.

Media planners are sometimes accused of not being close enough to the creative product, and for specifying channels on the incorrect assumption that the production costs will be minimal and thus not a barrier to their inclusion on the schedule. This is especially true of online media, where the 'culture of free' seems to have conditioned people to such a degree in their personal lives that they bring it with them to work! In fact, the development of websites, online display and search advertising, e-mails and mobile applications is like any other medium – it's always possible to fill them with lowest common denominator content, but this poor quality will reflect badly on any brand that's not positioned as a price fighter. And given that interactivity and the user experience are such essential aspects of the digital era, a clunky, slow performance that takes the brand out of the media flow is completely counter-productive. So media planners and content creators must have a regular dialogue to ensure the best possible fit between medium and message, and at a viable total cost.

Within the constraints of the budget, there is also the consideration of price negotiations with the media owners. Generally, this is a matter for individual negotiation between the media buyer and the media owner once the planning has been done. However, this can make the difference between making a media choice affordable or otherwise. Therefore, the ideal media plan may be modified in the light of pricing and cost considerations. (If clients and the media agency don't operate with this degree of flexibility they may end up paying somewhat more for their media than they should be!)

All this adds up to a complex matrix of challenges and opportunities in structuring the multi-media plan. It's not difficult to construct an effective plan with a sizeable budget, but it is rather more difficult when the budget is limited. In the old days, the answer was generally to put all the money into a single medium, but that is now undoubtedly the weakest option. And there is also the additional complication of how the public relations, sales promotion, search and e-commerce requirements are going to fit into the plan when these channels are quite often not under the control of the client marketing department. Clearly, in an ideal world all the brand's touch points with its customers should be part of the overall communications plan, and part of the skill of the modern-day media planner is to include all these channels in the master laydown, even if the budgets are separate.

# 4. Discerning the relevance to the brand's product category

Over the years, there have been two rules that can be applied to the process of matching brands with their relevant media:

Rule 1: There are some very well-established 'received wisdoms' as to which media are best suited to which product categories. These conventions are based largely on the various media's audience sizes and profiles, content and, very importantly, their creative properties. So TV became home for FMCG products; newspapers for retailers and financial; magazines for fashion and luxury items (cameras in camera titles etc). All very logical, perpetuated over many years, and still applicable today. For example, the UK literary magazine *Granta* wanted to increase the number of people subscribing to it and decided to use their eye-catching 'Sex' issue to get the attention of likely prospects. Given the photograph used on the front cover, which was a pun on price and sexual attraction, the choice of *RA Magazine* with its intelligent and visually aware readership was a natural place for their special offer ad to appear.

**FIGURE 11.6**   Perfect synergy between content, context and consumer

Reproduced by permission of Granta

Photograph by Billie Segal©

Design by Michael Salu

Rule 2: Any medium can work effectively for any product because breaking the product category media conventions can give the brand added stand-out. London Weekend Television used posters to promote programmes on a weekly basis; British Airways Business Class ran to great effect on mass market TV; Boddingtons used magazines to sell beer; radio launched the Carphone Warehouse; sponsorship has been a spearhead for mobile operator O$_2$; and The Macallan malt whisky brand started off with small ads placed on the back of *The Times*, beside the famous crossword, and later in *Private Eye* – hence the commemorative bottles celebrating the UK satirical magazine's 25th birthday.

**FIGURE 11.7**    *Private Eye* commemorative bottle of The Macallan malt whisky

Reproduced by permission of The Edrington Group

However, these rules (or lack of them!) apply to the use of a single medium, or at least a predominant lead medium. Now we are in a much more multi-media world. This is because consumers, who previously were happy to buy on the basis of seeing the advertising on just a single medium (eg 'as advertised on TV'), now expect much more contact with and from the brands they are interested in.

There are a number of major market research companies which have developed survey techniques used to address these issues. Their tools are able to discern, for any given market category and indeed brand within that, which media are the most relevant. Amongst the most commonly used by media agencies are: Integration's™ Market ContactAudit™, Millward Brown's ChannelConnect, BMRB's Compose, TNS Brand Media Monitor and ohal.

**FIGURE 11.8**    The key intersection within the flow

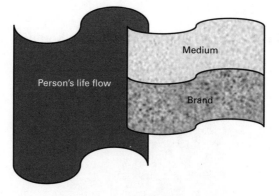

The philosophy that underpins these models is that by using market research to examine the relationship between brands, media and customers, it's possible to identify from the latter's point of view which are the most relevant contact points for them within a particular market category or indeed for the brand under consideration. For example, the customer decision-making process in the credit card market may involve a need for detailed information, and thus media which are judged right for delivering such information would seem the best channel choices in that market. The insights gained from this sort of research can enable the media planner to spot relevant channel opportunities which may be underutilized, and thus gain competitive advantage for the brand that they are managing.

What is clear is that relevance of media to the brand and product category is an important consideration. Some of the answers to this question can be found in basic audience research, which tells us who is watching which medium, in what numbers and where. Some of the answers can be found in more consumer-based research (eg TGI and the IPA's own TouchPoints), which tell us which media consumers specially choose and in what combination. Some of the answers can be found in very sophisticated research, such as MCA or ohal or even sources such as the Tesco-owned dunnhumby database, which try to provide the whole picture. But we have a sneaking suspicion that intuition, trial and error, and zagging when the established wisdoms zig will still continue to be as important as relying on the various research sources.

# 5. Realizing which media can enable the creative idea to flower

Now we come to the part of choosing a multi-media mix which becomes highly subjective, and where the art of media planning really comes into play. As we have seen, there are any number of proprietary research tools which can identify the most appropriate media for any given brand in any given market in relation to any given customer journey. So we can place our brand in the media flow with great precision, but the big question is what kind of creative 'bait' is to be used to catch our fish. And of course the notion of bait begs the question of the nature of the 'hooks' or, in other words, which media are best suited to the creative idea.

At the time that agency Abbott Mead Vickers developed the ground-breaking poster campaign for *The Economist*, with its distinctive white type on a red background, it was unprecedented for niche magazines with a tightly defined target audience to use a 'broadcast' medium such as outdoor. Similarly, TBWA's campaign for Wonderbra caused a sensation simply because a brand usually seen in the pages of women's magazines was suddenly out there on giant 48-sheet posters greeting the public with 'Hello Boys'. In both these examples the choice of medium – outdoor – gave already powerful creative ideas a massive injection of fame. More recently, the T-Mobile campaign based around the concept of filmed live events, such as the one in London's Liverpool Street station, is clearly an idea where medium and message are inextricably linked and where the audiovisual and sound requirement simply ruled out other media choices.

**FIGURE 11.9**    T-Mobile 'flash dance' at Liverpool Street station

Reproduced by permission of Saatchi & Saatchi

Clearly we've moved on from the world of linear channels, which were largely evaluated and used on a 'silo' basis, to a market that now involves bought, owned and earned media. What this in turn means is that 'starting with an ad' is not necessarily the best solution, and it could very often be the worst. This is because beginning with a particular creative execution, which entails the use of a specific medium, can lead to a pre-judgement which militates against a better-balanced media schedule. There is also the danger that the agency and the client fall in love with a creative idea which works very well in one medium, but less well in others. Critical to communication effectiveness is the ability to utilize and mix the various channels to their best effect, and create the optimum media flow for the brand. The ideal combination might include the client's own packaging, website, magazine or marketing event (owned media); a Facebook page, YouTube coverage or a word-of-mouth campaign (earned); TV, radio, press, outdoor, internet or search (bought); or, most likely, a combination of some or all of these.

In an era when integrated marketing communications are so important, this presents a challenge to media planners. Given that a multi-media mix of three or four channels is known to be optimal, should an idea that only really works in one or two of them be rejected? This goes to the heart of one of the trickiest of current debates, which is whether integration has to be achieved by means of slavish reproduction of a core creative idea in every single medium that is used – the so-called 'matching luggage' approach – or is it possible to achieve integration by using different creative executions which may not be linked in by anything other than a common attitude or tone of voice? The latter is suggested in IPA publication Datamine 3, *New Models of Marketing Effectiveness*, which showed that campaigns organized around a looser brand idea were more successful at delivering hard business effects than those organized around consistent creative executions, or 'matching luggage'.

While there are clearly exceptional exceptions, we believe that the evidence from behavioural economics reinforces our view that Keep It Simple Stupid or 'KISS' is the rule to follow. And, if we needed further evidence, behavioural economics shows pretty conclusively that people have an aversion to making any effort greater than absolutely necessary to carry out a given task or achieve a particular objective. So we need to make it as easy as possible for people to step into the media flow, to understand exactly what it is that we are trying to say and to engage with our brand as fluently as possible. In this context, using a core creative idea which works across all media, and employing devices such as visual and aural mnemonics to facilitate absorption of the message and create linkages with existing brand memories and associations, makes far more sense than using a more disparate and less cohesive approach.

In summary, let's return to the five customer considerations which cover their main product and purchasing needs and use FAIPA to sense-check the choice of media in the mix for the brand. Does the selection address the need to create brand *fame*, generate positive *advocacy*, provide necessary *information*, make an attractive *price* offer and tell the customer where the brand is *available* to buy? If it achieves all these five things, whether by bought, owned or earned media, then the brand will be well served within the flow.

# PART FOUR
# The strengths of each medium

# Introduction

**O**ur view of the media landscape is informed by a wealth of data and one of the most useful sources is IPA TouchPoints, the only UK media research which compares different media using a common methodology. The pie chart shows the breakdown of the media day for people. While it excludes outdoor, direct mail and other media unable to be recorded by time spent, it gives a pretty good idea. In the UK, broadcast TV accounts for 37 per cent of people's average daily media consumption, with out-of-home at 23 per cent, radio at 19 per cent, using the internet at 14 per cent, print media at 4 per cent and social networking at 3 per cent. So, on a robust quantitative basis we can see the relative importance on average of the main media from the customer's point of view, but that doesn't mean that's the only basis for selection or budget allocation.

**FIGURE P4.1**  Share of media day

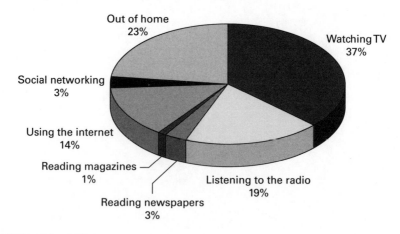

**SOURCE:** IPA TouchPoints3

As we have seen, there are five main needs of a brand in media terms and it's clear that each individual medium can have a claim for inclusion in the mix. That's why over the past decade there has been so much debate about the need for 'media neutrality' in the planning and buying of advertising and marketing communications. But the reality is that everybody, including the professionals, has opinions about media and, inevitably, their favourites. If this book were interactive – and maybe it should be, given that we are talking about media in the digital age – it would probably have asked a number of questions such as: 'What's your favourite medium, TV programme, magazine, website etc?' And these wouldn't have been difficult questions to answer because we all have an interest in the subject, not least because, after working and sleeping, consuming media is what occupies a large part of our waking hours. This makes us all expert on and opinionated about the media.

One of our clients used to say: 'Don't recommend posters to me, I'm allergic to posters.' Meanwhile, the creative director of the same client's agency would argue that large posters continued to be the only true broadcast medium and recommended them highly. And of course media, like most things in life, go in and out of fashion. Too often the pundits claim vociferously that a new medium will seriously damage or even 'kill off' an old medium. TV was supposed to be the end of cinema and radio but, as it turns out, all three now coexist happily in many a brand's media plan. There was a time when radio struggled to attract advertisers, followed by a period when it was everyone's favourite 'other medium'. In media planning parlance: 'Last year you were a loser if you planned radio onto your schedule, this year you're a loser if you don't.' Even the relatively new medium of the internet already has an impressive history of being a fashion victim, eg Facebook, LinkedIn, and Twitter may be great today, but whatever happened to Friends Reunited, Bebo and Second Life, and will foursquare be the next king of the hill? There are still some 'doom merchants' who are predicting that the internet and other smart digital technology will kill off newspapers, magazines, radio – even possibly TV! However, all the evidence suggests that online media work best, and certainly most effectively, in a symbiotic relationship with other media channels in the flow.

So in this section we aren't going to put 'value judgements' on the relative strengths and weaknesses of the available media. This is partly because it would be inappropriate to do so when we've invited key people to contribute to each of the individual chapters, one per medium, but also for the following three reasons:

1 Different customers consume different media and while there may be groups using the mass media there are others with more niche media habits.

2 People not only consume many different media, they do so increasingly at the same time, and this is particularly true of younger people.

3 So many predictions about a given medium, based on personal opinion, have turned out to be completely wrong.

Most importantly, irrespective of our own personal preferences and pre-judices, each and every medium does have its own particular characteristics and strengths, and especially in terms of advertising opportunities. Across the various media, the advertising opportunities are many and various and of course the skill of the media planner is in blending the optimal mix of owned and earned media for the brand, as well as bought. Clearly there will be some overlap, but each medium offers applications that give them, if not an entirely unique positioning, at least an ability to deliver specific benefits which will not be as readily or practicably available from their competitors, or at such an affordable price!

Each chapter begins with the 'elevator pitch' for the medium – so called because it is short enough to be delivered between the ground floor and the C suite – and then goes on to give more evidence as to why it deserves a place in the brand's media plan. IPA TouchPoints data are part of that support and wherever possible a summary of the best example of the use of each medium as a primary channel in an IPA Effectiveness Award-winning case has been included.

Before embarking on this medium-by-medium review there is an important caveat to be made. This is that there is no chapter on packaging. The reason for this is that it is such an extensive topic that it lies beyond the scope of this book. Having said that, it would be a gross omission not to make reference to the vital importance of the brand's presentation. This is not only in terms of its naming, its corporate identity and surface design, but of course its physical make-up too. Clearly packaging design is a repository of brand image and a trigger at the point-of-purchase for all the historical imagery that personal experience, peer group reputation, and advertising and market-ing communications have established. The trade press house ad opposite produced by agency jkr is an excellent summary of the purpose and power of good brand design which has a crucial part to play within the flow.

**FIGURE P4.2**    The power of packaging

1. I see what I want.

2. I like what I see.

3. I buy what I like.

These three points have guided our designs for almost twenty years.

1. Stand out. In a crowd of similar products make sure yours is noticed. You don't have to shout, you do have to be seen across a busy aisle.

2. Be likeable. This can mean being stylish and sexy or practical and informative. It always means being relevant, helpful and desirable.

In our experience get 1 and 2 right and you could, like Birds Eye, revive a flagging market.

It'll take more than good pack designs of course, but in this dog eat dog, fight all the way to the check-out world, one thing is certain:

Get one and two wrong and you can forget about number three. **jkr**

Reproduced by permission of Birds Eye Limited

## 12

# Contributors

## Cinema

**Martin Bowley,
formerly Managing Director,
Digital Cinema Media (DCM)**

Martin spent two years at DCM, creating a thriving sales house. With the development of new teams in client sales and creative development, DCM forged closer links with national advertisers and their creative and media agencies. DCM now leads the UK market in 3D, Digital and 2D cinema advertising.

**Fleur Castell,
Head of Marketing,
Digital Cinema Media (DCM)**

Fleur leads DCM's team of marketing, e-comms and PR specialists. She joined Carlton Screen Advertising in 2005 and oversaw the re-brand to Digital Cinema Media in 2008.

# Direct mail

### David Payne, Consultant Head of Direct Marketing, IPA

David Payne is an experienced direct marketer who is a consultant on direct marketing, data management, and CRM to the IPA and a number of other companies. He was chairman of Wunderman International in the UK prior to forming his agency Payne Stracey in 1988, acquired subsequently by Omnicom in 2000. He is a past chair of the Institute of Direct Marketing, of which he is an Honorary Fellow.

# Magazines

### Barry McIlheney, CEO, PPA

Following his successful involvement with *Smash Hits*, *Empire*, *Heat* and *French FHM* magazines, Barry became editor-in-chief of emap consumer media in 2003, leading the launch of *Zoo Weekly* in the UK, Australia and South Africa. Since 2007 he has consulted clients such as The Radio Times, The Word, Bauer Consumer Media, Haymarket Network, Sport Media Group, Attic Media Network and John Brown Media. He's a Fellow in the Creative Arts at Queen's University Belfast, and visiting lecturer at the University of Lincoln.

# National newspapers

### Claire Myerscough, Business Intelligence Director, NI Commercial

Claire began her career as a media assistant on the Procter & Gamble account at Saatchi & Saatchi. After 11 years at Saatchi's, she left to join the launch of Zenith Media as press buying director and then on to Zed Media when it was set up in 1998.

She moved to the commercial division at News International in 2003 first as business development director for *The Times* and *The Sunday Times* and then as business intelligence director across all titles, a role which embraces consumer insight, trade marketing and design.

Claire currently sits on the boards of the Newspaper Marketing Agency and the National Readership Survey.

# Local newspapers

### Robert Ray, Marketing Director, The Newspaper Society (NS)

The NS is the trade body for the UK's local media. Robert's team is focused on developing advertising from national brands/agencies by demonstrating the depth/breadth and effectiveness of local media. Before joining the NS in 2005, Robert ran a successful communications consultancy in the media/ advertising sector for UK and overseas companies. He spent 2000–03 as MD of Starcom Worldwide, a Publicis Groupe communications strategy division for P&G, across EMEA (Europe, Middle East and Africa) and before that was joint MD of MediaVest UK.

# Online

**Amy Kean,
Senior Marketing/PR Manager,
Internet Advertising Bureau**

Amy has been working at the Internet Advertising Bureau (IAB) since 2003, and has been responsible for building its brand and helping to put online on the agenda of advertisers across the UK. She provides PR and marketing support for every IAB initiative, from its landmark research projects to its regular educational events and the work of its many working groups, including search, social media, video, behavioural targeting, IASH and UKOM.

# Out-of-home

**Glen Wilson, Deputy Managing
Director, Posterscope Ltd**

Glen Wilson is managing director of Posterscope, the market-leading worldwide out-of-home communications agency. During his 20 years of involvement in the medium he has worked on some of OOH's most well-known brands, including Wonderbra and the famous 'Hello Boys' campaign. As well as conventional outdoor media, he has championed the use of new technology and production techniques: turning poster sites on their end for Pretty Polly, building ice rinks for Absolut and suspending Minis on banners.

# Point of purchase

### Martin Kingdon, Director General, POPAI UK & Ireland

Martin Kingdon has been involved in the display and shopper insight industries for more than 20 years and leading POPAI since 2000. In addition to this role Martin is involved in retail consultancy globally, specializing in the effectiveness of display and retail layouts, and recently brand and retailer attitudes to in-store communications. He has also set up a shopper insight company based in Cape Town, South Africa, focused on both the formal and informal markets there.

# PR

### Chris Satterthwaite, Group Chief Executive, Chime Communications

Since 2002, Chris has been group chief executive of the UK holding company whose divisions cover public relations, advertising and marketing communications, sports marketing and research & engagement. Chime's agencies include Bell Pottinger, Opinion Leader, Facts International VCCP, Teamspirit, Fast Track and Essentially Group. Chris is also a non-executive director of Centaur Media and a trustee of Dulwich Picture Gallery. He was chairman of the Marketing Society from 2007 to 2009.

# Radio

### Mark Barber, Planning Director, RadioCentre

Mark is the architect of the RAB's highly successful RadioGAUGE research project, and most recently was instrumental in developing and successfully launching the RAB's ground-breaking Online Multiplier project. Mark is also the co-author of *An Advertiser's Guide to Better Radio Advertising*.

### Andrew Harrison, CEO, RadioCentre

Andrew is also a board member of RAJAR and Digital Radio UK, as well as being chairman of Radioplayer Ltd. Andrew was voted Marketer of the Year in the 2003 Marketing Society Awards and was chairman of the MGGB in 2007/8. He is a Fellow of the Marketing Society and the Chartered Institute of Marketing.

# Sponsorship

### Karen Earl, Chairman, Synergy

Karen has worked in the sponsorship industry since the 1970s, starting her own business, Karen Earl Sponsorship (KES), in 1984. KES was renamed as Synergy in 2008 and is part of Engine, the UK's largest independent communications company. Synergy's clients include Aviva, Betfair, BMW, Bupa, Chivas, Coca-Cola, Diageo and RBS. Karen is also chairman of the European Sponsorship Association (ESA).

# TV

### Tess Alps, CEO, Thinkbox

Tess became the first chief executive of Thinkbox, the central marketing body for commercial TV, in July 2006. She is a past president of WACL, Fellow of the Marketing Society, trustee of NABS and a member of the MGGB. She sits on advisory boards for the Advertising Standards Authority and BBC magazines. She is a Fellow of the Royal Television Society and a member of BAFTA. In 2007 she won the Outstanding Achievement award from Women in Film and Television.

# Cinema

## 13

## The media owner's 'elevator pitch'

> The cinema audience is unique in that it is attentive, engaged, and comprised of highly desirable young, affluent, and well educated consumers who aren't distracted by telephones, remote-control devices, electronic media, or simply performing household activities away from broadcast media during commercial breaks. (Cinema Advertising Council)

Breaking this elevator pitch down into its constituent parts, the starting point is that cinema-goers are light viewers of television, so an advertiser can reach this important audience with another powerful and complementary audiovisual medium. Moreover, the cinema audience is extremely diverse. The large number of new movie releases, which in the UK averages 10 each week, entices a broad range of the population into the cinema. And this audience is 'captive' in the sense that cinema focuses people's attention and is arguably the most immersive medium. Because of this, and since cinema-goers also perceive the advertisements as part and parcel of the overall experience, cinema has one of the lowest ad-avoidance factors. According to a study by Pearl & Dean, 53 per cent of heavy cinema-goers believe that cinema commercials are a big part of the cinema experience and so viewers have a high attention to detail and a rich advertising take-out.

This advertising effect is enhanced because of the 'talkability' of cinema advertising – a visit to the cinema is a social event with, on average, a party of three people going together for a group experience. Both the movie and the advertising fuel word-of-mouth, ranging from 'water cooler' moments to conversations on social media sites such as Facebook and Twitter. These dialogues serve to spark a multiplying effect on the brands advertised.

## How do people engage with cinema?

The cinema's most distinctive feature as an advertising medium is its high degree of user focus and minimal amount of distraction. Whereas many other media are consumed in a multi-tasking mode, cinema receives almost undivided attention. Cinema offers a rare chance for retreat from the every-day grind. It has been described as a safe haven, total physical and mental relaxation, an antidote to real life, and a place of aspiration, fantasy and glamour.

The 'event' nature of cinema offers a unique bonding and social interaction. It's a catalyst for 'together time' for couples, friends and families and offers a rare opportunity to bond. Overall, the cinema audience makes an appoint-ment to view in its truest sense – they've chosen a film, purchased a ticket and set aside the time to surrender themselves to the experience. The typical cinema programme, with its preliminary sequence of trailers and advertising as people take their seats, with a progressive lowering of the lighting levels, is structured to create an escalating degree of audience excitement during the build-up to the featured movie. Once the lights go down the audience abides by 'cinema etiquette' and pays attention, becoming immersed in the film and formulating opinions for discussion later.

Cinema should be considered in the modern context of several media channels being consumed at the same time – the new 'media flow' environ-ment in which a medium can be switched from background to foreground and back again in seconds. For younger people nowadays an evening at home is typified by this multi-tasking and multi-media usage – dipping into magazines, newspapers and books, using mobiles, browsing the internet, watching TV and listening to music, often with the longest period of atten-tion being five minutes according to findings by DCM and Work Research.

**FIGURE 13.1**   Cinema attention process

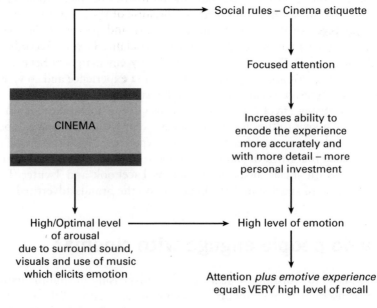

Reproduced by permission of DCM

By contrast, the high level of arousal the cinema experience creates through surround sound and powerful visuals elicits emotion in the audience members which increases their ability to recall what they have seen. This is the basis of cinema's strength as a largely single-task media experience, and one which provides a number of advantages to advertisers seeking stand-out in today's multi-media, multi-tasking world.

## How many and what sort of people engage with cinema?

The first and most important thing to take on board is that despite all the doom-mongers who forecast its demise at the hands of video, cinema admissions have grown steadily for over 25 years.

**FIGURE 13.2**    UK cinema admissions each year (millions)

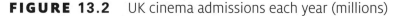
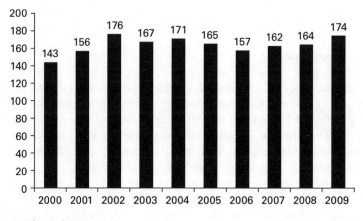

SOURCE: CAA/Rentrak EDI

Reproduced by permission of DCM

Indeed, the Cinema Advertising Association (CAA) estimated that approximately 172 million people would visit the cinema in 2010, which is the equivalent of filling the world's most successful music venue, the $O_2$ Arena, every single hour, 24 hours a day, every day of the year, with a captive audience.

IPA TouchPoints research data give us a very clear picture of what sorts of people comprise the cinema-going audience, and also provide insight into the reasons why they go. The focus is on the heavy users because this reveals where a medium's strengths lie and differentiates it more clearly from the other alternatives open to the advertiser and agency.

**FIGURE 13.3**    Profile of heavy cinema-goers compared to all adults

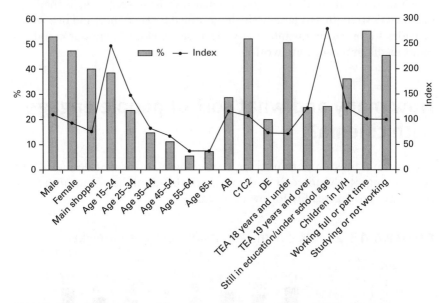

**SOURCE:** IPA TouchPoints3

Heavy cinema-goers are defined as people who go at least once a month, and we can see from the chart that there are significant spikes amongst young people aged 15 to 24, the AB social class and those who are still in education. The situation is rather similar in the United States where about two-thirds of the movie-going audience is under 35, with 88 per cent of the audience under 55, according to Nielsen Media Research.

In terms of the main reasons given for going to the cinema, the most important one by far is 'For entertainment', followed by 'To give me a night out', 'To spend time with friends and family' and 'To relax/escapism'. The heavy cinema-goer is also much more likely to agree with the following statements than the average adult: 'I often talk about films I've seen at the cinema with friends/family', 'There is no better place to watch films than the cinema' and 'When I really want to see a film I will go and see it as soon as it is released'. Americans share this social behaviour and see cinema as part of a night out, with 48 per cent of movie-goers dining at a restaurant and 31 per cent shopping before or after a movie, according to SV/Lieberman Research.

**FIGURE** 13.4   Main reasons to go to the cinema

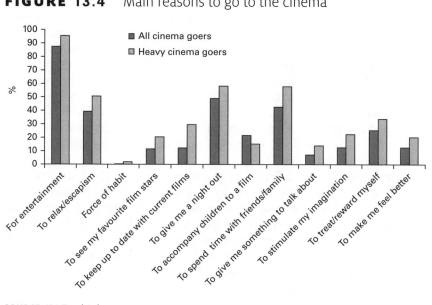

**SOURCE:** IPA TouchPoints3

# What advertising opportunities does cinema offer?

Cinema offers a wide range of creative opportunities, both in the auditorium and in the foyer. The so-called 'content platform' offers a pre-advertising reel position and an exceptional opportunity to showcase content in a proven environment. It also allows advertisers to broadcast longer lengths of content than the normal commercial. Advertisers who have successfully used this platform in the past include the BBC, who showcased their forth-coming programme releases, and Virgin Media, who ran a year-long national short film competition. DCM, one of the UK's two cinema advertising sales houses, has created 'From the Red Carpet', a movie-based entertainment show played within the advertising reel. Advertisers can sponsor this show using on-screen branding opportunities and related online content.

The 'advertising reel' is the part of the pre-show sequence where com-mercials are shown, much as in a television ad break, but with a greater degree of focus. This is where the bulk of cinema advertising appears, but there are also premium positions where commercials can be placed outside the ad reel and nearer to the start of the trailers and film. The current opportunities are the 'Silver Spot', which runs after the ad reel and before the trailers, and the 'Gold Spot' just before the film itself and made famous by Orange, the innovative mobile phone operator, with its long-running sponsorship of the 'switch off your mobile' message delivered by celebrity mini-movies which appear just before all non-family films.

An advertiser can also take fullest advantage of the captive cinema audience and create maximum impact by disrupting the usual programme sequence and transforming an on-screen advertisement into a face-to-face experience. Done well, the surprise of a live commercial can generate almost total recall and create a cascade of positive word-of-mouth. A good recent example is a Nintendo Wii ad with actors playing a mother and her son getting up from the audience and playing tennis on a Wii console projected on the big screen. Brands can also screen live key football and rugby matches, Formula 1 races, opera and computer gaming events. For example, Nike has used cinemas in this way to screen the Football World Cup, thus creating a close association between brand and event.

'Film seasons', when a brand sponsors a series of films at the cinema, are a highly effective way for advertisers to gain association with some of the most popular films of all time. Selecting the most appropriate genre for your audience allows this activity to be highly targeted. As part of their brand's disaster movie/entertainment campaign concept created by Grey London, Frijj staged a film season called 'Four Ridges', and even built a 2008 limited edition milkshake into the campaign by naming it 'Vanillaaaaarghh'. The Frijj case history by Ollie Gilmore won a Bronze IPA Effectiveness Award in 2009.

A variation on this theme is for a brand to sponsor preview screenings of a forthcoming movie in front of a specially invited audience; this enables them to become associated with a film before its official release, and also to advertise before it. There are also many standard sponsorship opportunities available within cinemas such as the Odeon Kids Club and Cineworld Movies for Juniors. These involve screenings of previously released films on Saturday mornings at pocket money prices and are an ideal opportunity for advertisers such as Butlins to appeal to both kids and their accompanying mums. Similarly the 'Big Scream' is run by the Picturehouse chain and caters exclusively for new parents with young babies so they can enjoy the latest releases without worrying about their little ones making a noise. At the other end of the age range, Odeon Senior Screen is a weekly cinema club held at Odeon sites nationwide and offers guests the chance to meet friends for a mid-morning screening of some recent and classic films.

Cinema foyers offer a high-traffic opportunity with a long dwell time. The average cinema-goer spends 18 minutes there before going into the auditorium and 93 per cent of cinemagoers claim to notice foyer advertising, which includes standees (large free-standing displays), ticket backs and popcorn boxes, the latter being ideal for adding a direct response mechanic to on-screen or other foyer activity. Sampling and product demonstrations can also work well, and given an average group of three there is also plenty of opportunity for talkability, especially if foyer and on-screen activities are linked. And of course there are many opportunities for brands to use other media channels in the build-up to a cinema visit. For example, Bluetooth is a mobile advertising platform across cinema networks and allows consumers to download trailer and brand information. In 2010 Pearl & Dean signed a deal with Tangible Media to deploy their interactive floor projections and 3D technologies to 50 UK cinemas. People can walk across this 'floor media' and their steps activate the surface with remarkably life-like imagery which can be tailored to a particular brand and linked to a cinema commercial or other in-foyer display.

Meanwhile, cinema's impressive ad revenue growth can be attributed in part to the advancement of the digital platform. Over the past few years, the shift from analogue to digital projection systems has reduced the barrier to entry caused by traditional production requirements. These involved the purchase and distribution of large numbers of expensive 35mm film prints of a commercial, which digital transmission renders obsolete. Unsurprisingly, this has been a primary contributor to the rapidly increasing use of the medium by national advertisers. In this context the potential of 3D is huge and 28 movies using this immersive technology were released in 2010. This number will increase in 2011.

# IPA Effectiveness Awards case study summary

*Gold Award Winner – IPA Effectiveness Awards 2009*

*Campaign: Cyclists should be seen and not hurt*

*Brand: Cycling Safety*

*Client: Transport for London (TfL)*

*Entrant: WCRS Ltd*

*Principal Author: Giselle Okin, WCRS*

*Contributing Authors: Fergus Adam, WCRS; Laurence Parkes, WCRS*

In 2007, 21 cyclists in London died because they weren't seen. The challenge was to find an idea that did not discourage cyclists from riding, or place blame for the accidents. The strategy therefore was not just to tell drivers that cyclists were not seen, but to actually prove it, by creating a test that enabled viewers to experience how easy it could be to look, but not see. Therefore, the 'Moonwalking Bear' video was born. The communications approach was to create a film showing the limitations of the viewers' own brains by asking them to count how many times the basketball is passed by the team in white. In taking the challenge, people concentrate so hard they simply do not notice the moon-walking bear as he wanders through the basketball game! Try it for yourself at **http://www.youtube.com/watch? v=xNSgmm9Fx2s**. Cinema was used, along with a London-only TV campaign, to generate word-of-mouth that would help the campaign to spread online.

The 'test' has been experienced by over 13 million people, saving an estimated £2.3m in human and administrative costs, and resulting in payback of £3.66 for every £1 spent. Perhaps more importantly, with a budget of only £600,000, TfL managed to reduce deaths on London roads by a third.

**FIGURE 13.5**    Did you see the moonwalking bear?

Reproduced by permission of WCRS

# Direct mail and e-mail

## 14

## The media owner's 'elevator pitch'

Since Lester Wunderman first used the term 'direct marketing' in 1967 to describe the practice of mail order selling (direct marketing via mail), it has become synonymous with direct mail. However, today e-mail is fast challenging direct mail as the primary medium of direct marketing. Both direct mail and e-mail are addressable media that allow the marketer to talk one-to-one to the recipient, thus targeting the message directly and personally to customers.

The key principle of each direct communication is its specific 'call to action', and this involves an overriding emphasis on trackable, measurable, positive response. In terms of cost per thousand, direct mail is the most expensive of all media. Having said that, a well-executed direct campaign can nearly always deliver a positive return on marketing investment (ROMI). Knowing the costs per response and per customer acquired, and with an estimate of their likely lifetime value, the marketer can calculate the incremental profitability of every mailing.

E-mail, because of its speed of delivery and low costs, has led the growth of digital direct media alongside search and pay per click (PPC). E-mail with click-through to a website or microsite, followed by either brochure download or product purchase, has led to lower costs for direct marketing and even better return on marketing investment, thus reaffirming the role of direct media in the advertising and marketing communications mix.

## How do people engage with direct mail?

People who are actually in the market for a particular product or service are especially amenable to direct communication which relates to their current need. Thus the brand which manages to put itself in the media flow in the places where its consumers step in can be very successful in capturing their attention, engaging them and providing the information and mechanism required to close the sale.

In a context where people are busy and inundated with television, radio, print, e-mail, web pop-ups and outdoor advertising, the US Postal Service's 'Gateway to the Household®' study examined the power of mail to enter the everyday lives of consumers relatively unobtrusively. They found that consumers have embraced the post as part of their lives and have come to anticipate what has been dubbed the 'Mail Moment'. This occurs in a personal space where people are comfortable and are able to devote time and attention to reading the mail. So advertisers using the medium can connect with consumers in a positive environment, and with careful targeting, can maximize the chances their message will be read by potential customers.

The 2007 UK Direct Marketing Association (DMA) report, *Participation Media: The Consumer Perspective of Direct Marketing*, suggested that respondents fell into one of four clusters in terms of their attitudes, which helps to explain the variation in responses:

- 'Open all hours': younger, more likely to be female, open to communications generally, most concerned about the quality of information and keen on customer magazines but quick to unsubscribe or reject communications that are not of interest.

- 'Pragmatists': more likely to be in the family life stage, balanced attitudes, mid-market, concerned with value for money and most responsive to direct mail.

- 'Time pressured butterflies': older, upmarket, more likely to be female, who value fast response and prefer newspapers and magazines as a source of information.

- 'Guarded privatists': more likely to be retired and male, they are generally negative about targeted communications and prefer broadcast media channels such as TV and radio.

The DMA report also states that in terms of general attitudes towards dealing directly with companies and marketing communications, consumer responses are often paradoxical – on the one hand 65 per cent of people feel overwhelmed by the number of commercial messages they are exposed to, while at the same time 66 per cent agree that they are happy to pick and choose between the ways they get information and services from companies. Thus the simple adage, 'a relevant message is a welcome message', seems true.

# How many and what sort of people engage with mail?

In the UK, the Direct Mail Information Service (DMIS) reports that 97 per cent of people sort their mail on the day it arrives, with 89 per cent looking at it immediately and 80 per cent claiming to be engaged in the mail they receive. Eighty-five per cent of people who sort the mail are the principal decision-makers on household spending. In two-thirds of households, women are the people with exclusive responsibility for sorting mail. Ninety-five per cent of these 'sorters' determine which advertising material is kept. Surprisingly perhaps, 60 per cent of consumer advertising mail is opened and 40 per cent is read. Understandably, because the sender is known to the recipient, 'warm' mailings perform best, with 38 per cent of consumers buying from these at some point.

Overall, men receive more direct mail than women (7 items vs. 5.6 items). In social class terms ABs continue to receive the most items of direct mail per week (7.9) whereas C2s (5.4) and DEs (5.4) receive the least. This is unsurprising given the relative value of these segments in terms of purchasing power. Similarly, receipt of direct mail tends to increase with age until 45–54, where it peaks. The proportion of super-heavy mail receivers (those receiving 6+ items per week) has slightly decreased. Super-heavies now constitute just over a third (32 per cent) of all respondents against 34 per cent in 2003.

Experian's latest research (2010) via its consumer classification system, Mosaic, shows that 15- to 24-year-olds are 'highly receptive' to direct mail, and are the demographic most likely to engage with it, after the over-65s. Teenagers are more open to direct mail than their parents, although they still lag behind the over-65s in their enthusiasm for leaflets, door drops and the like, and young consumers also prefer personal shopping to waiting for delivery. Their research also reports that although the younger generations spend a lot of time on the internet, they have a greater tendency to buy things in shops rather than ordering online. Experian attributes this to teenagers being part of the 'want it now' generation who use a cross-channel approach to optimize their purchasing experience.

IPA TouchPoints tells us a bit more about responses to direct mail. In the last 12 months, 43 per cent of people have used a voucher or coupon and 29 per cent have kept direct mail for later use or reference.

**FIGURE 14.1**    Response to DM in the last 12 months (Adults)

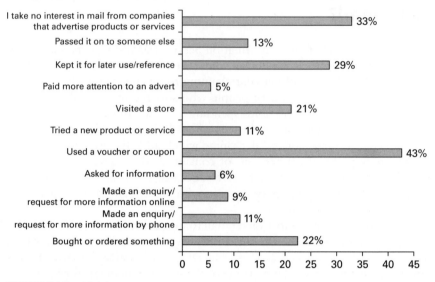

**SOURCE:** IPA TouchPoints3

In terms of the types of direct mail that consumers find useful, 74 per cent find discount coupons and offers valuable, 66 per cent appreciate product samples and 57 per cent believe they benefit from receiving government information.

**FIGURE 14.2**    Types of DM considered useful (Adults)

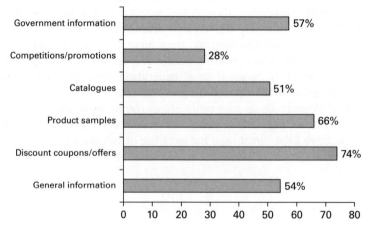

**SOURCE:** IPA TouchPoints3

# What advertising opportunities do direct mail and e-mail offer?

## *Direct mail*

It's fashionable nowadays to talk about 'owned' media and it's true that brand and corporate websites are providing a major new channel to market. However, one of the oldest and most important owned media is the personally addressed account mailing which has to be sent to customers either to secure payment, as in the case of a credit card or utility company, or to provide a statement, as in the case of a bank, savings institution or mortgage company. Typically the envelopes will carry the logo of the company, and as soon as the recipient sees that it is an official letter very likely concerning financial matters which have to be attended to, it gets opened pretty quickly! But of course each of these letters provides an opportunity to enclose additional marketing communications at very little additional cost, and these account mailings can be used to cross-sell other services using special offers or other introductory incentives.

The advertising opportunities presented by direct mail are at one level quite limited, but looked at in another way, almost infinite. The limitation is that the advertising material has to be delivered by a postman to the doorstep and usually posted through the letterbox or placed in a mailbox. This physical constraint, allied to the cost of postage in relation to the profitability of the product or service in question, clearly sets some tight parameters. However, on the other hand, postmen have vehicles and as long as the advertiser is prepared to pay the cost, any object whatsoever can be delivered to a household as part of a direct marketing campaign. There's a whole range of companies who use the postal services to deliver products to their customers at home or the office, and usually these packages not only contain the order but also re-marketing materials such as brochures, flyers or coupons designed to incentivize a further purchase. And of course 'guarantee cards' are a staple item within these delivery packages and though their completion, or not, has no bearing on the purchaser's statutory rights, nevertheless significant numbers of people fill in the details and return the cards, thus providing the company with valuable information for their customer database.

As we have seen, the core principle of direct mail is that it is a medium designed to elicit a response from the customer. So a very high proportion of the items posted or delivered to households contain an offer or some other enticement which is sufficiently compelling to generate action. These actions are many and various but would include accepting an invitation to apply for a catalogue, credit card account, join a book or wine club, test drive a new car, or sample a new food or toiletries product.

Because direct mail is at its most effective when it lands on the doormat of a household where an individual is actively in the market for a particular product or service, it's usually a good idea for the content of the mailing piece to be multifaceted. This is because the prospect is in research mode and hungry for information, including the basic facts and figures about the product, where it can be purchased and whether there are any special financial incentives on offer.

The largest category of unaddressed mail is door-to-door leaflet marketing. Distribution services are used extensively by the consumer goods and food industries, and many other businesses focusing on a local catchment area such as free newspapers and magazines. This method is targeted purely by area or postcode, and costs a fraction of the amount of a mail shot, saving the cost of stamps, envelopes and address lists with the names of home occupants. Taxi cab companies, estate agents, home decorating and maintenance contractors, and the home delivery services of pizza and curry restaurants are some of the mainstays of this sector.

## E-mail marketing

To many people, the term 'e-mail marketing' automatically means an e-mail intent on one thing: selling. In actual fact, there are a number of types of e-mail communications, some of which are just about customer relationship management.

The following are seven popular forms of e-mail marketing:

- E-mail postcards: These are short announcements, usually with a graphic, a simple layout and a clear message. They are mostly used to inform of special offers, new products and events. An example would be a 'new listing' postcard from an estate agent, informing potential buyers of a house that has just come on the market.

- E-mail invitations: These are similar to e-mail postcards, but the theme is all about 'inviting' you to some special event. For example, a car dealer might invite you to a special launch-night party to introduce its new car model.

- E-mail catalogues: These are electronic versions of print catalogues, although they will usually only list or promote a small selection of the products available. They usually contain pictures with short descriptions and links, and encourage the reader to click through to learn more and purchase.

- E-mail press releases: While this approach generally targets media contacts, it is widely used by businesses and charities to reach other audiences. A good example would be an animal shelter like Battersea Dogs Home that e-mails announcements regarding 'pets available for adoption'.

- E-mail newsletters: Also known as an eNewsletter, this is an increasingly popular customer relationship management (CRM) tool which helps a business or organization build a stronger relationship with its clients, prospects or membership group.

- E-mail surveys: This works particularly well for customer satisfaction or product development purposes. The company sends a questionnaire, perhaps offering a prize or free offer as an incentive for submitting the answers online.

- E-coupons: At one time, simple discounts or special offers sent by e-mail were the standard options to generate sales or encourage repeat business. But now, with the introduction of QR Code technology, new applications for redemption are available.

**FIGURE 14.3**    A QR code in action

# Done anything remarkable with a small budget?

Whether it's online, on TV or on a lamp-post, if you've had to work within a small budget (that's less than £2.5M to you and me), we'd like to see your submission to the IPA Effectiveness Awards 2011. Write a 3,000 word piece on 'How I achieved a handsome return on my marketing investment', signed off by April 15. To find out more visit ipaeffectivenessawards.co.uk

**SOURCE:** IPA

Each of these e-mail marketing techniques has specific advantages (and dis-advantages), and companies often have to experiment to find out which encourage customers to respond. Successful e-mail marketing is really pretty simple: get the right message to the right person at the right time and you will deliver more successful outcomes.

# IPA Effectiveness Awards case study summary

*Integration and Gold Award Winner – IPA Effectiveness Awards 2006*

*Campaign: 50 Pints or a TV Licence?*

*Brand: TV Licensing*

*Client: BBC*

*Entrant: Proximity London*

*Authors: Adrian Hoole, Debi Bester, Kate Harding, Paul Sturniolo, Arabel Thomson and Peter Kirk*

The BBC was concerned that many penny-pinching university students were watching television without paying for a £126.50 annual TV licence. To combat this problem, an integrated, ongoing campaign was launched which both raised awareness of the legal requirement to have a licence and also reinforced the consequences of evasion. Direct mail was a major part of this campaign, with a targeted mailing programme that sent letters to unregistered students, emphasizing the consequences of evasion as time went on. Owing to this campaign's personalized and honest approach, the vast majority of students bought a TV licence, with a year-on-year improvement of 10 per cent between 2003 and 2006. The campaign delivered an overall ROMI of 12:1 and illustrates the important role direct mail can play in encouraging positive action.

**FIGURE 14.4** Student TV licensing campaign

## FIGURE 14.5

A B Sample
Sample Address 2
Sample Address 3
Sample Address 4
Sample Address 5
Sample Address 6
Sample Address 7
Sample Address 8

### "You'll be needing a licence for that TV."

Dear Mrs Sample

You know as well as we do that it's not funny watching TV without a licence. While some students may make light of doing so, it's against the law. No doubt, that's why you've ordered these posters, leaflets and application forms.

Thank you for taking the time and trouble to distribute them in student accommodation and around campus, for example in common rooms, bars, the union and career offices.

It's fair to say that students, especially freshers, aren't used to having to think about such serious matters as obtaining TV Licences. That's why this campaign explains who needs one, how much it is, how many easy ways there are to pay, and how quickly they can get it all sorted.

continue overleaf

Reproduced by permission of Proximity London

# FIGURE 14.6

**Who needs a TV Licence?**

As you are aware, the law requires everyone who uses any device to receive television programmes to be covered by a TV Licence. But just in case you're asked, here's a recap at the start of the uni year of the finer points of the law.

A licence is required to use not only a TV, but also a video or DVD recorder, a set-top box or even a PC which you watch TV on.

If a student is living in a hall of residence and uses any of this equipment, then they need their own TV Licence. If a student rents a single room in a house under a separate tenancy agreement, once again they need to buy a licence of their own. However, if a group of students rent a house under a joint tenancy agreement, then only one TV Licence is needed for the house.

**A £1,000 fine – nothing funny in that.**

You'll see that the posters and leaflets also convey some of the serious consequences your students are risking if they continue to use a TV in student accommodation without a valid TV Licence.

- All unlicensed addresses are listed on our database.
- Unlicensed student addresses on and off campus face investigation by our Enforcement Team.
- Our latest electronic equipment can detect an unlicensed TV being used within 20 seconds.
- If caught using a TV without a licence, students may be interviewed under caution, and their statement taken as evidence.
- They then risk prosecution and a maximum fine of £1,000.

## Seriously, your students will be glad you encouraged them to get a TV Licence.

If you're asked by your students how they can get their licence sorted, the short answer is, go to **www.tvlicensing.co.uk/students** or call **0870 600 1236**.

You might also mention that once they've bought their licence, if they find they don't need their TV Licence for three consecutive months prior to it expiring (e.g. the three month summer break), they can apply for a refund for that period.

Finally, if you have any further questions or if you need more application forms, please don't hesitate to call us on the dedicated line we've set up especially for university officials, **0207 544 3116**.

After all, we'd rather help you encourage your students to get a TV Licence, than have them risk a visit from an Enforcement Officer this term.

Yours sincerely,

Nicky Barret
TV Licensing Student Campaign Manager

Reproduced by permission of Proximity London

# 15 Magazines

## The media owner's 'elevator pitch'

Magazines can offer a quality and depth of information and opinion that is unrivalled by most media. At the same time they are also highly personal, usually read for entertainment and relaxation in a person's leisure, pleasure time. As such, magazines play a dual role; they act as both friends and resources, so readers use them to gain guidance and support.

Because of this, magazines act as leaders and advocates for communities with common interests, engaging their audiences at a deeply emotional level and shaping their attitudes and actions in the process. As a result, the relationship between a magazine and its reader is potentially one of the most powerful tools an advertiser can utilize.

This relationship means that advertisers benefit from the de facto endorsement of the particular publication, as the influence a magazine holds over its readership means that they see its content, including advertising, as relevant to them. Indeed, advertisements are likely to be valued and read like other content, and viewed by readers as a vital part of the magazine experience.

## How do people engage with magazines?

Average magazine readers have a repertoire of around five titles and they are happy to part with their hard-earned cash and commit uninterrupted time to read them because a magazine is a treat they look forward to. This is why magazines take on the dimensions of a personal friend rather than serving as an impersonal information channel, as illustrated by research into consumer engagement undertaken by the Henley Centre.

**FIGURE 15.1** Magazines and 'My world'

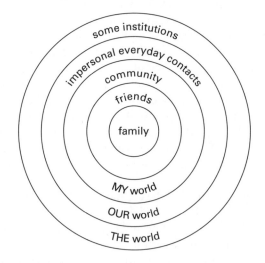

People's trust in traditional sources of authority continues to wane as their cynicism about government and corporate institutions grows. Instead, they are increasingly putting their faith in their closest, most immediate networks of friends and family. For individuals, belief and confidence today reside largely in what the Henley Centre terms 'MY world', rather than 'THE world'. This goes for commercial messages too. As a result, the most powerful piece of product promotion tends to be a recommendation from a personal source. Magazines dovetail well with the concept of 'MY world', because they enjoy many of the same characteristics of a close friend.

By understanding their readers, magazines are able to influence the choices they make, and magazine advertising can play a crucial role in this process as well. The unusual level of receptiveness that magazine readers display towards advertising is illustrated by research conducted by media agency Starcom. In this qualitative exercise readers were asked to select the 10 pages of their favourite magazine which most accurately captured the magazine's personality. Revealingly, 30 per cent of the pages selected were advertising as opposed to editorial. Clearly this is a mutually reinforcing and symbiotic relationship, as advertisers seek to address their target audiences through the pages of a magazine whose own editorial is designed to appeal to the same people. Indeed, according to IPA TouchPoints, people who read magazines are 33 per cent more likely than all adults to agree that they 'trust the advertising they see in magazines'. TouchPoints also tells us that 35 per cent of Conversation Catalysts™ are people who read magazines, so magazines not only influence conversation but also spur readers into action and can serve as a key bridge to both online and offline interaction. According to a PPA/TGI study in 2008, in 70 per cent of product categories magazines are the primary offline driver of online purchase, and they are unrivalled in categories such as fashion, travel, food and healthy living.

Specialist magazines, for example those concerning consumer durables such as computers and cameras and high-ticket infrequent purchases such as cars and property, are specifically sought out for the advertising they contain, and could be the first thing readers will look at. In such instances the advertising can itself provide a strong motivation for buying that magazine. Indeed, at the interface with annual directories such as *Yellow Pages* there is a genre of magazine that is purely composed of advertising, such as *AutoTrader* for cars, and *Daltons Weekly*, which lists business opportunities, holiday rentals and properties for sale. These are increasingly offline and online hybrids and *Exchange & Mart*, once a dominant player in the UK, went online-only in 2009.

The online world has enabled the creation of a whole new segment within the magazine market – webzines and e-zines – which live an entirely digital life. The relationship between online and hard copy print continues to evolve and a new trend is emerging which is the birth of magazines from brands which start online. Two of the most striking examples here are ASOS.com and Pistonheads. But of course the really exciting digital platform of the moment is applications or 'apps' for smart phones and tablet computers. These devices offer crisp and clear displays and the ease of use of touch-screen technology means that magazines can easily replicate their visually rich content in digital format for the first time. Technology magazine *Wired* serves as the perfect example here. The first edition on its app sold more than 73,000 copies, far more than its print edition, and shows that publishers can sell their content across multiple platforms and reach more readers in the process.

And of course there are other more traditional ways in which magazines have diversified to generate new revenue streams. One of the most famous examples is that of *Playboy* magazine, which started as a lifestyle magazine and then spawned an international network of clubs to make that lifestyle a reality. Indeed, the British casino revenues dwarfed those from publishing and financed the global Playboy empire. Some magazines have developed successful exhibition spin-offs, such as the *Country Living* magazine's bi-annual Christmas and Spring Fairs, and there are exhibition venues which have gone the other way and spawned magazines, such as the Royal Academy and its *RA Magazine* which, in addition to covering RA exhibitions and artists, covers art around London, Britain and abroad, art books and current debates in the arts.

**FIGURE 15.2** Country Living Magazine Christmas Fair

Reproduced by permission of Country Living

**FIGURE 15.3** RA Magazine

**SOURCE:** Reproduced by permission of RA Magazine

There's also the whole area of conferences and reader events which increase a magazine's points of engagement with its readership and create an even stronger sense of 'MY world' as per the Henley Centre research.

## How many and what sort of people engage with magazines?

Magazines remain a versatile and crucial mass market medium. Between September 2009 and October 2010, titles measured by NRS reached 76 per cent of the adult population of the UK. To put this reach into perspective, during the same period only 74 per cent of the population ever accessed the internet.

IPA TouchPoints3 gives further insight into who reads magazines and how they engage people. In terms of the heavy users, defined as people who spend more than 2.5 hours per week reading magazines, the peaks are amongst women and the 65+ age group, with the 15–24-year-olds and younger being the troughs.

**FIGURE 15.4**    Profile of heavy magazine readers compared to all adults

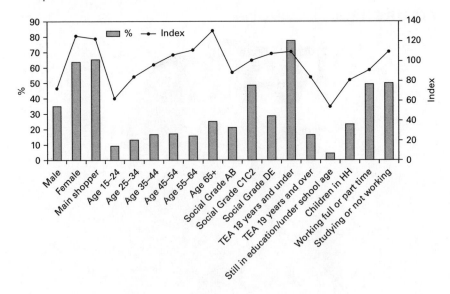

SOURCE: IPA TouchPoints3

By far the most important reasons for reading magazines are for entertainment and relaxation, followed by keeping informed about hobbies and the need to keep up to date.

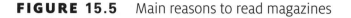

**FIGURE 15.5**  Main reasons to read magazines

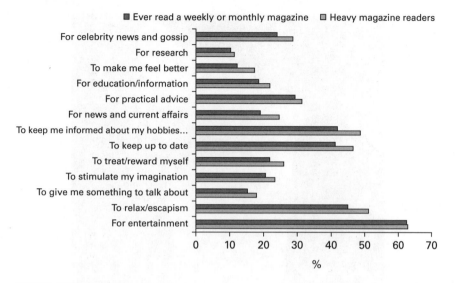

**SOURCE:** IPA TouchPoints3

In terms of purchasing behaviour, the TouchPoints lifestyle statements confirm the closeness of the relationship between reader and publication with their irresistibility clearly evident, as is their role as a voice of authority and also a source of relaxation. The pattern of readership through weekdays and weekends is also in line with the 'MY World' notion, with mini-peaks at break-times and mealtimes and most readership in the evenings and during weekends.

# What advertising opportunities do magazines offer?

In display advertising in magazines there are a couple of common strategies. Advertisers in monthlies may decide to occupy a constant presence by advertising consistently in the same titles. This will reinforce the brand to loyal readers over a long period of time. Advertisers using weeklies may advertise heavily in a few similar titles at the same time and then gradually wind down over a few weeks. However, there are many more variations on these themes. For example, there are special positions such as the outside back cover, used so successfully by agency BBH for Boddingtons beer to extol its distinctive golden colour, creamy head and Mancunian heritage.

**FIGURE 15.6**    Clever use of outside cover by BBH

Reproduced by permission of InBev

US advertising noting data from GfK MRI Starch Advertising Research is revealing. Firstly, their research shows that space size does matter, with larger-sized ads earning higher-than-average noting scores, which become lower than average for spaces less than a full page. Advertising position within a magazine also matters, to a degree: there is very little impact on noting scores when comparing left-hand versus right-hand spaces, while there is some impact in being in the first quarter of the magazine. But the real boost to noting scores comes from having a cover position. Indeed, the most noted space type in the research at 81 per cent of respondents is a 'second cover gatefold four pages in four color'. This is a gatefold where one opens the magazine and the attachment to the right-hand border of the front cover opens out to reveal two double-page spreads, making a total of four pages in colour. Clearly assessing the value trade-off of position versus price is a key role for media planning and buying agencies.

Going beyond display advertising space per se, the inventiveness of advertisers and their agencies can lead to all sorts of clever embellishments that can engage the reader with their brand. For example, one of the most successful promotional devices used to sell magazines is the cover mount, and according to TouchPoints, 22 per cent of people who read magazines agree that they are 'more likely to buy a magazine if a product sample is attached to it'. Toiletries and cosmetics companies use small sachets or fragrance strips stuck to their advertisement to give consumers a mini-trial of their new product. Loose inserts in magazines can also be very successful advertising vehicles, and sometimes advertisers will produce a substantial publication of their own which can be bagged up with the magazine, adding value from the purchaser's point of view.

While display advertising clearly has the lion's share of the business, the role of magazines as a source of information makes them a very fertile environment for semi-display and classified advertising, which comprises 17 per cent of revenues for consumer magazines and 25 per cent for business-to-business (B2B) ones. These advertisements create lively marketplaces for particular kinds of products and services which seek out the same target audiences as the publications themselves.

But we should not forget another very important category of commercial communication which magazines excel at. This is the advertorial article which is a paid-for piece of content that must be clearly identified as a 'promotional feature' in order to position it clearly in the middle ground between pure editorial and advertising. The benefit of an advertorial is that the advertiser gets its message more closely embedded in the magazine and has a more overt endorsement from the publisher as a result. Publishers and brands can also cooperate in producing joint competitions, sales promotions or reader offers not available elsewhere. In each case the media owner is adding value to its publication for its readers, while at the same time the brand owner is creating an opportunity for product trial. Perhaps the ultimate example of brand involvement in magazines is when it produces one of its own, either through a specialist agency or direct with a publishing house. Customer magazines have become an important segment of the market in their own right and account for £920 million, set to top £1 billion in the next year.

# Creative use of the magazine medium

Double-page spreads in colour are expensive but Ken New and David Abbott, then respectively media and creative directors of leading UK agency Abbott Mead Vickers, figured out a clever way to beat the system for their client, Sainsbury's, and Jeremy Miles, the account director, had little difficulty in selling the idea to the client. As Ken New recounts:

Sainsbury's was then the brand leader and we said that they should always behave like one, ie lead from the front, always be first, be dominant and be confident. So we always stipulated 'first supermarket in the issue'. We worked out that some magazines, because of technology limitations, always had a colour/b&w spread on pages 2 and 3 (ie the opening spread) which was reserved for a single page inside front cover facing contents editorial. We negotiated this space for the Sainsbury's colour/b&w spreads so, by definition, it was the first thing that readers saw when they opened the magazine. That's acting like a brand leader!

**FIGURE 15.7**    Ground-breaking advertising for a supermarket in the 1980s

Reproduced by permission of Sainsbury's and AMV BBDO

## Return on investment

In the current economic environment advertisers are placing more emphasis than ever on return on investment. Magazines not only enable advertisers to optimize the reach offered by traditional primary media, but can help to do so at a substantially lower cost. In 2005, research company TNS was commissioned by the PPA to investigate the return of investment the medium offers. The study focused on tracking 20 FMCG products and showed that magazines achieved a return on investment of 79 per cent during the length of the campaign, rising to 177 per cent over a 12-month period.

# IPA Effectiveness Awards case study summary

*Best Small Budget and Silver Award Winner – IPA Effectiveness Awards 2008*

*Campaign: From bags to riches*

*Brand: Radley + Co*

*Client: UKTV*

*Agency: DDB London*

*Authors: Julian Calderara, Les Binet, Sarah Carter and Monika Jakubczak*

In 2007, Radley had a small budget with which to expand its customer base. Many women had heard of the handbags but thought they were too quirky. Radley wanted to convert these women into customers while at the same time retaining their existing and loyal customer base. To do this, they decided to focus on the individuality of the bags, and introduced the slogan 'Truly Radley Deeply'. They placed double-page spreads in high-profile women's glossies, including *Elle*, *Grazia*, *Vogue* and *The Sunday Times' Style*. These ads focused attention directly on the bags themselves, emphasizing their distinctiveness as well as the design inspiration. The campaign tapped into the emotional attachment women have to their handbags, and within a year Radley had become the nation's favourite handbag designer, even trouncing high-end brands. The company's value tripled, and the campaign generated a payback of £5.57 per £1 spent, proving that magazines have the potential to produce large effects, even on relatively small budgets.

**FIGURE 15.8 and 15.9**    Radley tapped into the emotional connection women have with their handbags

Reproduced by permission of DDB UK

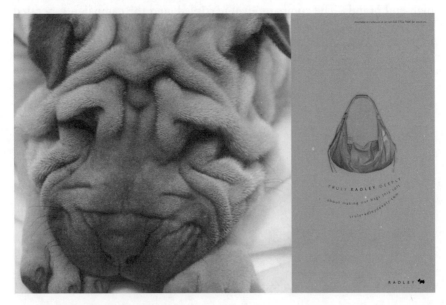

Reproduced by permission of DDB UK

# National newspapers

## 16

## The media owner's 'elevator pitch'

Newspapers have a special place in the life of the UK public: we bring them into our homes and our workplaces to accompany us through the working day and as we wind down in the evening and at weekends. We look to them for facts, analysis, commentary and opinion, choosing the title that best reflects our own views. When we are reading our paper, we are immersed in the experience, actively seeking information and entertainment while filtering out distractions. This makes newspapers an ideal forum for brands to reach people when they are highly engaged and receptive to new ideas.

National newspapers hold a one-to-one conversation with over half (55 per cent) of adults in the UK every day through print versions alone (October 2009–September 2010 NRS GB). This combination of mass market scale and precision-targeting capability allows brands to ensure their marketing budgets work as hard as possible. By identifying the exact demographic and mindset they want to address, marketers can minimize wastage and the overall impact of a campaign can be enhanced by increasing the resonance of each individual execution through tailoring it to its specific audience.

Brands can take advantage of the medium's logistical agility: relatively low product costs and short lead times enable marketers to be fast, responsive and as relevant to their audience's day-to-day lives as the newspapers are themselves. This means that newspapers are an efficient and cost-effective part of the media mix.

## How do people engage with national newspapers?

In 2007, the UK's Newspaper Marketing Agency analysed a wide range of research into how readers engage with their papers – this included findings from over 200 research groups, over 7,000 quantitative interviews and over 30,000 interviews from the NMA's in-market effectiveness tracking research.

The results show the powerful and involving experience papers create for their readers. Newspapers command attention: a newspaper is not a background medium, for while readers are engaged with their paper it is their sole focus. Respondents spoke of the intensity of the reading experience created by immersing oneself in a favourite title. Some referred to this as a bubble which excluded external distractions, allowing readers to dedicate time and attention to their paper (Emotional Connections research, NMA July 2007). The result of this high level of involvement was, respondents said, a much deeper connection with the content of a newspaper than that of some other media. To read something in a newspaper is to 'feel' it – information and ideas could 'sink in deeper' because of the high level of active engagement elicited by newspapers. One respondent summed this up by saying: 'It's more personal with the paper... you're taking it in more.' An example of the power of newspapers was *The Daily Telegraph* exposé of MP's expenses which dominated its pages for weeks during the summer of 2009 and contributed to the demise of the Labour government.

This touches on another important characteristic of the bond newspapers have with their readers: emotional proximity. Readers tend to choose the paper which most closely reflects their own opinions, so even before they start reading they are already receptive to the views they will find inside. This is enhanced by the one-to-one nature of the reading experience; for instance, respondents used phrases such as 'It's like a person close to me' to describe their paper. The implication for marketers is clear: reaching people in a trusted environment where they are receptive to views, facts and entertainment is a potent way for brands to engage readers and to ensure commercial messages are absorbed as part of the immersive newspaper experience.

The closeness readers feel with their favourite title allows papers to fulfil a broad range of need-states from entertainment and diversion to the provision of quick-fire facts. In 2002, News International conducted qualitative research called 'Reader NeedStates' to explore exactly which functional and emotional needs papers answer, and used a quantitative study to establish the relative size of each particular need. The study also showed that these need states can vary depending on the day of the week, time of day and type of paper being read:

1  'Feed Me' is the biggest need-state accounting for 37% of readers during the week and 30% at the weekend. It is driven by a desire to get under the skin of news and events that hold particular personal interest and relevance, and is characterized by active, focused reading and a desire for the level of detail provided by long articles, charts and diagrams. It occurs later in the day during the week and in the morning at weekends.

2  The 'What's New' need-state accounts for 28% of readers. People in this mindset want a quick and easy update on the latest news and events so they feel and sound informed. They tend to skim important facts and headlines, wanting bite-sized information to provide a

**FIGURE 16.1** The power of newspapers

# The Daily Telegraph

Saturday, May 16, 2009 ·· MS □ **BRITAIN'S BEST-SELLING QUALITY DAILY** No 47,884 £1.60

● Labour backbencher confesses to 'unforgivable' expenses claim

# The MP and the phantom £13,000 mortgage

David Chaytor: likely to be suspended by the Labour Party over his expenses claim

FREE BOOK INSIDE TODAY
GARDENING FOR SMALL SPACES

12 GREAT SECTIONS

FREE CD BB KING'S GREATEST
SEE PAGE 36
PLUS INTERVIEW IN MAGAZINE

JAMES CRACKNELL'S 50 GREATEST BRITISH ADVENTURES
WEEKEND

## THE EXPENSES FILES DAY 9

By Robert Winnett and Jon Swaine

A LABOUR backbencher admitted last night that he had claimed almost £13,000 in interest payments for a mortgage that he had already repaid.

David Chaytor, the second MP to be named as having made illegitimate mortgage claims, said that he had made an "unforgivable error".

He faces a criminal inquiry into his expenses and is likely to be suspended from the Parliamentary Labour Party. Mr Chaytor's statement is the frankest admission of wrongdoing by an MP since the Daily Telegraph's investigation into the parliamentary expenses system began. The scandal continued to have serious ramifications in Westminster yesterday.

Shahid Malik, the Justice Minister, was forced to step down and the Metropolitan Police began initial inquiries into questionable claims by several MPs.

The Telegraph has established that between September 2005 and August 2006, Mr Chaytor claimed £1,175 a month for mortgage interest on a Westminster flat. However, Land Registry records show that the mortgage on the flat had already been paid off in January 2004.

Last night, Mr Chaytor apologised "unreservedly". "In respect of mortgage interest payments, there has been an unforgivable error in my accounting procedures for which I apologise unreservedly," he said in a statement. "I will act immediately to ensure repayment is made to the fees office." Lawyers said that his claims, which were similar to those made by Elliot Morley, the former environment minister, could constitute a criminal offence under the 2006 Fraud Act and the 1968 Theft Act.

A Downing Street spokesman last night said: "This is a very serious matter. The Chief Whip will be urgently discussing the matter with the Member of Parliament."

The MP for Bury North has some of the most controversial arrangements of any parliamentarian examined by the Telegraph over the past nine days. Since 2004, he has claimed for five different properties, "flipping" his designated second home between London, Yorkshire and Bury. He claimed for one home where his son was the named occupant on council tax bills.

His prompt admission of wrongdoing underlined the concern in Westminster that there were serious abuses of the expenses system that MPs had failed to disclose to their party leaders or parliamentary whips.

Today, the Telegraph's Expenses Files disclose more details of "excessive" claims, with MPs switching between properties or buying expensive items for their homes. Although there is no suggestion of illegality, the claims push the limits of acceptability.

It can be disclosed that:
□ Sir Gerald Kaufman, the former Labour minister, charged £1,851 for a rug imported from New York and tried to claim £8,865 for a television. He also put in a claim for £28,834 – of which £15,329 was paid – for improvements to his London flat, telling officials that he was "living in a slum".
□ Chris Bryant, the deputy leader of the House of Commons, "flipped" his second home twice in two years, allowing him to claim almost £20,000 from expenses.
□ Anthony Steen, a long-standing Conservative MP, claimed tens of thousands of pounds for his country mansion, including expenses for looking after 500 trees.
□ Tam Dalyell, the former father of the House of Commons, attempted to claim £18,000 for bookcases two months before he retired as an MP in 2005.

Mr Chaytor checked out of the Fairfax Hotel in Washington last night, cutting short a taxpayer-funded trip with the children, schools and families select committee. He is expected back in Britain today.

In a statement, he said: "Changing and complex family circumstances have required me to live in different places during the last five years. During this time, I should have ensured that my mortgage had been switched to the flat in which I was temporarily living.

"Stupidly and inexplicably, and at a time of great personal and family stress, I failed to ensure that this was done."

Meanwhile, his wife said she was "flabbergasted" to be told of the expenses claim. Sheena Chaytor appealed to voters to believe it had been a genuine mistake.

"He has made a really stupid mistake – it was a mistake but I do not suppose anybody will believe him. I hope so though."

## Police set up panel to assess allegations against MPs

By Richard Edwards
Crime Correspondent

THE Metropolitan Police is making inquiries into MPs' expenses claims following disclosures by The Daily Telegraph.

In an unprecedented move, Sir Paul Stephenson, the Scotland Yard Commissioner, and Keir Starmer, the Director of Public Prosecutions, have set up a panel to assess allegations of misuse of expenses.

Police had been reluctant to get involved after several failed political investigations, but they have been left with little choice following serious allegations of fraud, and growing public anger.

A police source said: "We had to act as it has moved from snouts in the trough to fingers in the till."

The Metropolitan Police have received a number of complaints from members of the public about MPs, including the Cabinet members Alistair Darling and Geoff Hoon, the Labour peer Baroness Uddin and the former minister Elliot Morley. Criminal lawyers have said that Mr Morley's expenses claims could constitute a criminal offence under the 2006 Fraud Act and the 1968 Theft Act. He has been suspended from the Parliamentary Labour Party after it was disclosed that he was paid more than £16,000 in Commons expenses for a mortgage that no longer existed.

Mr Morley, a minister for nine years under Tony Blair, blamed his error on "sloppy accounting" and admitted that he claimed £800 a month for more than 18 months after his mortgage was repaid.

Police sources said that the allegations relating to Mr Morley were at the "most serious end" of complaints they were considering.

A joint statement issued by the Crown Prosecution *Continued on Page 4*

'We're scrapping ID cards.
We don't want anyone to
know we're MPs'

THE SAINTS
□ 10 MPs who refused
to join the gravy train
PAGE 9

## Malik steps down as Brown orders inquiry into his rent

By Robert Winnett, Gordon Rayner and Nigel Bunyan

SHAHID MALIK has become the first member of the Government to lose his job over the expenses row amid concerns that his living arrangements breached the ministerial code of conduct.

The Daily Telegraph disclosed yesterday that the Justice Minister benefited from a secret cut-price rental deal on his constituency home, which he designated as his "main home".

Meanwhile, he has claimed more than £66,000 in expenses – the maximum allowable amount – on his "second home" in London since becoming an MP in 2005. Mr Malik was forced to step down after Gordon Brown ordered a Whitehall inquiry into his rental agreement on his home in Dewsbury, West Yorks, where his landlord has said he pays well below the market rate.

Last night it was reported that any Labour MP found to have made improper expense claims would be automatically deselected.

The medical proposals, to be signed off by Labour's national executive next week, came as the Prime Minister was said to have given ministers a Monday night deadline to ensure expense claims over the past five years were lodged with the Parliamentary authorities and ready for publication.

Meanwhile, a poll found that almost two in three voters believed a general election should be called as soon as possible.

The ComRes survey for BBC Two's Daily Politics found 65 per cent agreed, compared with 33 percent who disagreed.

The ministerial code of conduct states that members of the Government must not accept any "gift or hospitality" which risks putting them under an "obligation". The arrangement had not been *Continued on Page 4*

EXCLUSIVE OFFER
15% OFF EVERYTHING AT HEAL'S
VOUCHER P30

ULTRA TRAVEL
YOUR GUIDE TO HEAVEN ON EARTH
FREE INSIDE

ISSN 0307-1235

Reproduced by permission of Barry Greenwood and *The Daily Telegraph* 16th May 2009 ©

**FIGURE 16.2**    Newspapers answer both functional and emotional needs

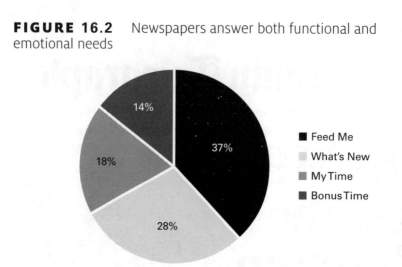

SOURCE: Reader NeedStates

quick link to what's happening in the world. The 'What's New' frame of mind tends to be seen more in the morning during the week and the afternoon at weekends.

**3** 'My Time' accounts for 18% of readers during the week and 21% during the weekend. It is characterized by wanting to relax and indulge in some personal time rather than absorbing need-to-know or current affairs. During the week, this mindset is strongest in the evening, while at weekends it is more prevalent in the morning for the quality titles and the afternoon for popular and mid-market papers.

**4** 'Bonus Time' accounts for 14% of readers and is typified by the weekday commute. Readers in this mindset want to fill some time and consequently have no set plan of what they will read – they look for stimulating content to draw them in. Most readers (62%) in this need-state will spend less than 20 minutes reading.

# How many and what sort of people engage with national newspapers?

Between October 2009 and September 2010, 55 per cent of the UK population read a national newspaper at least once a week (NRS GB). The average reach of national newspapers over a four-week period was 85.2 per cent of the population of the UK.

IPA TouchPoints provides important insight into the newspaper audience, specifically heavy users who spend more than 0.93 hours (56 minutes) per day reading newspapers. Among this group, the peaks are amongst men, the

**FIGURE 16.3** Four-weekly reach of national newspapers

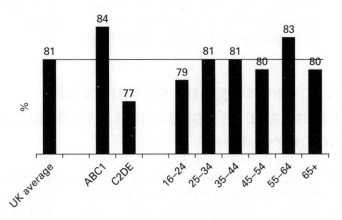

**SOURCE:** National Readership Surveys Ltd. (January–June 2010)

**FIGURE 16.4** Profile of heavy national newspaper readers compared to all adults

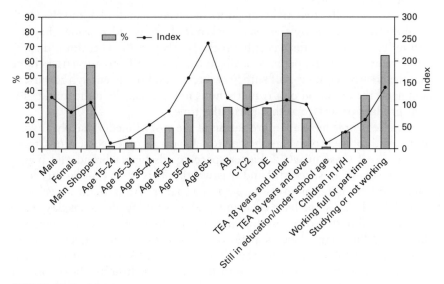

**SOURCE:** IPA TouchPoints3

55+ age group and those studying or not working, with 15–24-year-olds and those under school age being the troughs. In terms of social class, those in the AB social group are the most likely to be heavy newspaper readers.

TouchPoints also reveals the most important reasons for reading national newspapers, and these are consistent for both heavy and regular readers. Readers cite 'To keep up to date' and 'For news and current affairs' as their greatest motivations.

In terms of word-of-mouth, TouchPoints found that people who spent the greatest amount of time reading newspapers are most likely to be Conversation Catalysts™ for the following categories: 'financial services', 'public affairs or politics', 'gardening' and 'home appliances'.

# What advertising and commercial communications opportunities do national newspapers offer?

One of the main advertising benefits offered by newspapers is the medium's sheer agility. National newspapers can be used either to achieve UK-wide reach and a sense of scale for a brand, or to pinpoint specific audiences with bespoke, highly resonant creative work. The judicious use of titles and sections allows a brand to talk to very tightly defined demographics and mindsets. The very diverse nature of the newspaper medium can also provide advantages for advertisers who wish to address particular geographical regions of the country.

Newspapers offer two main categories of advertising: display and classified. Significantly, while people actively seek out classified advertising, they are naturally exposed to display advertising as they read. Therefore, display advertising in a newspaper is typically in the front half and advertisers hope that the creative content is of sufficient interest and offers enough reward to command the attention of a reader who is not necessarily in the market for their product or service at that particular time.

Because people have an appreciation of the cost of media (hardly anyone hasn't paid for their own classified ad to sell a car or other possession), there is a very real sense in which bigger space equals bigger brand and bigger brand means more successful and trustworthy. This is why ambitious companies will go as far as investing in a newspaper wraparound cover for a major launch and some have even gone as far as taking all the display space in a single edition in order to dominate it with their brand. Consumers use this 'brand body language' as a shorthand or heuristic and advertisers can take advantage of it to enhance their brand standing. And of course, because so many media buyers have come to the same conclusions, these sorts of spaces command a price premium.

Another great opportunity that newspapers offer to advertisers is their 'marketplace effect'. This is a function of particular editorial content which attracts readers specifically interested in that topic and thus related classified advertisements for brands in the market category, producing a virtuous circle whereby readers know where to go when they want to buy. That's why many newspapers have regular editorials on financial services, cars, fashion, property and food, to name but a few. A natural evolution of this idea is the creation of stand-alone sections of the newspaper with their own 'front covers' often bearing sub-brand names to establish their identity.

**FIGURE 16.5**    The sections of *The Sunday Times* newspaper

© The Times Online / nisyndication

There are now a number of well-established and successful newspaper-produced magazines, such as *The Sunday Times' Style*, and they have generated an additional source of advertising revenue. These special sections and magazines are often delivered in plastic bags within the newspaper and this has created even more advertising opportunities, from single sheet inserts to mini-catalogues.

Newspapers also present brand owners with the opportunity to create reader offers which are a three-way win: the newspaper is able to secure a special deal for its buyers, the advertiser is able to get a prominent position of a quasi-editorial or advertorial nature and the reader can take advantage of a competitive price. But there doesn't have to be a price discount to customers – advertisers can pay for an advertorial and this can achieve a sense of endorsement by the newspaper brand which is trusted by its readers. And newspapers, as one of the long-established mediums, were earliest into other platforms such as exhibitions, conferences and branded merchandise.

Clearly one of the biggest challenges facing the newspaper medium over the past few years has been the inexorable rise of the internet and the steady migration of classified and recruitment advertising away from offline publications to online ones. Perhaps a light has begun to glimmer at the end of this dark tunnel with the advent of smart phones and portable 'tablet' devices such as the iPhone and the iPad with their associated applications which facilitate the subscription to and reading of online newspapers. Data from comScore shows a dramatic increase in the numbers of people using mobiles to access news and information, and this trend is pan-European.

**FIGURE 16.6**   Number of UK users accessing news and information via mobile

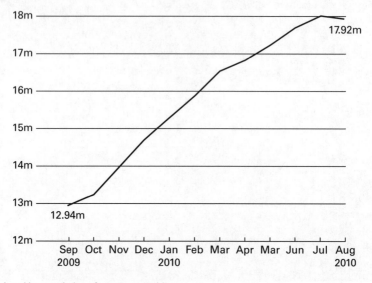

Reproduced by permission of comScore MobiLens

**FIGURE 16.7**   People accessing news via mobile, by country

Reproduced by permission of comScore MobiLens

While a few niche newspapers like the *Financial Times* and *The Wall Street Journal* have been trying to build their online subscription business for several years, and *The New York Times* launched a frequent users access charge in March 2011, the most daring move to date has been News Corporation's erecting of a 'paywall'.

**FIGURE 16.8**  *The Times'* online paywall

© The Times Online/nisyndication

This ground-breaking initiative is one of the most closely scrutinized developments in the media world ever, because of the implications for the whole online business model if News Corp can make it work. From the advertiser's point of view, introducing a subscription fee is likely to mean that online visitors will be those who are particularly engaged with their favourite newspaper title – and, therefore, even more receptive to the brands and messages it contains, now and in the future.

# IPA Effectiveness Awards case study summary

*Bronze Award Winner – IPA Effectiveness Awards 2010*

*Campaign: An unlikely David: Print and prosper,
the 2009 Kodak Inkjet Printer campaign*

*Brand: Kodak*

*Client: Kodak*

*Entrant: Ogilvy & Mather Advertising*

*Principal author: Adrian Zambardino, Ogilvy & Mather Advertising*

*Contributing author: Brent Vartan, Deutsch*

In 2009, Kodak was a small player in the printer marker, which was dominated by HP, Lexmark, Canon and Epson which together held 90 per cent of the market share. In order to combat low awareness and sales, Kodak created an alternative business model called 'print and prosper', which exposed the eye-wateringly high ink prices of its competitors and emphasized Kodak as a cheaper, high-quality alternative. The campaign made excellent use of newspaper advertising as part of its 'flashpoint' launch in the first week. Eye-catching ads which were 'splattered' with ink blots were taken out in different sizes and formats, often on facing and sequential pages. These were headed with concise questions encouraging people to consider the high cost of ink cartridges. This newspaper launch phase contributed to the overall success of this campaign, which achieved quadrupled sales, increased Kodak's market share by 10 percentage points compared to the previous year and generated a payback of £1.43 for every £1 invested.

**FIGURE 16.9**    Kodak ran 'ink-splattered' ads

Reproduced by permission of Kodak

# Local newspapers

## 17

## The media owner's 'elevator pitch'

Over 80 per cent of us spend half or more of our time and money within five miles of home (GFK/NOP '*the wanted ads*'). Home is where we live our lives, where we work, where we spend time with friends and family, and where we shop. And our appetite for local news and information is an important factor that helps us in our local life.

There are around 1,200 local newspapers across the UK, regularly read by nearly 38 million adults (Kantar Media TGI 2010 – average issue readership). These range from large metropolitan daily titles through to small community titles. But irrespective of size or population centre, what links them is their unique content and connection with their audiences. These local newspaper businesses are rapidly evolving to become local *media* businesses delivering local news and information across print, online, mobile and broadcast platforms. In addition to the 1,200 core local newspapers, there are around 1,500 local newspaper websites with some 37 million unique web users a month and 600 niche/hyper-local newspaper products.

**FIGURE 17.1**   Most people continue to live their lives locally...

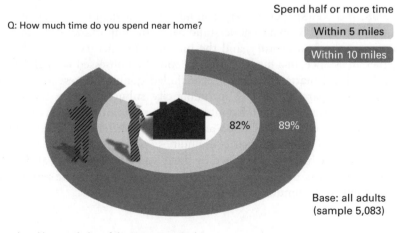

Q: How much time do you spend near home?

Spend half or more time

Within 5 miles
Within 10 miles

82%   89%

Base: all adults
(sample 5,083)

Reproduced by permission of the Newspaper Society

Local newspaper editorial is relevant to people's lives; it is highly trusted and acted upon. It is the medium that for 65 per cent of people best represents their locality – significantly ahead of the next-nearest media channel, radio, at just 13 per cent (GFK/NOP 'the wanted ads'). The same core values apply to advertising in local newspapers (and their websites) and this provides a powerful platform for both national and local advertisers. People find the advertising content helpful and not an unwanted intrusion. Over 70 per cent of people have acted upon the advertising they have seen in their local newspaper – a figure which is very consistent across both age and income levels (GFK/NOP 'the wanted ads').

Advertisers can tap into the unique and trusted values of local newspapers and their ability to target specific geographic communities. In a nutshell, local newspapers deliver mass reach across the UK with flexibility to target individual villages, towns and cities in a highly relevant, trusted and action-oriented advertising environment.

# How do people engage with local newspapers?

Local newspapers (and their websites and other product extensions) deliver unique local news and information to people across the UK. Their continued success and mass reach is down to people's attachment to their local community and the vital role that local newspapers play in people's lives.

A report by Ofcom concluded:

Local and regional newspapers play a particularly important role in informing, representing, campaigning and interrogating and thus underpinning awareness and participation in the democratic process. Newspaper journalism is also a crucial part of the local and regional media ecology because it supports journalism on other platforms. (Ofcom – Local and regional media in the UK; September 2009)

In 2008, the Newspaper Society commissioned a major research project through Millward Brown to understand better the importance of local communities in the 21st century, and the fundamental factors that bind them together. In essence, in a media landscape too often obsessed with globalization, does local matter? The project included qualitative research groups across various parts of the UK, including city, suburban, town and village population centres. This then fed into a 5,000+ sample quantitative study to isolate the key drivers of cohesion and the role of differing media channels in engaging with people in their communities.

The project, which was launched by the NS as 'Local Matters' at the IPA, identified six areas of importance to communities. These were termed the 'six segments of community cohesion'.

**FIGURE 17.2** The six segments of community cohesion

**SOURCE:** Millward Brown/Newspaper Society 2008

Unsurprisingly, the importance of each segment varied by age, life stage, region and the type of population centre. However, what was clear is the real importance of community and local life to people throughout the UK. This was well illustrated by the difference in attitudes towards national and local issues. While the UK economy faced challenging times after the research fieldwork was completed, the contrast in attitudes towards 'national' versus 'local' is significant:

**FIGURE 17.3** Issues are more positive at a local level

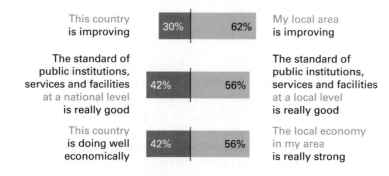

Reproduced by permission of the Newspaper Society

The '*Local Matters*' research showed that the concept of local community means different things for people at different stages of life. The qualitative work implied that 'Pre-Family' is quite a selfish time of selective connections with the community (social life, sport, entertainment etc), although it was interesting that nearly 40 per cent of this group did feel 'part of/integrated into the local community'. In fact they had very positive opinions about it, which gives every reason to believe that even the young 'i' generation will connect more locally as they grow up.

This becomes even more apparent when one sees just how relevant the local community becomes once people have had children. It is a time of discovery and as one mum from Woodley said, 'A door was opened to a whole new world'. This life stage sees a step change in involvement in the local community – with the arrival of children comes a practical and less selfish engagement with it. At the 'Teen Family' stage there is a new focus on the local community as different family members develop individual networks and activities and operate less as the family unit. 'Empty nesters' become more self-focused again, while retaining a high level of community engagement.

**FIGURE 17.4**    Selection and needs for community engagement vary by life stage

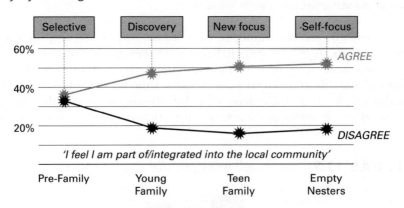

Reproduced by permission of the Newspaper Society

Local newspapers and their websites are hugely important across all aspects of community life. The content is by definition relevant to people's engagement with their community and reflects what is important within the local newspapers' catchment area – real life, real people and real local issues that matter. The Millward Brown research went on to quantify the importance of the various media channels across the six segments of community cohesion. The dominant strength of local newspapers and their websites – collectively referred to as 'local media' – in facilitating community cohesion reflects their unique and single-minded focus on local news and information. For example, when looking specifically at respondents with families at home:

**FIGURE 17.5**    Engaging families in the local community

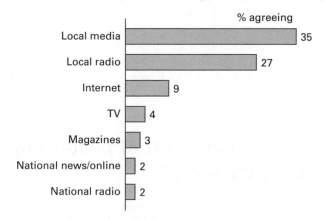

Which sources are important in feeling part of your community?

% agreeing

| Source | |
| --- | --- |
| Local media | 35 |
| Local radio | 27 |
| Internet | 9 |
| TV | 4 |
| Magazines | 3 |
| National news/online | 2 |
| National radio | 2 |

Reproduced by permission of the Newspaper Society

Research has quantified just what it is that people see as the core reasons for engagement with their local newspaper. It helps them feel part of their community, helps them get the best out of their locality and provides unique local news and information that they cannot get elsewhere. The trust and integrity of local newspapers was also quantified as dominant versus other media channels.

**FIGURE 17.6**    Five essential beliefs about local press

Helps me feel part of the community

Helps me get the best out of where I live

Honest and believable

Their 5 essential beliefs about local press...

More accurate & reliable than other media

Rely on it for news that can't get elsewhere

**SOURCE:** Newspaper Society with GFK/NOP Media – 'the wanted ads'

Local media are an environment where real action takes place. People act upon the advertising they see in their local newspaper and the GFK/NOP Media research identified that nearly 40 per cent, or 14.2 million 16–65-year-olds, have used a product or service as a result of local press advertising; over 50 per cent, or 19.5 million, have used a coupon or money-off voucher; and 56 per cent, or nearly 22 million, have visited a store or outlet due to an ad in the local press. This gave a net of 27.2 million or 71 per cent of the 16–65-year-old population who have taken action due to local press advertising.

## How many and what sort of people engage with local newspapers?

Nearly 38 million adults read a local newspaper every week (GB TGI 2010 Q3) – representing 76 per cent of the UK adult population. Local press remains the largest print advertising medium, taking £1.7 billion a year and accounting for 12 per cent of all UK advertising revenue. Online recruitment advertising in the regional press accounted for another £55.8 million in 2009 and according to the Advertising Association the total spend in the regional press is more than four times the total spend on radio, and more than the combined total for radio, outdoor and cinema. Given such a mass audience reach, local newspapers engage with all sectors of society – across all age groups and income levels.

**FIGURE 17.7**    Readership of local newspapers

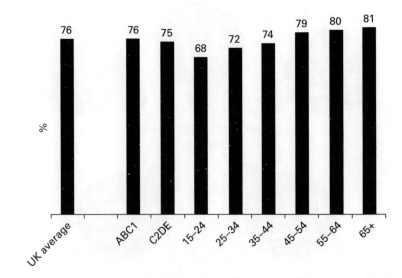

**SOURCE:** TGI 2010

The rapid growth of local newspaper websites, now reaching around 37 million unique users every month, is further extending the scale and depth of engagement with communities across the UK.

In terms of heavy local newspaper readers, which are defined as reading for at least 0.35 hours per day (21 minutes), TouchPoints tells us that, as with national newspapers, the peaks are amongst the over-55s and those studying or not working. Interestingly, although the 'main shoppers' in a household are more likely than all adults to read any kind of newspaper, they are even more likely to read local newspapers, which gives local advertisers an important opportunity.

**FIGURE 17.8**  Profile of heavy local newspaper readers compared to all adults

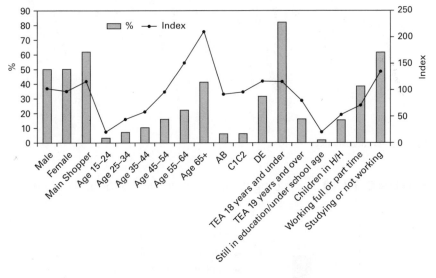

SOURCE: IPA TouchPoints3

The main reasons why people read local newspapers are very similar to the reasons why people read national newspapers, but with a local focus: 'To keep up to date with local news' and 'To keep up to date on local issues'.

The local newspaper readership survey, JICREG, provides metrics on individual local newspaper readership right down to postcode sector level. Building upon this, the industry has recently integrated online reach metrics into JICREG to quantify the combined audiences of local print and online. Endorsed by the IPA, the JICREG 'Locally Connected' tool is the UK's – and probably the world's – first integrated print/online reach evaluation. Just how local media audiences are extending through print and online is illustrated across some example locations below.

**FIGURE 17.9**    Main reasons to read local newspapers

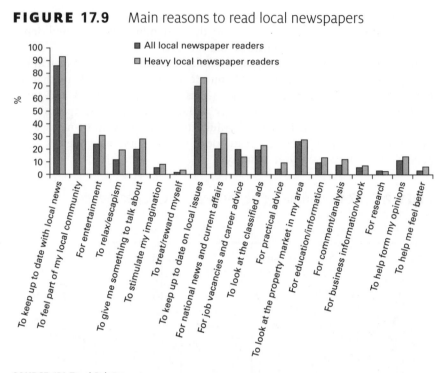

**SOURCE:** IPA TouchPoints3

**FIGURE 17.10**    Building local coverage with print and online

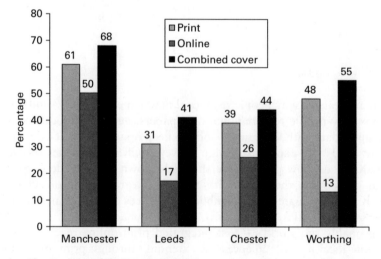

# What advertising and commercial communications opportunities do local newspapers offer?

Local newspapers and their digital extensions offer advertisers a unique opportunity to connect with local communities across the UK. There is simply no other media channel with the depth of local engagement offered by local media. Advertisers can use the medium nationally, across regions, or right down to very local or hyper-local targeted campaigns as both media and creative can be highly targeted to specific geographic locations. This is of huge benefit to advertisers across all categories – retailers can target specific store locations (or those of their competitors!) with product offers relevant to that store's individual catchment area; brands can target areas of particular strength or opportunity, again targeting the message as appropriate; and issue-based advertising (eg government, charities etc) can target specific hotspots. All of this makes for relevant and targeted communication, minimizing unnecessary wastage.

With a portfolio covering local newspapers, websites, niche magazines and mobile applications, the possibilities for connecting with local audiences are limitless. Creative messaging has a real opportunity to target the unique role and audience relationship of local newspapers. Some examples of campaigns which have leveraged local newspapers and their portfolio demonstrate just how national advertisers are effectively connecting with communities.

Honda used local newspapers and their websites to launch its new hybrid car, the Insight. By linking with a volunteering organization, Do-It, Honda was able to attach itself to green issues, and by communicating this in a local media environment it could target specific dealer catchments and tap into the affinity that communities have with environmental issues. The campaign coupled print editorial and advertising with a bespoke web campaign which integrated the Honda Do-It website into individual local newspaper websites. The campaign ran across 150 locations and saw highly positive shifts in brand metrics and dealer footfall.

Trade and DIY retailer ScrewFix used a combination of product advertising in the well-read local classified sections, coupled with grassroots sport sponsorship in print and online to create greater affinity and relevance to local tradesmen across various store locations. This highly targeted approach saw store traffic increase significantly amongst both existing and new/lapsed customers, with a very positive response from tradesmen: '... it's exactly where they should be, what they should be doing' (Jim, tradesman, Barnstaple).

The channels available from local newspapers provide endless opportunities. Ikea used the full breadth of print and digital platforms to successfully launch their store in Ashton. These ranged from advertorials and promotions to wrap-arounds (wrapping the whole paper), an online treasure hunt and even the use of delivery vans and newsagents' promotional boards. Major supermarkets such as Tesco have built their relationship with local communities using local press. They use a highly targeted approach to local store marketing, for example in promoting a Tesco Metro in Notting Hill Gate.

**FIGURE 17.11**    Tesco target their advertising to local communities

Reproduced by permission of Tesco

Birds Eye used local newspapers to promote a cooking event for mothers with children, a life stage which we know is closely connected with community. Their executions were tailored to individual localities in the style of a party invitation, while global super-brand Coca-Cola used local press to connect their football sponsorship closer to individual teams' fans. Sport is one of the strengths of local newspapers, which have a very close relationship with the clubs and teams in their catchment areas. Coca-Cola leveraged this insight to great effect by running targeted ads in specific papers prior to the play-offs which were, at that stage, taking place in Cardiff. The ads gave each team their own chant in Welsh!

# IPA Effectiveness Awards case study summary

*Silver Award Winner – IPA Effectiveness Awards 2004*

*Campaign: Police Officer Recruitment*

*Client: Hertfordshire Constabulary*

*Entrant: Bernard Hodes Group*

*Authors: Martin Homent, John Wardle, Marc Rothman, Helen Rosethorn and Cathy Reid*

When Hertfordshire Constabulary's constituency was increased due to a border change by the Home Office, the Constabulary was faced with the difficult task of recruiting a large number of additional officers in an area of low unemployment and competitive starting salaries. Therefore the campaign had to convey the essence and appeal of the role in order to attract members of the community who might never have considered a career in the police service. Thus, the creative strategy was centred around the idea of 'a life less predictable' – an alternative to the 'nine to five' daily grind. Local newspapers were an important aspect of the media strategy, and were utilized throughout the campaign period. The campaign was a runaway success, and the recruitment target was achieved within three years – four years ahead of schedule!

## 18

# Online

## The media owner's 'elevator pitch'

As an entertaining, educational and interactive medium, the internet is now one of the first places people turn to when seeking information and peer-to-peer recommendations. What sets the internet apart from other media is its unique place within the purchase path and its ability to take the user from the initial point of interest right through to the sale, and thereafter to online customer service and electronic customer relationship management (eCRM).

With over 80 per cent of internet sessions beginning with a search, and results pages for brands receiving more visits than corporate websites themselves, online marks the very start of the purchasing process on a fast-increasing number of occasions. For this reason online has become a core component in almost all UK advertising campaigns, for example through search, display advertising, a corporate website or a simple online conversation. At the 2009 Internet Advertising Bureau's Engage Conference, Mark Lund, then CEO of the UK government's Central Office for Information, described digital as 'a joiner upper, an enabler of government and other media channels. It's the plasma that runs through media ecology.'

## How do people engage with online?

Driven by vastly increased broadband speeds and innovative internet technologies, the Web 2.0 era is synonymous with interactivity, feedback, and two-way, immediate communication online. Brands are experimenting with appropriate ways of participating in this new space by using engagement, social or word-of-mouth marketing. The proliferation of blogs, social networking sites and user-generated content on platforms such as Wikipedia, Flickr and YouTube has created new depth in the online experience. This has blurred the line between people's online and offline lives as they step in and out of the media flow at will.

As the web becomes increasingly social, online activities are becoming more dominated by peers and by sharing content. The chart below shows the average internet 'hour', which gives us a 60-second snapshot of how Britons like to spend their time online.

**FIGURE 18.1**  If all April 2010 UK internet time was condensed into one hour, how much time would be spent in the most heavily used sectors?

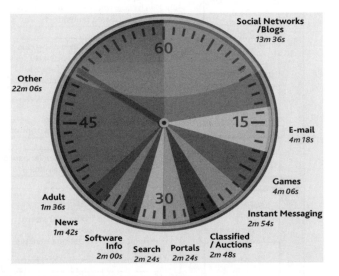

Reproduced by permission of UKOM and Nielsen online

In tandem with this increasing reliance on the internet, advertisers have followed their audiences, and as a result online advertising expenditure in the past 10 years has seen exponential growth. Based on the US population, Forrester's Social Technographics survey of 2009 illustrates that more than four in five online adults participate socially.

# How many and what sort of people engage with online?

In early 2010 the first online media owner contract was awarded to Nielsen by the UK Online Measurement Company to carry out research on the size of the internet audience on behalf of the major online media owners. The first data, published in April 2010, showed that the majority of the UK population was shown to be online, with over 40.5 million active internet users – a 10 per cent increase from 2009 – and the figure continues to increase at a steady pace. Moreover, of those internet users, 8 out of 10 go online every day or most days, and 92 per cent have broadband. The UKOM research also showed that the online population is split relatively equally

**FIGURE** 18.2   Breakdown of online participation

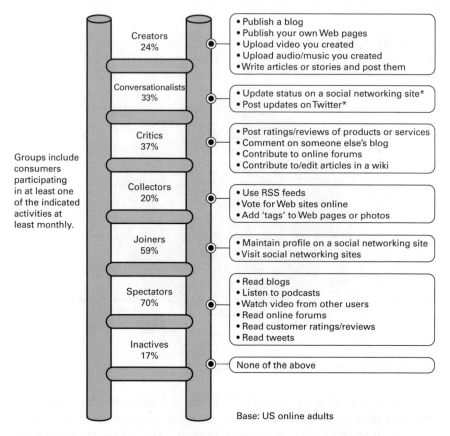

Groups include consumers participating in at least one of the indicated activities at least monthly.

Base: US online adults

* Conversationalists participate in at least one of the indicated activities at least weekly.

**SOURCE:** A Global Update Of Social Technographics®, Forrester Research, Inc, September 28, 2010

male/female, and that one in four Britons accessing the web regularly are aged between 50 and 64 years.

IPA TouchPoints tells us more about the profile of heavy internet users, defined as those who spend over three hours online daily, and shows that there are peaks among males, 15–44-year-olds, the AB social groups and those in work.

The behaviour of heavy users varies greatly between weekdays and weekends: Monday to Friday use is almost double that of weekends and is at its highest during the standard working day, with a dip at lunchtime.

Unsurprisingly, given the extraordinarily wide-ranging nature of the internet, users give many different reasons for using it, as can be seen in the chart below. 'For entertainment', 'To communicate with others', 'To keep up to date', 'To keep in touch with family and friends', 'For information' and 'For company information/work' are just some of the main motivations.

**FIGURE 18.3**    Profile of heavy internet users compared to all adults

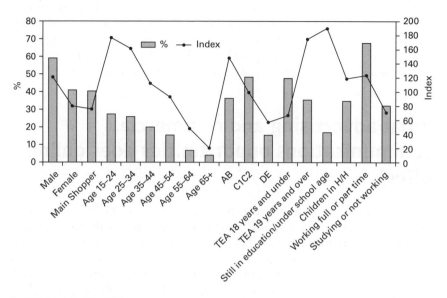

**SOURCE:** IPA TouchPoints3

**FIGURE 18.4**    Main reasons for using the internet

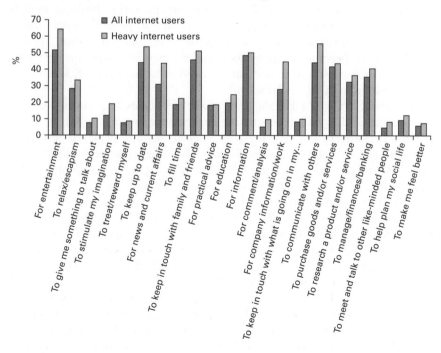

**SOURCE:** IPA TouchPoints3

For heavy users who are leading the way forward, there are a couple of noticeable trends. People are enjoying the convenience of downloading content that they can watch at a later time. In fact, 'convenience' is a major theme, as many of the top statements refer to the mobility and immediacy of access to the internet afforded by mobile phones. In terms of advertising, it seems clear that users respond well to interaction, with many agreeing: 'I find online adverts more interesting if I can interact with them'.

# What advertising and commercial communications opportunities does online offer?

There is a wide spectrum of advertising 'real estate' available online. This includes not only the traditional genres of classified and display, but also newer ones including pay per click (PPC) and search engine optimization (SEO), which is a highly specialized communications activity unique to online. E-mail and paid-for search advertising were the original low-risk entry products; these highly accountable tools were the foundation of performance-based marketing online and developed rapidly towards the end of the 1990s. Affiliate marketing in particular – a technique that relies on online partnerships and sales-driven commission – now comprises a vast network of relevantly matched sites and content. Other business models came later, including price comparison sites and lead-generation sites which pay commercial partners based on consumer leads and acquisition. Affiliate marketing has become a huge business and the process of driving user traffic to a retailer's website on a cost per acquisition basis in the UK was worth £72.6 million in 2009 (IAB/PwC).

However, PPC still takes the lion's share of budgets, accounting for 59.9 per cent of all UK online advertising expenditure in the first half of 2010. With PPC, advertisers pay for their website to be displayed alongside 'organic' search results as sponsored links. Because consumers only click on their ad if they are already interested in the offering, advertisers only pay for the number of clicks on their ad, not how many people view it. PPC is often used as a complementary strategy to SEO, which has also been an increasingly important aspect of the marketer's agenda. SEO relates to natural search results, which are of huge importance as they capture 70 per cent of the overall search traffic. Natural search results cannot be bought outright; search engines incorporate a wide range of undisclosed factors into their ranking algorithms, and according to their particular methodologies the most relevant websites will appear at the top. Therefore, achieving SEO is a longer-term solution than PPC. For the most cost-effective and favourable results, websites must be built from the ground upwards with search compliance in mind, thus ensuring that the website's relevance is recognized by search engines. There is intense competition for both the number-one spot in the search results and also for the first page of results, as most consumers do not venture beyond these.

Classified advertising has also developed a strong online presence. Online classifieds are often longer than their print counterparts because the cost is not typically done on a per-line basis. They are also searchable so relevant listings are easy to find, whether the focus is local or more widespread. A number of companies now provide a specialized service helping clients to design and distribute their ads to online ad directories.

Online display took an 18.1 per cent share of all online advertising revenues in 2009, and remains an effective way to achieve sales and brand engagement. The traditional display formats have long been employed to attract the attention of consumers while complementing their online session. The intrusive 'pop-up' formats that dogged the early days of online advertising and tarnished its reputation for some years are now all but extinct, and have given way to much more polite, relevant creative work that enables internet users to interact on their own terms. The image below shows the standard measurements for online display advertising.

**FIGURE 18.5**   IAB Display Ad Standards 2010

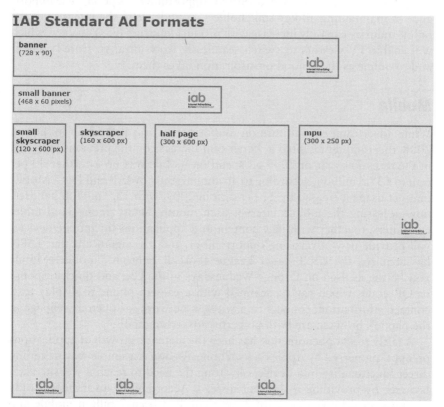

Reproduced by permission of IAB

Marketers are able to achieve greater return on investment by targeting internet users who are more likely to buy. Shared interests are grouped together based upon previous web browsing activity and web users are then served advertising which matches their shared interests. In this way, advertising can be made as relevant and useful as possible. This technique is known as interest-based or online behavioural advertising (OBA). In such a potentially sensitive area it is essential for best practice to be promoted, particularly when dealing with issues of consumer privacy, and all providers of behavioural advertising have to comply with UK laws. In most cases, the information used for targeting adverts is not personal, in that it does not identify the user in the real world but instead relates only to the computer's IP address. Thus data about browsing activity is collected and analysed anonymously. If this analysis allows an inference to be drawn as to a particular interest, a cookie is placed in the computer and it is this cookie (*not* browsing data) which determines what advertising is received.

In March 2009, the Internet Advertising Bureau – in partnership with its members – launched Good Practice Principles for online behavioural advertising. These principles, which providers of behavioural advertising are required to sign up to, ensure that consumers' privacy is protected and that they are given notice when targeted advertising is taking place, educated about the process, and provided with the opportunity to opt out. The importance of maintaining all key stakeholders' confidence in the integrity of the online industry can only increase with product launches like YouView, which will enable TV viewers to switch seamlessly from linear to stored content and to online as their mood or inspiration takes them.

## Mobile

While advertising expenditure on mobile was worth just £26.8 million in 2008, this total represented a 99 per cent increase on the previous year, and in the recession year of 2009 ad spend on mobile was up a further 40 per cent to £37.6 million, according to an annual study by IAB and PwC. Mobile internet usage increased by 21 per cent in 2009, with 18.9 million handsets now accessing the mobile internet each month. Smart phones and tablet computers, together with new content and applications for mobile devices, will provide new advertising opportunities, and it is significant that ESPN has acquired the UK Premier League football rights for mobile. Mobile vouchering as used on Orange Wednesdays in the UK, and quick response or QR codes which can be scanned with a camera phone to display text, contact information, connect to a wireless network, or open a webpage in the phone's browser, are both powerful advertising tools.

A fairly recent phenomenon has been the meteoric growth of applications or 'apps' pioneered by Apple on its iPhone. An app is a simple way of adding direct functionality to a device, obviating the need to reach a website via a browser by providing a shortcut instead. According to an industry study commissioned by Getjar, as of 2009 there had been 7 billion mobile app downloads. This number is expected to increase to 50 billion by 2012, and the revenue from mobile apps is expected to increase from $4.1 billion to $17.5 billion. Following Apple's announcement in April 2010 that it will now allow advertising within apps, this advertising will grow together with the increasing penetration of smart-phones and devices.

As advertisers become more confident with such experimentation, and even more consumers refuse to exist without their broadband, continuing to live their lives both on and offline, this will inevitably secure the medium's place as the 'plasma' that Mark Lund described.

## Creative use of online

As online technology has developed, so too has creative thinking to enhance the impact of online display. Agency Weapon7's banner ad enlisted Google Maps to illustrate how the Smart fortwo diesel car can travel up to 621 miles on one tiny 33 litre tank. Within the banner, internet users were able to discover exactly how far the car could take them, simply entering their postcode and finding out exactly where in the world they could travel on one tank.

**FIGURE 18.6** Creative, interactive ad for the smart fortwo

Many other advertisers, including the COI on behalf of government, Virgin, Yell.com and Sony, have been amongst those leading the way in online display, producing eye-catching creative to engage consumers and win awards. The very best examples can be found at **www.creativeshowcase.net**, the home of the IAB and Microsoft Advertising's Creative Showcase Awards.

# IPA Effectiveness Awards case study summary

*Bronze Award Winner – IPA Effectiveness Awards 2009*

*Campaign: ghd – Creating a premium shopping experience online*

*Brand: ghd*

*Client: ghd*

*Entrant: TBWA\Manchester Limited*

*Authors: Andrew Hovells, Peter Harris and Dawn Williams*

In 2008, hair styling iron ghd (Good Hair Day) was faced with a decline in retail sales and the booming online retail environment was putting pressure on both margins and the exclusivity of the brand. The solution was to increase ghd's online sales by improving the website so that traffic was converted efficiently. This included warning customers of counterfeit stock if bought elsewhere, making the purchasing process easier (the need to register was removed) and making the site easier to navigate. Site visits were up by 80 per cent and revenue increased by 175 per cent. As a result of this increased attention by consumers, the website re-design generated a payback of £2.01 per every £1 spent.

**FIGURE 18.7**    ghd's website redesign ensured traffic was converted efficiently

Reproduced by permission of ghd (Jemella Ltd)

# Out-of-home

## 19

## The communication agency's 'elevator pitch'

There are two especially compelling things about out-of-home (OOH) as an advertising medium. Firstly, there is its ability to build near-universal coverage of the UK population within a fortnight. Indeed, it's been said that in the age of multi-channel TV, posters are the last 'broadcast' medium available to marketers. OOH is also inherently complementary to TV given that light viewers tend to be heavy OOH viewers and vice versa. Advertisements placed OOH can enhance TV's creative content on a huge scale, to produce the kind of impact that generates enormous word-of-mouth, thus adding to the 'broadcast' effect.

Secondly, OOH has the ability to place commercial messages in front of customers in close proximity to the point of purchase or consumption. Creative content can be tailored very precisely to the particular position in which it will be placed, and also to the people who will see it there. Many poster locations can add a level of implied trustworthiness and credibility to an advertiser's brand via the 'editorial' context they provide; for example, hair and beauty products can be advertised near well-regarded hair salons, and healthy products can be advertised close to popular gyms. OOH can deliver the last message a consumer sees before entering a shop, and once in the retail environment, digital screens can offer a further advertising connection very close to the actual point of purchase. These continue to be the two core strengths of OOH and, unlike any other medium, you don't have to turn it on, tune it in, log on or turn over the page: it's just there in front of you when you are out-of-home.

## How do people engage with OOH media?

The huge diversity of OOH formats means that there is an equally huge range of ways in which consumers can and do engage with the medium. And

OOH is not carried along on the coattails of editorial content like many other types of media – people can simply be attracted to a brand's message as they go about their daily routine. We are creatures of habit, and many OOH formats allow advertisers to benefit from this fact, using a sequence of messages to build a relationship with consumers who pass the same sites at virtually the same time every day. Research for the Advertising Standards Authority (ASA) in 2002 showed that OOH media is welcomed by the vast majority of consumers as a pleasant, entertaining or informative alternative to the boredom of commuting or other journeys.

In this context an excellent example of the public's regard for the best of OOH is the early example of 'kinetic' advertising for Lucozade. This poster for a sports drink made by Beecham Products was positioned by the elevated section of the M4 motorway with the company's offices on both sides of the Great West Road below. The fluorescent poster sign saying 'Lucozade replaces lost energy' and displaying the temperature (a reference to the brand's previous history as a health tonic) welcomed drivers back into London for 50 years until the building was demolished for redevelopment in 2004. However, in a display of positive affection for this advertising, local people campaigned for it to be put back on display and eventually the local council, and Margaret Hodge, the Labour Party minister then responsible, gave permission for a replica to be put back on the side of the new building. It was reinstated on 15 February 2010.

**FIGURE 19.1**  A poster reinstated by popular demand

Lucozade is a trade mark of the GlaxoSmithKline Group of Companies

# How many and what sort of people engage with OOH media?

OOH is truly a 'broadcast' medium which can achieve huge coverage and frequency very rapidly. For example, a two-week bus campaign will reach 88 per cent of all adults in London, while a roadside six-sheet campaign for the same period will reach 80 per cent of adults in the UK. A campaign that uses a multi-format approach will achieve the cut-through necessary to reach over 90 per cent of the UK population.

IPA TouchPoints data give us a very clear picture of what sorts of people comprise the OOH audience, with a focus on the heavy consumers of the medium. In this instance they are defined as people who are out-of-home for more than 22 hours a week, and we can see from the chart that their profile, and the index versus all adults, is relatively flat, though slightly biased towards men, people aged 35 to 44 and those who stayed in education past the age of 19.

**FIGURE 19.2**   Profile of heavy OOH consumers compared to all adults

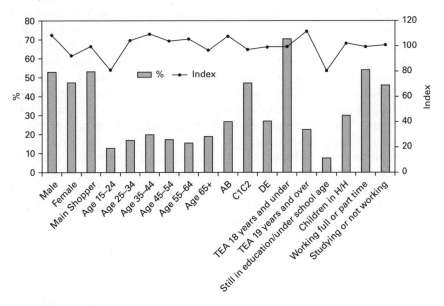

**SOURCE:** IPA TouchPoints3

Exposure to OOH is higher at the weekends than during the week, but given that campaigns are rarely shorter than a week in length this does not make much difference in practical terms. In terms of generating word-of-mouth, it's interesting to note that Conversation Catalysts™ spend more time OOH than the average person. Thus, OOH is perfectly placed to generate discussion, especially about certain topics. TouchPoints data show that these valuable originators of word-of-mouth who spend a lot of time OOH are very likely to influence others about 'sport and hobbies', 'cars', 'financial services' and 'holidays and travel'.

# What advertising opportunities does OOH offer?

By definition, anyone who leaves their home is likely to see an advertising message, as the range of OOH formats and the locations where they can be seen are almost limitless. The reason for this is that almost anyone with a surface to sell and who can get permission to do so can become an OOH site owner. In the United States it is estimated that there are more than 2,000 operators, and these OOH media companies range from major corporations with massive inventories all the way down to small businesses with a handful of sites.

Overall it is possible to categorize OOH into four broad types: traditional roadside billboards, posters on street furniture such as bus shelters and telephone kiosks, advertising on and inside vehicles such as buses and taxis, and miscellaneous sites of almost infinite variety. Street furniture, transit, and alternative media formats comprise 34 per cent of total OOH revenue in the United States, so traditional billboards are still the mainstay of the industry. '6 sheets', which are 1.8 × 1.2 metres in size, are the most prolific UK format in OOH, with distribution across multiple environments including gyms, cinemas, malls and supermarkets as well as extensive roadside coverage. They offer high frequency and are better at reaching people in city centres. '48 sheets', which are 3 × 6 metres in size, are a large format with distribution across roadside, rail and underground tube/metro locations. These offer good levels of impact, cover, frequency and stature. '96 sheets' are 3 × 12 metres and are predominantly a roadside format with a small number available on the London Underground. Their size delivers great impact and can be used to cover major towns and cities.

Public transport buses offer extensive coverage, especially in key conurbations, with good penetration into both city centres and outlying districts. There are two main formats: the pavement-facing 'super-side' format delivers the pedestrian audience, and the 'T-side' shape with drop-down 'stem' to the same scale as a 6 sheet is ideal for a product pack shot and targets both the pedestrian and the motorist. Traditionally the 'ear pieces' on the top corners of a London double-decker bus have been used to promote theatrical productions, and more recently giant wrap-around posters covering the entire rear of the vehicle have become popular for the launch of big movies and video games. Similarly, taxi cabs offer various OOH opportunities, with sites on the doors, inside on the backs of the jump seats or even all-over designs aimed at pedestrians and other motorists. In-cab TV is another possibility, and can be used for longer communications. In the UK 38.4 million trips by taxi are taken every month and thus advertisers have the potential to reach 30 million consumers per week.

Where planning authorities allow them, banners can have colossal impact and add stature to a brand. Each position is unique, which means that the approach must be site specific, and this can enable even greater creativity when the content plays off against the context. MINI is a contemporary example of this timeless idea, the OOH 'special build'. Even without any clever technology, customizing a billboard with 3D objects can still be extremely impressive, engaging and fun. In MINI's case, the sheer scale of this build is what made the difference – a vastly long poster featuring a life-size MINI apparently loaded into a giant catapult, at full stretch and ready to fire. It communicated with people at a key moment of boredom – commuting on the train – as the site was viewed from out of carriage windows shortly after the train had left the station and was still moving quite slowly.

**FIGURE 19.3**  MINI's 3D poster was well placed to entertain commuters

Reproduced by permission of MINI

People can be reached virtually everywhere they go and the long list of available OOH advertising environments includes airports, theme parks, shopping malls, supermarkets, petrol stations (including the pump handles themselves), schools, leisure centres, gyms, doctors' and dentists' surgeries, hairdressers, pharmacies, bars, cinemas and toilets anywhere.

Meanwhile, developments in technology and innovation by media owners have provided advertisers with much more versatile ways of targeting consumers. Digital out-of-home (DOOH) is an exciting and fast-developing sector and in 2009 represented an 11.3 per cent share of OOH spend, up 24 per cent year on year despite the economic downturn.

**FIGURE 19.4**   The growth of digital

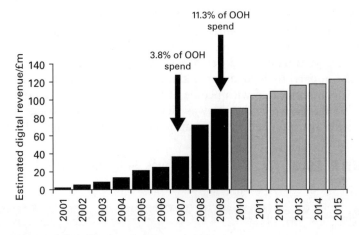

Reproduced by permission of Posterscope UK

Data produced by the OAA

DOOH covers many different opportunities, including screens (LED, plasma, LCD/TFT screens) and projections (2D, 3D holographic, static and animated, interactive). At the last count there were 62 different media owners offering digital opportunities in the UK, selling across a total of 48 different OOH environments, and there are a total of 196,000+ screens and growing. Over two weeks, DOOH has the potential to deliver 360 million+ impacts, which is roughly equivalent to a week's activity in the national press, and it allows people to be exposed to more engaging advertising when they are commuting, shopping, doing the school run or out and about at leisure. For example, digital screens in the London Underground can display different creative work depending on the station and the time of travel. Clever sequences of images on digital escalator panels can also be very involving.

Today, people spend more time away from home than ever before, and thanks to the rapid rise of mobile technology they can do much more when they are out and about. This has opened up the potential for great media synergies between OOH and mobile media which can prompt online search and purchase of products for home delivery, and not just in the shops as previously. The OOH medium is also being transformed by emerging technologies such as radio frequency identification, near field communications, image recognition and augmented reality, which will allow for both more interaction with the consumer and also greater accountability.

# Creative uses of OOH media

The power of the OOH medium was initially challenged by the arrival of commercial TV in the 1950s, but landmark creative work in the 1970s, like CDP's surreal Benson & Hedges 'gold box' posters, re-established OOH's importance. Campaigns for Araldite, Birds Eye, Fiat, Wonderbra, Pretty Polly and both the Conservative and Labour political parties further raised the profile of the medium, and technical innovations continue to enable eye-catching creativity. For example, bus shelters were customized for Cadbury's Creme Eggs to include a touchscreen on which a game could be played. The rules were simple: 'splat' as many eggs as possible in a given time, and over one million eggs were splatted across 20 sites. Consumer reaction was hugely positive and significant PR coverage was generated.

**FIGURE 19.5**   Interactive touch screen in a bus shelter

Reproduced by permission of Saatchi and Saatchi

Similarly, the UK charity Barnardo's utilized customized bus shelters with screens and a donation collection box. Audiences were able to watch a looped clip of a young female crying, with a call to action prompting the viewer to make a cash donation. Inserting coins prompted the video to change, calming the girl and displaying a 'thank you' message to the donor.

To launch the TV channel Five USA, OOH work brought the channel's strapline 'Are you watching America?' to life. Live video footage from a camera placed on the streets of New York was streamed to the cross-track projection screens on London Underground. In another creative under-taking, people working for Glacéau Vitaminwater sat anonymously in cafés and bars near a 'Transvision' screen on a station concourse, observing people in the area. Using mini-laptops they typed messages that appeared instanta-neously on the giant screens. These messages were personalized and encour-aged the people nearby to do fun things such as waving at the screen or doing a dance. Several groups danced the conga all around Piccadilly Circus and others went and bought the product to 'show' to the screen!

# IPA Effectiveness Awards case study summary

*Gold Award Winner – IPA Effectiveness Awards 2008*

*Campaign: Now everyone has a mate called Dave*

*Brand: Dave*

*Client: UKTV*

*Agencies: Red Bee Media, UKTV*

*Authors: Hannah Yelin and Jonathan Wise, Red Bee Media*

The aim was to make the channel, originally named UKTV G2, the most popular digital channel for men aged 16–44, an ambitious target for a repeats channel. The broadcaster's target audience was males who needed more 'banter' back in their lives, banter that had been missing since the addition of responsibilities that arrive with adulthood. When re-launching the brand as 'Dave' (ironically a name thought up by an employee called Steve!), the UKTV media strategy was to concentrate the entire budget into a tightly focused two-week outdoor burst. High-impact, large-scale back-lit sites emblazoned Dave across the UK's major cities, making its arrival unmissable. This strategy worked, and audience share increased 35 per cent within a single month. The campaign's success attracted an additional eight million viewers to the channel and generated payback of £2.99 for every £1 spent.

**FIGURE 19.6**    Dave underground

Reproduced with permission of UKTV and Red Bee Media Limited

# Point of purchase

## 20

## The media owner's 'elevator pitch'

Point-of-purchase (P-O-P) advertising is the medium that is closest to the moment of truth when the shopper is in-store. All other media will have had their effects on brand image and messaging earlier on and will rely on shopper recall being effective when they come to make a buying decision. However, only P-O-P can trigger shopper recall of a brand's previous investment in advertising and marketing communications, and influence their buying decisions when shoppers are actively engaged in the purchasing process.

Drawing attention to one brand and away from another is an important means of gaining competitive advantage in-store. Since many people buy across a portfolio of brands in a product or service category, the purchase decisions of a significant proportion of customers can be affected while they are shopping. Even in these days of extensive pre-purchase research by shoppers online and the growth in comparison websites, brands are still able to influence the buyer in-store by using a range of P-O-P solutions. These can be used to reinforce the brand message, provide product information, highlight product comparisons, make promotional offers and thus create an exciting, engaging and more enjoyable shopping experience. Thus P-O-P performs an important role in enabling brands and retailers to inform and educate shoppers about key product features and benefits within the retail environment. But it also plays a vital role in driving impulse sales for retailers and brands.

## How do consumers engage with P-O-P?

Each of us has our own set of memories and associations connected to a particular brand, especially if it's one we buy and use regularly. Advertising and marketing communications add richness to this brand image, as does word-of-mouth from friends and acquaintances and information gleaned from newspapers, magazines and broadcast media. So, when a customer is close to buying something, a well-designed and positioned piece of P-O-P can trigger all this imagery and remind the person of all the emotional and rational benefits of the brand in view.

It is almost impossible to step inside a modern UK retail outlet without being exposed to some kind of P-O-P material and messaging – even here people are within the media flow. According to Point-of-Purchase Advertising International (POPAI), the industry's trade association, and its Marketing at Retail Initiative (MARI) study within the grocery sector, there are, on average, a minimum of 5,500 items of display in-store at any one time. This may rise to well over 12,000 in larger stores. POPAI has identified more than 50 individual display mechanics that may be used by marketers in a retail environment.

Overall it takes a shopper just under one second to view a piece of display material and make a decision as to whether to engage or not. Within super-markets, POPAI's MARI research highlighted that the average person then spends an initial time of around 3–4 seconds looking at P-O-P messaging, before either being sufficiently engaged to dwell for longer, or choosing to move on to the next item in their scanning process. Within other types of retailer, such as consumer electronics, telecommunications and DIY, this time is often considerably greater.

The breadth of P-O-P solutions available offers a diverse range of oppor-tunities for marketers who are able to target different shopper demographics by altering the creative design, mechanics and messaging of the medium. They are also able to target shoppers at different stages of their journey in-store, as well as to deliver different commercial communications that reflect the frequency of purchase and the level of involvement required by the shopper within their purchase process.

The increasing use of digital technology within P-O-P solutions means that brands are now in a position to target specific communication content to different audiences, at different times of the day, rather than hoping to reach an audience that might be attracted by the use of more generic mes-saging. For example, a P-O-P display within a mobile phone retailer can promote features and benefits of a phone range to business-users during a lunch period and then to a younger audience after school. The majority of P-O-P solutions are able to house the product physically or are situated on-shelf, meaning that shoppers can make a direct purchase after engaging with the medium. New technology allows for an even deeper level of engagement and interaction with shoppers, and also helps to act as an invaluable tool for retail store teams who can deliver an immediate, human extension to the selling process.

## How many and what sort of people engage with P-O-P?

P-O-P is in almost universal use in retail outlets and thus as a medium it's 'on all the time' and accessible to the entire population, with the exception of the relatively small number of people who are unable to go shopping for themselves.

**FIGURE 20.1** Average hours per day spent shopping

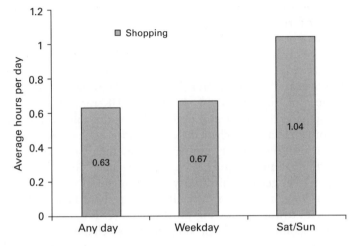

**SOURCE:** IPA TouchPoints3

As we can see from the TouchPoints survey, the average person spends over 40 minutes shopping each day during the week, and at weekends this rises to over an hour. Thus, every brand needs to consider its presence at the point-of-purchase, as that is where it frequently encounters its customers.

# What advertising and commercial communications opportunities does P-O-P offer?

Brand owners and their agencies are now thinking in terms of 'bought', 'owned' and 'earned' media and structuring their plans in the light of these three categories. In this context P-O-P is interesting because it straddles both 'bought' and 'owned'. The brand is in complete control of the point-of-purchase communications material it produces but very often has to take into account the varying in-store policies of retailers and wider issues concerning promotion of the category instead of just individual brands, as well as negotiating the cost of P-O-P placement in-store with the retailer.

P-O-P is one of a brand's most powerful communicators to shoppers and thus great attention needs to be paid to make sure this 'owned' medium performs to its full potential. Today many retailers, such as supermarkets and brand stores, are themselves brand owners, and can deploy P-O-P material for their own-brand products within their own outlets without third-party restrictions. A study by Deloitte and the Grocery Manufacturers Association found that the number of brand owners with a dedicated shopper marketing division rose by 23 per cent between 2007 and 2008. Some 60 per cent of retailers have also increased their own capacity in this area, and they predicted that in-store communications will continue to grow at a faster rate than any other form of marketing.

The only limitations on the possibilities for P-O-P are the imagination of the marketer or creative agencies, budgets, and any restrictions imposed by the retailer. Clearly, the retailer owns all the 'real estate' that could be occupied by a brand's P-O-P material and is fully aware of its value. Thus placing a piece of third-party P-O-P within a UK retailer can sometimes form part and parcel of the overall negotiation on the volume and pricing of goods, and other elements such as the contribution to the store's advertising or securing a position in their catalogue. In the highly controlled environment of a major multiple retailer, such as a consumer electronics retailer or grocery superstore, getting third-party P-O-P material placed in-store can often prove a long, sometimes difficult and expensive process for brands. Retailer policies towards allowing third-party P-O-P material in-store can also vary considerably, across both competing retail chains and sectors. Many overseas retailers, particularly those in mainland Europe and the United States, take a far less restrictive approach to the type of P-O-P solutions they allow into their stores and this presents international brand marketers with an opportunity.

Given the sheer volume of competing messages in-store and the premium value attached to retail floor or shelf space, the key requirement of the brand owner is to come up with a compelling solution that will engage and inform shoppers.

**FIGURE 20.2**    P-O-P must overcome the plethora of choice

Photograph by Hamish Pringle

Retailers are ultimately interested in P-O-P solutions that will both drive sales of the brand's products and also strengthen and grow that particular category. P-O-P has also proven to be a highly effective method of brand building and raising awareness of a new consumer product. It may be used to promote new features of established products, or to communicate offers and promotions such as Buy One Get One Free (BOGOF), to help the retailer enhance its reputation for value for money. Or it could be used to further enhance the shopper experience by making the product or category easier and more enjoyable to shop. P-O-P can also highlight which products staff should be talking to shoppers about, once they have established what is driving the need for purchase, while acting as a key driver for maximizing add-on sales and linked services, such as warranties and product insurance, which are often purchased with consumer durables such as televisions and washing machines.

In markets with even longer lead times for purchase frequency, such as retail banking, P-O-P can be used to prompt shoppers for consideration of products and services and provide 'take-ones' or explanatory leaflets. In such instances, purchase decisions may be driven by life stage rather than impulse, and so P-O-P offers brands and retailers the chance to sow the 'seed of need' and steer shoppers to having a conversation with a member of staff.

P-O-P material ranges from sophisticated stand-alone permanent display fixtures, encompassing the latest digital interactive screens, to high-impact temporary P-O-P campaigns incorporating everything from gondola ends or product trays to shelf talkers, in-store posters and floor graphics. The diverse range of materials and production techniques available to creative agencies and P-O-P manufacturers – such as woods, plastics, metals, print and various finishes, not to mention digital screen integration – means that marketers can develop an enormous suite of tactical P-O-P solutions for their brands.

Within supermarkets, gondola ends offer the prime selling space at the end of a run of shelving, at right angles to the main run, where products are placed for sale. These highly visible in-store locations, especially the ones facing customers as they enter the store, are competed for intensely and the retailer can charge brand owners a premium for having their promotional messages placed on them. Another ubiquitous variation on the P-O-P theme is the in-store poster, often used to carry key retailer and promotional messages, for example multi-buy offers, store event-related promotions such as Halloween, Back to School and Christmas, and information on the retailer's extended offer, including financial or home delivery services.

## Digital media in retail

According to the sixth edition of Samsung's UK Retail Digital Signage Survey, there are 14,475 outlets using digital screens within the UK, with approximately 102,582 screens in use. Supermarkets, leisure and entertainment outlets and telecoms stores continue to have the highest total numbers of screens overall. In terms of network technology, the medium is already starting to see a raft of 'ready out of the box' products that are completely interoperable coming to the fore. This new generation of digital screen networks is also seeing a shift away from passive screens to the use of smaller screens, located at eye level amongst products and built into fixtures and shelving, with shopper interaction encouraged through touchscreens, mobile phones and the latest radio frequency identification (RFID) technology.

The digital screen network provided by Amscreen within BP retail demonstrates how retailers and brands can now deliver highly effective, affordable digital P-O-P solutions in-store on a vast scale, combining their own content scheduling with information messaging, as well as their own and third-party advertising. Digital screens are also used extensively within retail banking to occupy, inform and even entertain customers in seated waiting areas, with supporting printed collateral available for customers to browse, thus integrating in-store with above-the-line activity.

Within FMCG retailers, digital screens are increasingly being sited within branded fixtures to create a seamless solution. They can also be used at kiosk till points to remind customers of behind-the-counter services. The latest digital technology is helping to improve the immediacy and relevance of in-store communications. For example, displays can play back product-specific video, which is triggered when shoppers pick up a product, along with showcasing cross-recommendations to other products in the range. And with next-generation smart phones and pads all capable of being an end device that can be targeted, digital media in retail is no longer simply restricted to a screen on a shelf or wall – it can be any web-enabled touch point. Smart phones can already scan prices to facilitate comparison shopping, placing shoppers in a powerful position to demand more competitive prices.

# POPAI Awards Display of the Year Award 2010 summary

*Gold Award Winner – POPAI Awards 2010*

*Campaign: 'Playing the game'*

*Brand: National Lottery*

*Client: Camelot*

*Agency: Checkland Kindleysides*

With The National Lottery played by around 70 per cent of UK adults on a regular basis, Camelot operates four of the top grocery brands in the UK, with one of those – Lotto – the single biggest brand in the country. As a key part of a £16.5 million investment by Camelot to improve its permanent P-O-P in its 28,500 National Lottery retail outlets, a new 'bubble' design concept was created and introduced. As well as refreshing the consumer experience of playing The National Lottery, the new play station design created a fresh, eye-catching new look for The National Lottery in-store, while capitalizing on the strengths of its iconic brand, to reinforce it on the high street. The campaign included other media tie-ins, including advertising and editorial copy in the trade media to drive awareness of the new play station, as well as TV advertising to promote specific games and rollover jackpots. Since the launch of the play station, the bubble design concept has also been incorporated into the set design for the BBC National Lottery draw programme, increasing public familiarity with the concept.

**FIGURE 20.3**   An in-store National Lottery play station

Reproduced by permission of POPAI

## 21

# Public relations

## PR's 'elevator pitch'

The reputation of a brand is the sum of the total relationships it holds with its customers and other stakeholders, and reputation is a 'social' evaluation of people or organizations. 'It's what people say about you when you've left the room.' If advertising seeks coverage, awareness or salience as the benefit to its paying customers, then public relations has a single goal: building reputation.

Therefore, a good PR strategy seeks to add value to all the key relationships brands and companies have, and in so doing to improve the reputation they have amongst these key third parties. Third parties are not only journalists working in the media, but also opinion leaders, politicians, regulators, pressure groups, customers, bloggers and members of the company's own staff. All of these people comprise the 'medium' through which public relations disseminates its messages and they can repeat these messages, modulated by their own interpretation for good or bad, via writing, broadcasting or simple word-of-mouth.

As the internet continues to drive change in our media, it will also drive connectedness and transparency. People are generally only one click away from finding out what they want to know about any individual, brand, company or country through web search or social search. It is for this reason that reputation has become one of the greatest factors in success or failure for many organizations. Thus public relations, the management of reputation, is becoming a key adjunct to brand management, since reputation is one of the most important 'intangible' discriminators between competing brands, companies or even nations.

## How do people engage with PR?

In nearly all respects the process of public relations is virtually identical to that of advertising: you receive a brief, you develop a strategy, and you create an idea to bring that strategy to life. However, when it comes to execution, the disciplines diverge. In advertising you 'buy' the distribution of your idea; in public relations you act through third-party endorsement and 'earn' your communications coverage. Diagrammatically this can be expressed as follows:

**FIGURE 21.1**    Advertising vs. public relations

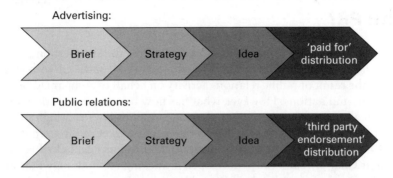

Brands have always had to deal with three main categories of communications: bought, owned and earned. In the pre-internet era these three would have been typified by a brand's paid-for advertising (bought), its packaging, point-of-sale and catalogue or customer magazine (owned) and its media coverage generated by public relations (earned). However, nowadays, with the advent of brand and corporate websites and online social media, the categories of 'owned' and 'earned' have taken on massively greater significance. One of the key outcomes of effective public relations activity is the word-of-mouth that's generated by it, and this has become a significant component of brand communications activity. Personal recommendation has always been very important, as we all know from our personal experience; here's the sequence which led to one happy customer who had been looking for someone to make window blinds:

**FIGURE 21.2**    Word of mouth in action

**Finding someone to make some blinds**

Vivienne Pringle recommended to Dorothy Richardson by her friend,

↓

Dr. Elizabeth Hockney, who was recommended by her business partner,

↓

Dr. Rosemary Flood, who was recommended by her hairdresser,

↓

Vivienne Alexander, who was recommended by another of her clients,

↓

Cathy Richardson, who is a friend of

↓

Irene Mead, who is sister to

↓

Dorothy Richardson the curtain lady

# How many and what sort of people engage with PR?

It's almost impossible to put a limit on the answer to this question because the media that people watch, listen to or read are all suffused with stories that are the result of public relations activity on behalf of companies, brands, politicians and nations. However, what has now become clear is that a relatively small percentage of the population is responsible for a high proportion of the word-of-mouth that affects the main product of PR – reputation. Dr Walter Carl of Northeastern University and founder and chief research officer at Chat Threads Corp. developed a tracking methodology that identifies the word-of-mouth relay effect. He found that one unit of advocacy results in, on average, 62 conversations. In other words, if 1,000 influencers are affected by a campaign, they will generate 62,000 conversations about the product or service. Crucially, these influencers, or Conversation Catalysts™, speak more regularly with more people, and about a larger range of topics, than the rest of the population. IPA TouchPoints tells us that, while the majority of adults speak regularly to 15 people, Conversation Catalysts™ will speak to 21. Moreover, they will influence others across five categories, instead of the average three. According to consultancy Keller Fay Group, 54 per cent of these conversations about brands include references to marketing or media, with advertising at 26 per cent followed by programming and editorial at 14 per cent, which it would seem reasonable to attribute to PR activity.

**FIGURE 21.3**    Marketing and media are tools for encouraging WOM

60% of influencers' brand conversations include references to marketing or media

...led by advertising (29%)
editorial (16%)
point of sale (11%)
promotion (10%)
websites (10%)
direct mail/email (6%)

**SOURCE:** Keller Fay's Talktrack®US 2010

Despite our improving understanding of its mechanisms, measuring the worth of PR coverage can be tricky and difficult to put a price on. People estimating its value use varying techniques, but generally speaking, the standard method used in the PR industry is to work out the advertising equivalent value (AVE) and multiply it by three. Three, because it is accepted that as a rule of thumb a PR story is worth three times the value of an advertisement because the audience believes the messages in editorial coverage and view them as news and, therefore, fact. This is why it is generally believed that PR carries more weight and resonates more strongly with audiences. There is a continuing debate as to the accuracy and appropriateness of AVEs as a measure. This is for two main reasons: firstly, a significant amount of PR activity is not directed at getting a story into the media; indeed, some practitioners are valued highly for their ability to keep a client's bad news under wraps. Secondly, not everyone agrees with Oscar Wilde that the only thing worse than being talked about is not being talked about. They believe that any coverage of a client will have a range of value depending on whether it is in the context of positive, neutral or negative editorial comment, and thus to apply a blanket 'three times AVE' to all of it is superficial.

# What commercial communications opportunities does PR offer?

If the primary activity of the PR business is securing third-party endorsement distribution to build reputation, then one of the key aims is getting the company, brand or individual's story understood, picked up and repeated by other people. With advertising, the medium in which space or time is bought has an image impact on the advertisement, and the same applies to PR. The more authoritative and influential the re-teller of the story, and the more relevant or prestigious the media context in which it is read or heard, the greater the positive impact on the company's, brand's or individual's reputation will be. For example, strategic PR activity which leads to the production of a documentary supporting a client's business that's then broadcast on national television can have a huge impact on its reputation. By the same token, a more localized programme of public relations can still have a significant effect on the light in which a planning application might be viewed.

An important element of public relations has been providing stories to journalists working for print and broadcast media owners on either an employed or freelance basis. This is a symbiotic relationship, but that does not make it an easy one, and the most successful PR practitioners work closely with the media in a collaborative manner rather than by 'pitching' stories at any journalist who will listen. This appreciation enables a PR practitioner to judge a piece of brand news, calculate to whom it will be of most value, based on previous experience, market knowledge, and relationships, and then present it to elicit the most interest from the target journalist.

Clearly some stories, such as a new product release by Apple, are of such interest that the carrot of exclusivity does not need to be dangled. On the other hand, PR is going to have to work very hard to excite a jaded journalistic palate with a story about a new type of yoghurt. Thus a spectrum of public relations tools has evolved, broadly corresponding to the news value of the story and the degree of inventiveness and creativity that will be required to engage and excite interest. Like many other media, public relations works against the whole range of demographics and target markets, but broadly speaking the business splits into two main segments: business to business (B2B) and business to consumer (B2C).

**FIGURE 21.4**    PR spectrum

Thus a high-interest, high-value story can be the subject of a public press conference, an investor road show or a widely distributed press release or report, whereas a low-interest item may require value enhancement by being given exclusively to just one journalist.

PR also has a vital role in suppressing, minimizing or containing a story. Alastair Campbell, the notorious Labour Party 'spin doctor', spent as much of his time briefing against enemies as he did in favour of allies. Burying bad news on a big news day has become part and parcel of political news management, a dark art made famous by Jo Moore, a special adviser to a UK government minister, who sent the following e-mail as the twin towers of the World Trade Center were burning on 9/11: 'It's now a very good day to get out anything we want to bury. Councillors' expenses?'

Meanwhile, in the corporate arena, crisis management has become a well-established public relations discipline ever since the Tylenol murders in Chicago in 1982 and in New York in 1986 when owner Johnson & Johnson's exemplary handling of mass product recalls was seen to have saved the brand's reputation, and arguably the business itself. There are many forms of crisis which can strike unexpectedly and with devastating effect, such as the 2010 BP oil spill in the Gulf of Mexico, and a significant part of the top-tier public relations industry focuses on investor relations in good times as well as bad. A company embarking on an aggressive mergers and acquisitions strategy needs to work hard on managing market sentiment in order to ensure a successful outcome. In the year 2000 UK mobile phone operator Vodafone succeeded in its audacious bid for Germany's Mannesman, whereas 10 years later UK insurer Prudential came unstuck in its equally brave bid for AIG's Asian business. More recently, BP's reputation and share price have taken a battering, and some observers believe that deficiencies in the company's public relations have resulted in a number of avoidable gaffes. In each of these cases, public relations was a decisive factor in managing the market and the investors' expectations, for better or worse, and both fleetness and sureness of foot are vital.

A key element in the Labour Party's three successful UK General Election campaigns was its 24-hour newsroom whose mantra was 'to win the daily majority'. This communications hub operated as the nerve centre of the election campaign. It monitored all media outlets day and night and used voter focus groups and opinion polls repeatedly to assess the Party's grip on the key issues. One vital practical benefit of this newsroom was the way in which it enabled almost instant rebuttal of any adverse story before it gained momentum in the media. In the same way, the internet is enabling 'real-time planning' by public relations and other agencies that can use 'search' and social media as a means of analysing public and media interest.

The online environment, and especially social media websites such as Facebook, has increased hugely the potential for the core activity of public relations, which is securing third-party support. In this context, earning a positive endorsement can most easily be gained through outstanding brand performance. Online travel enthusiasts are happy to endorse a hotel on Trip Advisor only if they have had an exceptional experience, and if they have not they will make that equally clear. Toyota has seen the negative impact of vehicle recalls, not just on its brand, but also on its overall corporate reputation and share price. Amazon and eBay seek feedback on every transaction as a key part of their relentless focus on customer satisfaction and continuous service improvement.

Any brand or company with a website is a media owner and has thus expanded its ability to communicate with its customers and other stakeholders much more easily and cost-effectively than was possible in the era of hard copy. Brands that understand this build relationships with online audiences by treating the online medium as if it were a magazine or even a TV station. BMW was one of the first brands to commission high-quality short films which showcased its cars going through their paces in a way which at that time, prior to the extension of self-regulation online, would have been illegal on TV due to the requirement for seat belts and safe driving in commercials! Dove has an editorial policy in the way it develops its web presence. Diesel has gone further and developed a radio station. These brands recognize that they can build direct relationships with their target audiences. Increasing numbers of brands aid and abet consumers in participating in their bought advertising properties and thus earn valuable third-party endorsement. The humble press release has been transformed into a 'multi-media news release'.

# IPA Effectiveness Awards case study summary

*Silver Award Winner – IPA Effectiveness Awards 2008*

*Campaign: Dove's big ideal – From real curves to growth curves*

*Brand: Dove*

*Client: Unilever*

*Agencies: Ogilvy Advertising, MindShare Media UK*

*Authors: Nicolette Robinson, Ogilvy Advertising; Haruna McWilliams, Ogilvy Advertising; Felix Bullinger, Simon Dudworth; Clay Schouest, MindShare Media UK*

Evidence suggested that projecting images of perfect beauty has a negative impact on a woman's self-esteem. Dove broke its category norm to 'make women feel beautiful every day by inspiring them to take greater care of themselves'. The 'Big Ideal' campaign engaged consumers by using women of all shapes, sizes, ages and races to project a more accessible notion of beauty. The PR side of the campaign was massively successful, being picked up and featured heavily in many major press publications. Overall it generated $38 million in sales revenue and payback of US$3 for every US$1 spent.

**FIGURE 21.5**     The Dove campaign for real beauty

new Dove Firming.
As tested on real curves.

Dove
Firming Range

new Dove Firming.                    As tested on real curves.

Dove
Firming Range

Reproduced by permission of Mindshare

# 22 Radio

## The media owner's 'elevator pitch'

Radio is the sole medium to communicate purely through sound, so it can be enjoyed as an accompaniment to other primary activities, complementing the listener's mood and connecting them in real time to the outside world. Hence radio can be both a background and a foreground medium, enabling both high-attention and low-attention processing of communications information as listeners are immersed in its flow. It has also been said that radio encourages people to 'paint pictures in their minds' and this intrinsic interactivity of the medium gives it real power. As Ernst Hoffman said: 'Hearing is seeing from the inside.'

Eighty per cent of all radio listening is to music-based stations, and since the vast majority of people tune in for an average of three hours daily, the medium can be said to provide the soundtrack to their lives, with all the emotional connection that implies. For the 20 per cent of listening that is to speech-based radio, the listeners can be said to be benefiting from the comforting familiarity of 'the friend in the room'. In the UK, radio broadcasters such as Neil Fox, Nick Ferrari, Tony Blackburn, Vanessa Feltz and Chris Moyles have become famous as a result of the on-air relationships they establish with their audiences. Some radio programmes such as *The Big Top 40 Show* (networked on stations across the country), *Rock and Roll Football* on Absolute and Classic FM's *Most Wanted*, together with the BBC's *Desert Island Discs* and *The Archers*, have developed lasting appeal and a loyal following over the many years that they have been broadcast.

Radio can be accessed, unedited and unchanged, through almost any mobile media device: mobile phone, MP3 player, online streaming to a PC, or digital television, in addition to the stand-alone digital or analogue radio. This makes it currently one of the most widely available and portable media, and especially immediate when it comes to breaking news. So radio is uplifting, complementary and spontaneous. It is a unique and extraordinary medium, which complements and enhances any other channel in a media mix.

# How do people engage with radio?

The Radio Advertising Bureau (RAB) research has revealed a consistent pattern to listening behaviour, with nuances that have evolved as radio has become available through new devices and platforms. For instance, quite a high percentage of radio listening takes place when people are on their own and IPA TouchPoints data confirm that 46 per cent of radio listening is solitary. Because of this, many listeners are consuming stations that they selected personally as compared with, for example, shared TV viewing. And whether the listening is solitary or not, radio is most common in a personal space such as the bedroom, bathroom, study, kitchen or car.

The vast majority of radio listening is habitual, with 79 per cent of adults claiming that radio listening is part of their daily routine, occurring at the same time every day, especially during the working week. Moreover, TouchPoints reveals that radio is unique in being the leading media up until lunchtime. In 9 out of 10 listening situations radio is an accompaniment for people engaged in another primary activity, and this is a unique characteristic of radio as it is the only medium that people can consume completely while involved in doing something else. So people use radio to help them wake up and then listen while they wash, dress, eat breakfast and browse the internet. This habitual listening extends to people in cars on the way to work or during the school run, and also extends to station selection. Despite the huge proliferation in station choice (there are 360 commercial radio stations in the UK), people's station selections are still relatively limited, with the average listener choosing from a repertoire of fewer than three stations.

These standardized listening patterns have a strong effect on how listeners relate to radio as a medium. This is because radio stations are seen as playing a positive emotional role in people's lives, keeping them company, giving them information, entertaining them, lifting their mood and connecting them to what's going on in the wider world. Habitual listening, when combined with the emotional support role that radio plays, means that listeners develop a close relationship with their favourite station, which is often characterized as a trusted friend.

# How many and what sort of people engage with radio?

According to UK industry research by RAJAR in Q1 2010, just over 90 per cent of the adult population (46 million people) tuned into radio each week, listening for an average of over three hours every day. Within this overall listening figure over 31 million adults listen to commercial radio for an average of 13.4 hours per week. These high levels of consumption are reinforced by IPA TouchPoints, which demonstrates that the average adult spends 20 per cent of his or her time spent with media listening to radio.

When RAJAR first posted listening figures in 1992 commercial radio was particularly strong in reaching the 15–44 age group. This demographic became known as the 'commercial radio generation'. In recent years, however, a number of factors have helped to increase commercial listening amongst older demographics. The first of these is the cohort effect – people who have grown up as commercial listeners continuing as such, even as they enter demographic segments traditionally associated with listening to the non-commercial BBC stations. Another important factor has been the development of a greater variety of station formats catering for a broader set of tastes. For instance, Smooth, Jazz FM and Planet Rock all have core appeal amongst listeners at the upper end of the traditional commercial radio generation age range (35–54-year-olds), while Xfm, Choice and Kiss cater for younger 'urbanites' (15–34-year-olds). In recent years the radio owners and groups have done much to explore these audiences in depth to understand the relationships which listeners have with their stations of choice, and how these insights can develop effective campaign laydowns, the use of sponsorship, promotions, events and online planning.

IPA TouchPoints gives some useful insight into the radio medium. Heavy radio listeners are defined as people who listen to at least 3.5 hours per day, and we can see from the chart below that their profile, and its index versus all adults, has significant spikes amongst men, people over 35 and those working full or part time, while there is not a significant difference in terms of social class, with only a slight peak in the C1C2 category.

**FIGURE 22.1**    Profile of heavy radio listeners compared to all adults

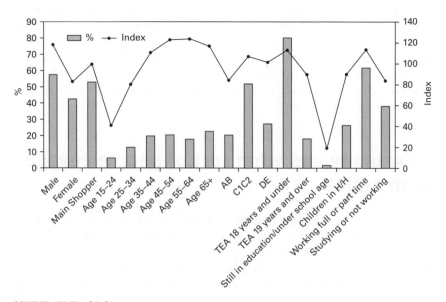

**SOURCE:** IPA TouchPoints3

In terms of the main reasons given for listening to the radio, the most important one by far is 'For entertainment', followed by 'For news and current
affairs', 'To keep up to date', 'As background' and 'To relax/escapism'. These
numbers reflect the qualitative research summarized earlier on and exemplify
the particular characteristics of radio listening as the context for advertising.

**FIGURE 22.2**   Main reasons to listen to the radio

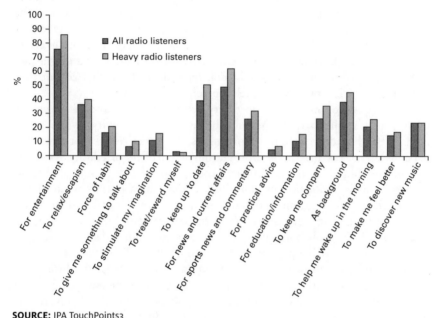

**SOURCE:** IPA TouchPoints3

There are notable differences in listening patterns between weekdays and
weekends. Between Monday and Friday, listening peaks at around 8.00 am
and remains relatively high until about 4.00 pm, when it begins to decline
quite steeply. On Saturday and Sunday the audience is much smaller and
rises to a peak around 9.30 am and then falls away by 2.30 pm. Clearly
these differences have implications for media planners and present opportunities for brands, for example a retailer needing to build traffic at the
weekend.

# What advertising and commercial opportunities does radio offer?

Radio offers a variety of powerful opportunities for advertisers to communicate with listeners. The first and largest commercial opportunity in terms
of the proportion of overall revenue it commands is spot advertising, and

listeners can be targeted by day of week or time of day to connect at the most appropriate time for the brand to deliver optimum effect. In addition to national and regional opportunities, radio can be planned and bought on a local level to provide optimum efficiency in targeting terms.

There has been much debate in recent years about the 'interruption' model of advertising as opposed to the 'engagement' one. Radio's role as an accompaniment to other primary tasks means that it's part of life's flow as opposed to an intrusion into it. Therefore, levels of advertising avoidance are lower for radio than for all other media except cinema, as shown in the 'You Can't Close Your Ears' advertising avoidance study, conducted by Clark Chapman in 2005. This means that radio listeners are more likely to stay tuned in and engaged while a commercial runs its course and thus are exposed to advertising messages in full, regardless of whether or not they are currently in the market for such a product or service.

The second commercial opportunity with radio is branded content, a term which applies to any beyond-the-spot on-air activity. While many media offer branded content opportunities, the effectiveness of these often depends upon how predisposed programme controllers or editors are to incorporating brands into the editorial product. As a lot of commercial radio reflects what is happening in daily life, within which brands often play a major role, radio programmers tend to be more open-minded in their thinking about brands appearing outside of the commercial breaks. Indeed, the radio stations themselves use on-air promotions to retain and attract listeners, so they are very much a part of the medium's culture. This is especially true when compared to most television programmers or newspaper editors. It is not surprising, therefore, that branded content is a particularly important revenue stream for radio, accounting for 20 per cent of all advertising income – a higher proportion than any other traditional medium.

Branded content on radio takes three main forms:

*Sponsorship* – In its basic form this involves attaching the name of a guest brand to an existing part of the station output, as in: 'Now here is the travel and weather, brought to you in association with Brand X.' Sponsorship is particularly effective at building awareness of, and affinity with, a brand over time.

*Promotions* – In general these are interactive, competition-based segments within station editorial such as: 'Win a luxury holiday to the Italian Lakes with Holiday Company Y.' Promotions are usually short-term exercises used to generate immediate high cut-through and listener involvement related to a brand event. They are often valuable as data collection exercises.

*Advertiser-funded programming (AFP)* – When a brand's objectives align with a station's programming goals, the station may decide to create original content to run on-air. AFP can be particularly effective in reinforcing or altering existing attitudes towards a brand. In the minds of the listeners, the guest brand can be seen to have made the programming possible, which naturally enhances perceptions.

The third and fastest-growing set of commercial opportunities allows brands to connect with listeners off-air. Station websites have evolved from solely reflecting the broadcast product to become the centre of the radio station listener community. Beyond the standard web advertising formats such as banners, or multiple purpose units (MPU), the square online ad usually found embedded in a web page in a fixed placement, station websites offer a range of effective communication routes, including audio-visual pre-roll within the station's streaming radio player, branded micro-sites and sponsored podcasts. Off-air opportunities are often combined with on-air activity to create an all-encompassing multiple touchpoint brand experience for the listener.

So, radio already offers a variety of communication routes for advertisers to connect with listeners in relevant and effective ways. But what of the future and how will advertising to the radio listener community develop as the medium evolves? RadioDNS is a new technology that has been specifically developed for radio to allow FM and DAB broadcast radio receivers to link to relevant content online. The application of this technology will soon open up new communication opportunities for brands. For example, radio is now incorporated into many media devices that feature a screen (eg mobile phone, iPod, PC etc) and many radio stations are exploring use of visuals to enhance both editorial and advertising on an ongoing basis. 'Radio with pictures' will allow brands the chance to reinforce their audio communication with a logo, pack shot or other appropriate images.

In addition, the adoption of RadioDNS will allow listeners to 'tag' any radio content that they find of interest – editorial or advertising – to revisit in more detail at a later stage. 'Tagging' will open up opportunities for brands to provide longer-form audio or visual content for listeners to interact with. This process also creates a collection of meta-data which will ultimately allow advertisers to apply web-like analytics to their radio communication, leading to enhanced accountability for the medium.

# IPA Effectiveness Awards case study summary

*Bronze Award Winner – IPA Effectiveness Awards 2008*

*Campaign: Making a small budget go a long way*

*Brand: Trident*

*Client: Metropolitan Police Service*

*Agencies: Miles Calcraft Briginshaw Duffy, MediaCom*

*Authors: Andy Nairn, Miles Calcraft Briginshaw Duffy; Matt Buttrick, MediaCom; Duncan Snowden, MediaCom*

Research had shown that black teenagers aged 12–16 were susceptible to gun crime's glamorous imagery, so a strategy was developed to demonstrate a different reality. Using the rallying cry 'Stop the guns', communications dramatized the effects of gun crime. Radio endorsements by Kiss and Choice FM were used in order to promote and support the messages provided by other media to the appropriate target audience. In order to emphasize the seriousness of the situation, commercials ran on Kiss and Choice FM, featuring victims' families talking about how guns had ripped their lives apart. It was then used to extend the reach of the next leg of their campaign, which emphasized that if you stay silent and do not report gun crime you will end up with blood on your hands. This message was endorsed by DJs of the aforementioned radio stations, and followed by another string of ads warning that guns will lead you to an early grave. As a result, calls with intelligence on gun crime have trebled, arrests of offenders have increased, and Trident officers seized 908 guns in 2007, more than the previous four years combined.

**FIGURE 22.3**   Radio script from Trident's campaign

RADIO SCRIPT

CLIENT: Trident
TITLE: Walls
LENGTH: 40's
DATE:

MILES
CALCRAFT
BRIGINSHAW
DUFFY

The MVO in this ad would be a black teenager.

MVO:  It's when you get back in here and the doors shut, that's when it hits you.

SFX:  *Thud*

MVO:  To begin with you don't want to speak to no one – you're just thinking about what you were gonna do that week. And then you think about how long it's gonna be till you can do them tings again.

MVO:  Tings like you won't be rolling with your guys no more.

MVO:  You won't be wearing all them clothes no more.

MVO:  Can't even spit bars on a track no more.

MVO:  And you're going to have to live life like that from now on.

VO:  Murder with a firearm carries a life sentence.

VO:  Don't blow your life away.
Trident. Stop the guns.org

# Sponsorship

## 23

## The media owner's 'elevator pitch'

The success of sponsorship derives from its ability to create image associations and establish a dialogue with audiences and customers through their personal enthusiasms and passions. In effect, sponsorship is the brand in action in their lives. While many other forms of communication *interrupt* what consumers are interested in, sponsorship helps brands become *part of* what people are engaged in through the association created with a particular sponsorship property.

**FIGURE 23.1**   Sponsorship: interruption to interest

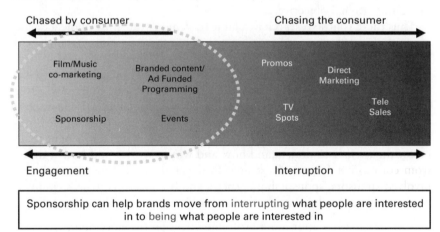

Sponsorship can help brands move from interrupting what people are interested in to being what people are interested in

Reproduced by permission of Synergy

Because there are so many sponsorship opportunities, whether of individuals, teams, institutions or events, it's possible for a sponsoring brand to interweave itself into people's lives in a welcome manner because it's both supporting their enthusiasm and sharing it. Perhaps not surprisingly, over 79 per cent of sponsorship money is invested in sport. This is because sport enjoys the near-tribal allegiance of millions, so a brand can embed itself with the fans and benefit from the passionate association.

Very often sponsorship properties are showcases for star performers so there's a celebrity halo effect which can give added burnish to the corporate, product or service brand attached to them. In a sense the sponsorship property is the 'editorial context' in which the brand is viewed, and this can have a powerful impact if the juxtaposition is well chosen.

# How do people engage with sponsorship?

If the sponsorship property is the editorial context in which the brand is viewed then the most important thing is how the target audience feel about the particular property and the degree to which they see an appropriate fit with the company, product or service and a sponsor of it. There may be an obvious and clearly defined affinity – for example male football fans who are also lager drinkers – or an inferred one such as the link between high net worth individuals who are big buyers of financial services products and also keen gardeners. So a good deal of research is commissioned by brands to determine the level of engagement of audiences with particular sponsorship properties and the effect of that sponsorship on predetermined business objectives. It is usual practice for a brand to draw up a list of criteria against which a prospective sponsorship is benchmarked and sponsorships are then researched before, during and after their life cycle to determine results relating to the original objectives.

Thus there is little research available to demonstrate how audiences engage with the medium of sponsorship per se, but there are close parallels with broadcast sponsorship from which we can learn. A broadcast sponsorship is where a brand pays to be associated with a TV programme, as opposed to taking spot advertising within it, and is an area of growing interest to advertisers. In 2008, Thinkbox, the marketing body for commercial television in the UK, commissioned independent research company Duckfoot to look into audience relationships with broadcast sponsorship. They sought to dig below the surface to understand how and why it works, and how it differs from conventional spot advertising. In order to inform the research they involved sponsors, sponsorship agencies and broadcasters in cross-industry working groups to elucidate the findings, which were summarized as follows:

1  Broadcast has a far more profound effect on the emotional, sub-conscious mind than on the rational, conscious one.

2  The stronger the viewer's relationship with the programme being sponsored, the more effective it is in attaching positive emotions to the brand.

3  Sponsorship credits need to make the relationship between the brand and programme clear. The best results come about when the credits integrate the brand successfully into the emotional relationship that the viewer has with their programme.

4 As a rule, the longer a broadcast sponsorship has to establish and maintain the relationship between the programme and the brand, the better it performs.

5 Brands can take on aspects of the personality of the programmes they sponsor, with resultant enhancement of their image.

6 Broadcast sponsorship can make brands famous by associating them with television programmes and creating a sense that the brands are bigger and better known than they really are.

Source: Duckfoot research for Thinkbox

Clearly, sponsorship at its heart is all about a brand benefiting from the association with a TV programme or event which its customers and prospects are fans of, or with sporting heroes, and getting the halo effect of the attributes of that sponsorship property. The fans recognize that the financial support of the brand is helping the thing they love – for example Emirates sponsoring Arsenal football club's new stadium – but it's also possible for a sponsorship to be used to bring tangible benefits to the fans themselves.

**FIGURE 23.2** Sponsorship creating added value for customers

Reproduced by permission of O₂

An innovative aspect of mobile brand O₂'s sponsorship of the AEG-owned Millennium Dome was the creation of 'Priority' which puts its customers to the front of the queue for event tickets, gig tickets, one-off competitions and notifications of forthcoming attractions. The most valuable of these perks is the $O_2$ customer privilege of being able to buy Priority Tickets up to 48 hours before general release. Top music acts sell out almost immediately, so when the likes of the Rolling Stones, Bon Jovi or Beyoncé have played the $O_2$, those who subscribe to the $O_2$ network have had a huge competitive advantage over other fans in securing tickets (more on this later). The outstanding success of the relationship between the $O_2$ brand and the AEG property is summarized as follows and shows how best to engage the customer through a brand sponsorship: 'Be a partner, not a sponsor. Make sure it is integral, rather than ancillary, to the business plan. Own it rather than badge it. Deliver and enhance a differentiated customer experience' (Charles Vallance, founding partner of VCCP, lead agency for $O_2$).

## How many and what sort of people engage with sponsorship?

IPA TouchPoints research provides good insight into how people feel about sponsorship. The chart below shows the percentage of all adults agreeing with various statements and first of all it's clear that people do see sponsorship as 'just another form of advertising'.

**FIGURE 23.3**    Attitudes to sponsorship

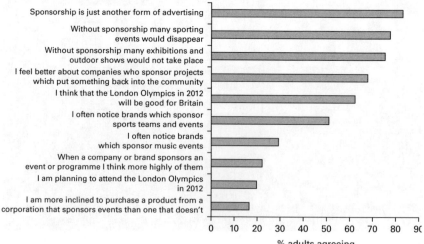

**SOURCE:** IPA TouchPoints3

Having said that, it's also apparent that there's an understanding of how important sponsorship is to the very existence of sporting events, exhibitions and outdoor shows, and this is reflected in the positive attitude to the companies involved in 'putting something back into the community'.

A sponsorship works best when audiences are engaged through activities they like, and so sponsorships are researched in terms of their popularity with their audiences. Most commonly, suitability for a brand will be determined using TGI (or similar) statistics, matched against interest in certain leisure activities. For example, a brand with a specific male target audience, aged between 35 and 55, time-scarce and in a higher income bracket would be measured against a range of leisure pursuits to establish those most likely to appeal. Another brand wanting maximum media exposure across a wide target male/female audience and appealing to all age groups would be measured against a different set of criteria. Here again the TouchPoints data are useful in getting a picture of the broad range of leisure activities people are involved in.

**FIGURE 23.4**  Percentage of all adults who have attended or watched certain events

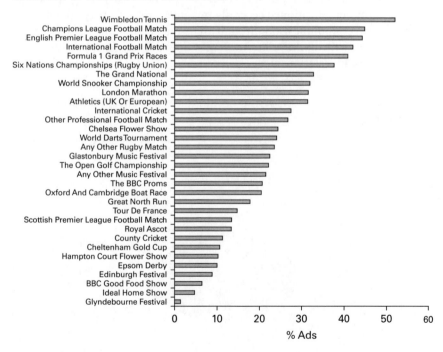

**SOURCE:** IPA TouchPoints3

This chart shows the percentage of all UK adults who have attended an event or watched it on TV. At one end of the spectrum is an elitist activity such as going to the opera at the Glyndebourne Festival, with less than 2 per cent of all adults involved, while at the other end there's Wimbledon, with over half the UK population going to a tennis match or watching one on television. Similarly, just under 45 per cent of adults have watched a football match in the UK Champions and Premier Leagues. Clearly, given the enormous range of opportunities, the choice of sponsorship must be determined by business objectives and target audience preferences. Relevance is also key: there would be little point in a digital game manufacturer targeting an opera audience.

# What advertising and communications opportunities does the sponsorship medium offer?

Used properly, sponsorship can become one of the most powerful tools in a brand's armoury. Positioned centrally in a marketing strategy, sponsorship enables brand communication through all its business channels, targeting its key audiences with appropriate messages and delivering opportunities to create meaningful relationships.

**FIGURE 23.5**    Sponsorship can take the central position in a marketing strategy

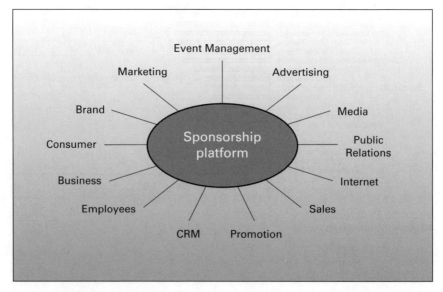

Reproduced by permission of Synergy

A number of marketing objectives can be achieved through sponsorship. These include increasing brand name awareness and changing brand imagery; influencing key opinion-formers and enhancing corporate reputation; enabling corporate entertainment for key and potential customers and creating employee engagement. Some sponsorships are designed to deliver only one or two specific objectives while others are used to underpin all forms of brand communication. Some national brands wanting to project themselves globally have chosen sponsorship as the means to do so, for example Aon's sponsorship of Manchester United. As Aon's chief marketing and communications officer, Philip B Clement, said on the announcement of the £80 million, four-year deal: 'The sponsorship is an efficient and effective way of building the Aon brand. We would have had to spend significantly more on media to match the exposure the deal will bring.'

Brands can also use sponsorship to launch in specific new markets. In Shaun Watling's book, *Defining Sponsorship*, David Wheldon then global director of brand at Vodafone, is quoted as saying that:

> For a business like Vodafone, which has partly grown through acquisition globally, there's nothing better for building name awareness than sponsorship. Across borders it's more efficient at awareness generation than advertising. Take Ghana for example, a new market for us – awareness of Vodafone as a brand already stood at over 50 per cent before we even entered the market, and this can only come from our sponsorship.

Celebrity endorsement is one of the most powerful forms of sponsorship when there is a good 'fit' between the brand, the star and the target audience. David Beckham is one of the more successful sponsorship vehicles because he and his wife Victoria have relevance not just to the world of football, but also to fashion, family and music. 'Brand Beckham' is reputed to have earned tens of millions through sponsorship deals over the years with brands such as adidas, Brylcreem, Coty, Gillette, Motorola, Pepsi and Vodafone. Despite the potential risks, celebrity sponsorships will continue because they drive sales so successfully. Nike is sticking with Tiger Woods in the belief that he will continue to shift its products as he has done since 1996 when the brand signed him for $40 million. At that time Nike had just 1 per cent of the global golf equipment market. When it re-signed the deal with Woods in 2000 for $90 million it had captured a 15 per cent share – an achievement Nike attributed largely to the sponsorship deal and clearly worth considerably more than the outlay.

In September 2008, following the European Championships, IPSOS ASI commissioned research examining sponsor recognition surrounding the event. The results showed that sponsors' ROMI is increased when investment is made in paid-for advertising as well as in the 'broadcast touchpoints', which are those brand identification assets purchased through the sponsorship contract. This is a good example of how sponsorship can be combined with other media to better effect.

**FIGURE 23.6**    Surrounding the broadcast is crucial to sponsorship awareness

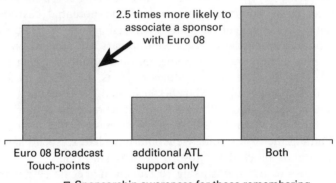

Euro 08 Broadcast Touch-points | additional ATL support only | Both

2.5 times more likely to associate a sponsor with Euro 08

☐ Sponsorship awareness for those remembering...

Broadcast Touchpoints: perimeter boards/interview backdrops/sponsor idents

Reproduced by permission of Ipsos ASI UK

The rapidly evolving technology driving the development of social media is already having an effect and, increasingly, sponsors are extending their reach through digital communications. This ability to create social groups with similar interests enables brands to connect more effectively with consumers through sponsorship platforms. Popular music, particularly, has been used by brands such as Samsung, T-Mobile and BlackBerry to enhance their connection with consumers and provide added value, thus increasing the influence and reach of their sponsorship. In 2009, as part of its 'Fan v Fan' campaign during the Ashes Test cricket match between England and Australia, Betfair mounted a digital campaign which aimed to obtain 750 brand messages within mainstream social media outlets and to gain 5,000 Twitter followers. By using cricketing legends Phil Tufnell and Jason Gillespie in a series of amusing challenges, over 3,000 brand mentions and 16,000 Twitter followers were obtained.

# IPA Effectiveness Awards case study summary

*Best Media, Gold Award Winner – IPA Effectiveness Awards 2010*

*Campaign: The $O_2$: a new blueprint for sponsorship*

*Brand: $O_2$*

*Client: Telefónica*

*Entrant: VCCP*

*Principal author: Andrew Perkins, VCCP*

*Contributing authors: Nick Milne, VCCP; Louise Cook, Holmes & Cook; Paul Feldwick*

In 2007 $O_2$, which had just been bought by Telefonica, found itself in a highly competitive market against such high-profile rivals as Vodafone and Orange. It decided to focus on sponsorship, buying the naming rights to the former Millennium Dome, which was being transformed into a music venue. This was a risky move considering the widespread disparagement of the empty and neglected 'Dome of Doom'. However, $O_2$ became fully involved with the sponsorship, and completely reversed public perception of the dome. Instead of merely badging the venue with its brand, $O_2$ took care to become an integral part of the customer experience, even ensuring that $O_2$ customers received special treatment for their loyalty, thus building trust and an emotional attachment. Today, The $O_2$ is the world's most popular entertainment venue, selling 2.35 million tickets in 2009. As of December 2009, the sponsorship's ROMI was 6.3:1.

**FIGURE 23.7**    From 'dome of doom' to The O$_2$

Reproduced by permission of O$_2$

# Television

## 24

## The media owner's 'elevator pitch'

Ask anyone of any age about their favourite ad and 9 times out of 10 they will pick one from TV. Just as TV programmes make people famous, TV advertising makes brands famous. It remains the only medium that can do this almost immediately, since each day commercial TV reaches 70 per cent of people in the UK, each seeing 45 TV ads, totalling 2.5 billion ads. People then talk about the products and services advertised, search for them and then buy, both online and off, sometimes straight away.

The reason for this powerful effect is that television uses sight, sound and motion to engage us more effectively than any other medium. With engaging story-telling, beautiful filmic images and stirring music, TV ads are not just accepted but are often sought out and keenly anticipated. Indeed, commercials are arguably one of the most enjoyable forms of advertising because of the reward they provide the viewer, over and above their 'selling' component. And of course, television provides the closest parallel to real life and thus the most powerful stream that people can enter when they step into the media flow.

The most important thing to say about TV advertising is that it is the best profit generator for brands, both in absolute volume and efficiency. There is a wealth of econometric data and brand case studies which prove TV's effectiveness and its supreme short- and long-term return on investment, such as the 10-year analysis of 708 brands undertaken by PwC which found that TV delivered 4.55 times the investment in incremental turnover. However, the evidence suggests that TV works even better when integrated with other media or marketing tactics and this is because of the leveraging effect that it has. The most effective campaigns of all are where TV ignites desire and excitement and other media complete the consumer journey, be that radio, outdoor, point of sale or, most dramatically, online media. Thus in many campaigns TV starts a powerful process and its description as 'lead medium' is usually justified: although all types of media have important roles to play, they often have the potential to perform better with TV in the brand's multi-media mix. It seems pretty clear that TV advertising is important commercial as well as cultural 'glue'.

# How do people engage with TV?

TV is a vital and enjoyable part of most people's days: it forms part of their routine but is also something looked forward to, and is often a big event with opportunities to participate, such as voting on contestants in 'reality' shows. Time spent relaxing and sharing TV is, for many people, the way they express being a couple or a family. Indeed, TV is the second most popular topic of conversation after friends and family. The heightened emotion and relaxed nature of shared TV viewing enhances TV advertising's effectiveness. Thinkbox's Engagement Study and BARB data show that shared TV is very much the norm, with over two-thirds of viewing happening with other people. And of course watching TV with other people provides an ideal opportunity to talk about advertising in the same time and space as the advertising itself (one of the original forms of viral marketing). When people discuss ads together, and what they might wish to buy or do, deep processing embeds the effect more deeply in the brain.

But these brand conversations are no longer limited by time or physical space. Technology has liberated TV advertising. From Sony Bravia balls bouncing down San Francisco to Nike's Wayne Rooney in a caravan, favourite TV ads can be searched for and re-watched at the click of a mouse, e-mailed across continents, discussed in real time online and blogged. So the internet gives us a great window into the effect that broadcast TV creates, for the comments on Twitter, Facebook groups and pastiches on YouTube are easier to observe than the private chat in front of the telly. But there are two important things to remember when using the internet as a gauge for the success of TV advertising. Firstly, we shouldn't confuse cause and effect. When commenting on a popular TV ad such as Cadbury Gorilla the pundits only ever seem to write about the millions of YouTube viewings; and they usually forget to mention the 520 million broadcast viewings that sent people looking online in the first place. Old Spice is another example of how the interest sparked by a brilliant TV campaign (which was first seen approximately 1.2 billion times on US TV) can then be extended online to allow interaction.

Secondly, online activity is only the tip of the iceberg. Conversations about TV commercials take place in homes, offices and pubs, not just online. In 2010, Keller Fay, the US word-of-mouth specialists, estimated that 81 per cent of conversations about brands happen face to face and only 7 per cent online, albeit more visibly.

The word-of-mouth element contributes to TV's unique ability to make brands famous. Its ability to hit large volumes of people in a short space of time has always been a key unique selling proposition (USP), but it can also serve to make brands seem bigger than they really are, instilling a sense of authority and stature. And, with the dawn of the internet bringing the high street into the living room, people can talk about and act on what they've just seen on TV immediately. Watching TV while also using the internet

**FIGURE 24.1**    The Cadbury Gorilla phenomenon

Reproduced by permission of Fallon and Stan Winston Studio

Performers: Garon Michael, Lindsay MacGowan and Landon Richard

represents only 5.4 per cent of viewing time according to the IPA's Touch-Points3, but it is an exciting and growing trend that advertisers should be exploiting. Mediacom's recent study into TV responses discovered that web response has now overtaken phone response, that 46 per cent of ad-driven responses to the web come from TV advertising and that over a third (35 per cent) of that happens within 10 minutes of seeing the TV ad. In their words, TV has become a 'point of sale' medium.

In recent years technology has enhanced further the experience for viewers and advertisers. TV, television and 'telly' are the default words that people use for professionally made, immersive, audio-visual content – whether viewed on a TV set, on a mobile or on a computer screen. In fact, pretty much anything with a glass screen and audio speakers can bring you TV. Early research suggests that, if TV is viewed on a device other than the TV set, it is likely to be incremental viewing, mostly displacing other media activity. We are just at the start of the 'on-demand' TV revolution.

At the heart of TV's power is how human minds process it. Put simply, TV stimulates the parts of the brain that other media don't reach as effectively, namely those responsible for emotions and long-term memory. This is why people can remember commercials they loved from decades ago, and why TV ads can make them fall in love with brands: just think of Honda, Apple, Budweiser, Sony, Nike, Cadbury, Hovis, John Lewis or Guinness – and the business success that those loved TV ads created. Thinkbox's Engagement Study, which monitored people watching TV in their own homes, provided fascinating insights into how TV advertising actually works. It showed that an engaged viewer is more likely to have a positive emotional association with the brand and is more likely to consider purchasing it in the future. The IPA's monograph, *Marketing in Era of Accountability* by Les Binet and Peter Field, has also revealed that emotional campaigns are more effective than those with a rational focus, and TV is a powerful creator of emotions. This meta-analysis of 26 years of IPA Effectiveness Award winners also proved that campaigns which included TV as the lead medium were 35 per cent more efficient at driving market share growth.

## How many and what sort of people engage with TV?

Only a small percentage of the population never watches TV. All ages, all demographics and all locations are exposed to commercial TV, which reaches 95 per cent of the population each month. The official figures for TV viewing in 2009 from the Broadcasters' Audience Research Board (BARB) show that the average person in the UK watched 26 hours, 15 minutes of broadcast TV a week, up 4.2 minutes from 2008. Importantly for advertisers, this growth – seen across all age groups – has been driven by commercial TV channels, which account for 64 per cent of all broadcast TV viewing. In the past 10 years, commercial TV viewing alone has increased by one hour, seven minutes a week. Inevitably, those with most spare time watch TV for longer but, even for light TV viewing groups such as ABC1 adults or 15–24s, watching linear TV constitutes the highest percentage of their media time, with 31 per cent for 15–24s and 34 per cent for ABC1s.

**FIGURE 24.2**    15–24s – media time allocation

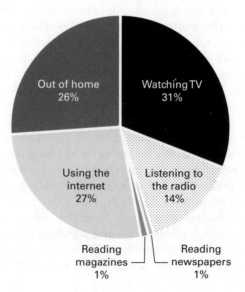

SOURCE: IPA TouchPoints3

**FIGURE 24.3** ABC₁s – media time allocation

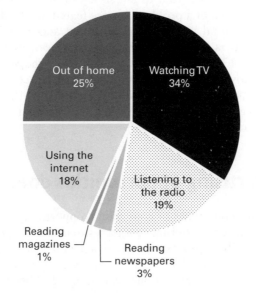

**SOURCE:** IPA TouchPoints3

In terms of the main reasons why people watch television, IPA TouchPoints confirms that the main motivations are: 'For entertainment', 'For news and current affairs', 'To relax/escapism' and 'To keep up to date'.

**FIGURE 24.4** Main reasons for watching television

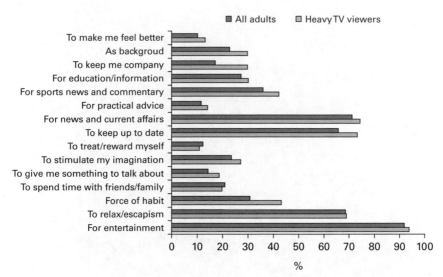

**SOURCE:** IPA TouchPoints3

In this context it's worth noting that it has never been easier for viewers to avoid TV ads if they really want to but so far, in the UK at least, this does not seem to be as much of a problem as once feared. BARB data shows that only 7 per cent of total viewing is time-shifted and even in homes with digital video recorders (DTRs) such as Sky+ or Freeview+ the time-shifted percentage is only 13 per cent. Moreover, data from the Sky View panel of 33,000 homes shows that Sky+ owners watch 15 per cent more TV than before they had it and 30 per cent of all the recorded ad breaks are not fast forwarded. Hence, households with Sky+ actually watch a net increase of 3 per cent more ads than previously.

## What advertising opportunities does TV offer?

In terms of the different types of commercial opportunity available via TV, the spot ad, shown before, during or after a broadcast TV programme on a national or regionally targeted basis, remains the bread and butter of broadcast TV advertising and the backbone of any TV campaign. Spots can range from pure brand-building ads to ones encouraging a direct response from the viewer (DRTV) and can be in standard definition or in high definition (HD). Longer spots can be major events generating significant PR, like the Honda live sky-dive broadcast on Channel 4 on 29 May 2008 or the T-Mobile 'flash dance' at London's Liverpool Street Station.

**FIGURE 24.5**  First 'live' ad for Honda – a skydive

Reproduced by permission of Honda UK

There's also the rapidly growing market of TV broadcast sponsorship, where brands align themselves with a programme or a series of programmes, a programme segment or even a whole channel. Sponsorship enables a brand to associate itself even more directly with TV, and to build its personality through implicit association with the brand values of the programme and the broadcast environment. One stage beyond sponsorship is advertiser-funded content, where the advertiser makes a direct investment in the commissioned programme in exchange for enhanced rights to that content.

A related area is product placement, which recently opened up within the EU and came officially to the UK in 2011. This will be a small market in the UK for many years but is well developed in the United States. Recent research from Nielsen indicates that TV viewers in both the United States and the UK have a generally positive view of product placements. Sixty-six per cent and 63 per cent respectively found them 'Natural and seamless' or 'Somewhat natural', with only 3 per cent in both countries seeing them as 'Somewhat forced' and just 1 per cent in the United States regarding them as 'Forced and awkward'.

**FIGURE 24.6**   Viewers don't object to product placement

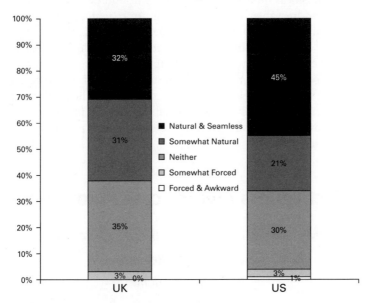

Reproduced by permission of The Nielsen Company

Interactive advertising was initially marketed as a largely tactical, technology-led, response-driven mechanic, but the past five years have seen a shift towards using it to deliver long-form brand engagement through the TV. Not only does the red button present an opportunity to be less time-constrained in the delivery of brand narratives, but with precise measurement tools such as Sky View, it also allows for even greater accountability. Interactive branded games work well in this arena. The red button is very successful for interactive programme content and brands can successfully become part of this by using the interactivity of the red button technology to provide links to other information, their website or response materials.

Another exciting recent development in TV advertising is 'green button' functionality. This allows users to bookmark advertising content that they want to watch again later. The ad content is recorded to their hard drive for them to refer to whenever they want. On-demand TV also offers other ways to target and to interact. Sky Anytime is an on-demand service using local storage through the Sky+ HD box. UK Sky+ viewers who got their set-top box after August 2005 are able to access the best of Sky programming on a discrete part of their hard drive, with 35 hours of programming available for viewing in a largely ad-free environment. On-demand TV services available on the open web, such as ITV Player, 4OD, Demand Five and Sky Player, or delivered direct to the TV set, such as the catch-up services that will be part of the upcoming YouView service, allow pre- and mid-roll advertisers to have clickable ads which take viewers directly to a brand's website, opening an era of transactional advertising via TV in addition to the exposure business model which currently dominates.

The era of 'addressable' TV advertising is approaching, via broadcast TV, not just web or IPTV. In 2010 on Sky Player and in 2011/12 on Sky broadcast TV, it will be possible for advertisers to buy a single spot, but to tailor and deliver the creativity to segments that they co-create, using legitimate and volunteered information about Sky households. This could be anything from tailoring the voiceover regionally or segmenting the audience for different products or offers. Sky AdSmart will be just the first system to offer all the power of TV advertising with the personalization normally associated with direct mail or online.

# IPA Effectiveness Awards case study summary

*Silver Award Winner – IPA Effectiveness Awards 2010*

*Campaign: Still Red Hot*

*Brand: Virgin Atlantic*

*Client: Virgin Atlantic*

*Entrant: RKCR/Y&R*

*Principal author: Richard Cordiner*

*Contributory authors: Joanna Bamford and Tom Barnes, RKCR/Y&R; Zehra Chatoo, Manning Gottlieb OMD; Tosin Osho and Paul Sturgeon, Brand Science*

In mid-2008, Virgin Atlantic was suffering due to a combination of the global credit crunch and an increasingly weakened brand image. Bookings were down 13 per cent from the previous year and market share was rapidly being lost to British Airways. To combat this problem, Virgin Atlantic decided to re-energize and reinforce its core brand attributes with the hope of regaining its position as the preferred 'challenger' airline.

In January 2009, Virgin launched its 'Still Red Hot' campaign, which celebrated the brand's 25th birthday. TV spots placed around high-profile programmes such as *Big Brother* and the FA Cup celebrated Virgin Atlantic's inaugural flight in 1984, and featured a confident cabin crew striding through the airport to the sound of Frankie Goes to Hollywood's *Relax*. Larger than life, glamorous and nostalgic, these commercials reminded consumers of Virgin's core beliefs and positioning, and conveyed the idea that flying could still be fun. Crucially, Virgin Atlantic increased its media budget while its major competitors reduced theirs, thus leading to a significant increase in share of voice.

This approach paid off, and Virgin Atlantic reported a £68m profit in May 2009. ROMI was £10.58 for each £1 spent, and the campaign was responsible for an impressive 20 per cent of Virgin Atlantic's total revenue over the period. Moreover, by the end of the campaign, research showed that preference for Virgin Atlantic had overtaken British Airways.

**FIGURE 24.7**   After 25 years, Virgin Atlantic is 'Still Red Hot'

Reproduced by permission of RKCR/Y&R

# PART FIVE
## Where's it all going?

# Introduction

The future is of course digital. The new digital environment has not only brought with it fundamental changes to the way that media is distributed and used but also the way that advertising is now developed, planned and placed across the various media channels and platforms. Korean-born American conceptual artist Nam June Paik (1932–2006) was credited with saying 'the future is now' and the world of UK media is very clearly entering a 'third wave' in its development. As we have already explained, the first wave was created by the newspaper medium, the second wave by television and now the third wave by digital which has produced a whole range of new communication channels and opportunities.

Additionally, it has broken down the boundaries between the various traditional media channels and we have moved on from the world of linear channels, which was largely evaluated and used on a 'silo' basis, to a market that now involves 'bought', 'owned' and 'earned' media. This has in turn created the new phenomenon of the 'media flow' which is running in parallel with people's life flows, and with which they intermingle both willingly and subconsciously as they move endlessly from not deciding to deciding, and not buying to buying.

Of course, the new media world of digital is still in a process of evolving, driven at an ever-increasing rate by the underlying technologies, as predicted by Gordon Moore, the co-founder of Intel: 'The number of transistors incorporated in a chip will approximately double every 24 months.' This is accelerating the speed with which data are processed and transmitted, aided and abetted by the increasing bandwidth which is making the customer experience so much easier and more enjoyable.

While we have witnessed the emergence of search, social networks and e-commerce – all of which are predominantly 21st century phenomena – large sections of the media community continue to operate in a similar manner to some 20 or 30 years ago. For example, the main TV channels are planned, traded and evaluated in largely the same way as they were in the 1980s. And the majority of the other 'traditional' media are no different to TV in that they have hardly changed their approach. Even so, we would contend that overall the media world is at something of a crossroads today and the next three to five years are going to define its structure for the longer

**FIGURE P5.1**  Faster broadband changes behaviour

Photograph by Hamish Pringle

term. There will be a new hierarchy of media and media owners emerging; advertising and media agencies are going to develop different skills, configurations and operating processes. Many advertisers are going to be asking for different kinds of services from their media agency partners and evaluating them with different and more sophisticated measures of accountability.

This is not only because of the 'digital revolution'. It is also because the UK, along with the rest of the world, has encountered a major economic recession, which started during 2008 and ran through 2009. Even though the recovery in 2010 has been rather better than anyone might have expected, the recession had a harsh impact on advertising budgets and, as a further consequence, even today advertising in its traditional sense is too often regarded as a cost as opposed to an investment by manufacturers and brand owners. As a result, advertising budgets, which are still required to fund much of the UK media scene, are neither as resilient as has been the case in the past, nor as likely to grow significantly in real terms in the foreseeable future. For a media world that is increasing its advertising inventory at a dramatic rate, this is creating a major financial challenge for the business.

It is against this background of digitalization and financial uncertainty that we are reviewing the future in this part of the book: firstly, looking at the likely developments in the media, secondly, the implications for media ownership, and thirdly, looking at how we believe media agencies will be structured to service their customers in this digital future. Clearly we are going to be making quite a few predictions. We can guarantee that they will be wrong, but, to draw on an American saying, we're confident that we'll be in the right ballpark, though the precise score may be wrong!

# 25 Media channels in future

If the future of UK media is all about digital, it's as well to understand exactly what is meant by digital media! The term has become a much-overused descriptor for pretty well anything that is new and electronic, from the internet to new television channels and from mobile phones to electronic posters. Digital is a technology that enables content to be distributed faster, in greater volumes, more flexibly and with better quality than the old analogue systems. It also offers the potential for interactivity. But it is still only a distribution device and, while the media industry likes to talk about 'digital media' as a catch-all phrase, consumers still think in terms of television, newspapers, magazines, radio, posters etc and of course the internet. It is just that through digital technology all media content is more widely and flexibly available – the *Coronation Street* viewer is no longer confined to watching the programme at a specific time on ITV, they can now choose to watch it on a number of other devices (the internet, ITV Player, iPad, PDAs etc) at a time of their choosing. But nevertheless they are still watching *Coronation Street*. So we should never underestimate the continued or indeed arguably increased importance of content versus technology and the fact that technology means nothing without content. Sky struggled in the UK until it started airing *The Simpsons* and new media platforms will need appetizing content – bits and bytes alone are not enough to attract an audience.

Similarly, many people will still watch *The X Factor* live on Saturday night on ITV, but some will watch it on different channels, at different times and in different formats. And when watching *The X Factor* they will also be doing a lot of other things at the same time – chatting with friends, watching other programmes, reading a magazine or a newspaper, checking on news updates and even buying stuff which they might have seen advertised or recommended in the various content they have been looking at. And not just some, but all of this, and possibly all on the same screen, and not even necessarily at home – they could be travelling, be at a friend's or relative's house or even be on holiday abroad. Phew! A very different environment, made possible by digital technology and the growth of the new media channels – the converged life and media flow of the future.

**FIGURE 25.1**   Great content helped sky get established

Photo by Hamish Pringle

While recognizing that digital is just an enabling technology, its impact and implications on all media have already been far reaching and it is starting to reshape the way the entire industry is structured. So how has it changed the shape of media and how is it going to reshape the future media world? Firstly, digital has created the internet and the world wide web, which sits on the internet and enables the transfer of data. The internet in turn has created entirely new communication and advertising channels: e-mail, search, social media and social networking sites and of course websites, many of which contain e-commerce opportunities. Because these are now all so fundamental to the way we live our lives it's easy to forget that the first e-mails only became common from the mid-1990s with Microsoft Windows, providing an integrated browser, server and internet service and making the internet universally available and usable, first launching in 1998, less than 15 years ago.

Secondly, digital facilitates convergence. Again this is a much-used term but media convergence doesn't seem to have happened quite as quickly or dramatically as some were predicting – most of us are still watching TV on dedicated screens in living rooms, reading newspapers and magazines on trains, at home and even in the bath, listening to the radio (possibly also in the bath!) amongst other places in and out of the home, and going to the cinema to see the latest Harry Potter film. But the lines between media are becoming increasingly blurred and next generation devices are going to speed up the process of convergence. The iPad has already had a significant impact – most newspaper publishers are calculating the costs and returns on publishing their products electronically and the iPad is also ideal for getting iPlayer and video on demand services. But the two devices that are going to accelerate convergence most dramatically are smart phones and connected TV. In fact smart phones, giving instant access to the internet and allowing customers to search and transact online, are already having a marked impact, particularly on younger adults. In 2009, around a quarter of UK mobile phones had 'smart phone' technology and this is anticipated to rise to at least double that (probably over 50 per cent) by the end of 2011. Connected TV is set to launch seriously into the UK in 2011. This will provide immediate access to the internet, via the television set. The chief executive of Sony, Howard Stringer, said recently: 'The next evolution is upon us: the marriage of the television and the internet.'

**FIGURE 25.2**    PC World – an Aladdin's Cave of digital devices

Photograph by Hamish Pringle

The joint potential of smart phones and connected TV should not be under-estimated in turning the world of previously 'silo' media into a genuinely converged environment, because the mobile phone and the TV set are argu-ably amongst the most personal and important devices in people's social and leisure lives today.

**FIGURE 25.3**   TVs proliferate and get bigger and better

Photograph by Hamish Pringle

Thirdly, digital provides an almost limitless number of channels on which to distribute content – whether from existing broadcasters and publishers, or from new/aspiring content providers. For the existing broadcasters, used to a limited and highly regulated spectrum of channels, this provides an array of opportunities to leverage their library of existing content and develop new content and schedule formats. Clearly this is already in evidence on TV, as all the broadcasters have launched a variety of digital channels and are developing catch-up and VOD services. The next stage of development will be in radio. The government is aiming for a 2015 digital switch-over for radio. However, this will only be achieved if digital penetration is at a minimum of 50 per cent of UK homes two years before handover (ie 2013). The government is hoping this will be the case but realistically it is anticipated that 2017 is a more likely earliest date. To date, commercial radio has had only a single fully national FM station, Classic FM, because of the limited spectrum – the BBC has all the other national channels. The introduction of digital radio will change all of this and the commercial radio broadcasters will be able to turn their 'networks' (eg Capital, Heart, Magic, Smooth etc) into genuine national stations, though because of funding pressures it may be a year or two after the switch-over.

Finally, digital provides connectivity and interactivity. Arguably this is the real power of digital. It has opened up a new world of two-way, commerce and data/information for media owners, advertisers and consumers. And this alone has revolutionized the way the media now operates, how media are used and (not to underestimate its impact) the way people can organize their lives.

**FIGURE 25.4**    Telephone exchange to let

Photograph by Hamish Pringle

So, given the impact of digital, what will the media world look like in the next five years or so? There is an old saying: 'No media ever dies.' (And it doesn't even just fade away.) In our view all the media that we know today will continue to exist in 5 and indeed 50 years' time. This includes newspapers, which some commentators have tipped to disappear; Professor Roy Greenslade noted pessimistically in the *London Evening Standard*:

> To get a handle on the longer-term trend I dug out the (ABC) figures for October 2000. They show the 10 dailies selling an average of 12,673,462 copies compared with last month's total (October 2010) of 9,679,622. It means that in the course of a decade there has been a market fall of 23.6 per cent.

However, we believe that the various media will be distributed and accessed by consumers on an increasing array of different devices and in different formats, as well as their current formats. Thus television will be viewed on computer screens, laptops, tablets, PDAs, mobiles, posters, games consoles and satellite navigators – in fact potentially any device with a screen. But it will also continue to be viewed on TV screens – never forget the installed base, which means that the average US household now has 2.93 TV sets, according to Nielsen's Television Audience Report in May 2010.

Newspapers and magazines will continue to appear in print but will also be available and read on other, albeit larger, screened devices, including potentially (and ironically) the TV screen. Cinema? The same, and in fact films are already widely distributed across any number of screened devices and have been for many years.

But we don't believe that media will converge onto a single 'universal' device, even in the longer term. Why? Because human behaviour suggests otherwise – for example, why would the wristwatch continue to exist when time is displayed on any number of other personal and public devices, including the mobile phone? Maybe it's partly about having a fashion item but it's mainly because people's continued personal preference is to check the time on a watch of their own choice on their wrists! Similarly, just about everybody now owns a mobile and many possess two as they find it convenient to use one as a phone and another for web access, often simultaneously. People possess both a book reader and a laptop or tablet. There's clearly a human desire for the division of labour with their personal devices.

We believe that the television screen in the front room, the printed newspaper, the copy of the personally chosen magazine (always bought on a certain day) are no different – they simply have a utility that people prefer in certain circumstances. So our view is that, in 5 years' time and even in 25 years' time, people will still read a printed version of *The Times* and watch TV on a main 'dedicated' TV screen in the home – admittedly by no means everybody and not all the time. In what proportion is impossible to predict and, arguably, will it really matter from a media owner or an advertiser's point of view if they continue to consume the same content and see the same advertising that it carries, but now across a range of devices?

While no medium ever dies, new media are born and then grow and develop. The new digital age has already parented a number of hugely influential new media which have not only added to the existing media landscape but are also influencing and changing the way that people use and interact with their media. These are search, social media and mobile.

# Search and search engine marketing

During the 1990s, as the world wide web began to grow substantially in scale and complexity, attempts were made to help the growing number of web users find the content they wanted. These initial attempts relied largely upon human input and categorization: selections of edited content would be pushed via web portals (the initial point of entry to the web) like AOL, or content would be collated on web directories like Yahoo!, organized by category and sub-category. Over time, as the number of websites continued to grow, the emphasis shifted towards the use of 'search engines'. These are online tools for searching that rely predominantly or solely on programs that comb the web methodically, indexing web content and using proprietary algorithms to list what are deemed the most relevant results for specific enquiries or keywords. Pioneering search engines that became widely known to the public include WebCrawler (1994), Lycos (1994), AltaVista (1995), Inktomi (1996) and most notably Google (1998).

Google's superior algorithm, PageRank, and its continued commitment to improving speed and accuracy of response have made it far and away the dominant search engine globally. When an individual makes an enquiry using keywords the resulting 'organic' or 'natural' search return provides information which is designed to be the most relevant response to the enquiry, whether it's trying to locate the nearest plumber or the latest developments in nuclear physics. Brands can benefit from a specialism within digital marketing called search engine optimization, whereby their web content is designed and built with search engines as well as people in mind – this can help websites to appear higher up relevant page rankings in search results.

Along with 'organic search' there's 'paid search' (PPC – pay per click), which enables an advertiser to buy certain keywords that will result in their ads appearing when people use those words in their search. However, unlike organic search, the prominence of the position in which the advertiser appears in the ranking will depend on what price they pay for the words, as well as their relevance, and is calculated on the basis of a ranking measure called a 'Quality Score', introduced by Google.

It is of course far more than a directory service and, though search engine marketing (SEM) has only really existed in the past decade, it is now a fundamental part of most advertisers' marketing and communication strategy – and, if it isn't, arguably it should be! Search now works on a number of levels, from identifying brands and services in a specific product sector through to acting as a 'gateway' to detailed information on products and brands, and from providing basic location information through to providing consumers with access to full online purchasing opportunities (with price and quality comparisons). Though SEM is hardly 10 years old, it is difficult to imagine that most modern brands could now exist without it, and a number of very significant e-commerce businesses have been built with the significant help of search engine marketing, eg eBay and Amazon for a start.

The future will inevitably see further growth of search, particularly with the impact of smart phones and connected TV. Google, who dominates the UK search market with a share of some 85 per cent, continues to innovate and grow its business and wider media interests – it now also owns YouTube. What is a particularly interesting characteristic of Google is its very different approach to trading – it sells paid-for search on an auction basis where the advertiser bids for keywords on a 'pay per click' basis. In other words, the advertiser pays only when an ad is clicked on rather than when it is displayed.

The future of search will be about ever more sophisticated targeting and use of data, which in turn will provide increasingly efficient ways of identifying and securing customers. The challenge for advertisers and their media agencies is to incorporate the process of search into their wider advertising and communication strategies, whether in support of traditional paid-for advertising or as their part of an e-commerce strategy or both. It is also very possible that its trading approach could start to be at least in part adopted by the more established and traditional media.

# Social media

To social scientists, social networks are as old as humanity itself. They are social structures made of individuals or organizations that are connected through various familiarities ranging from casual acquaintance to close familial bonds. However, in the 21st century the phrase 'social network' has become a widely used abbreviation of 'online social networks' or 'social network services'. These are websites that provide profiles of and connections between individuals. The term 'social media' applies to web-based technologies offering people the opportunity to generate and share content, and to interact with other users through discussion and comment. According to the latest IPA TouchPoints research, over 33 million people in the UK use social media, slightly over two-thirds of the adult population. Social networking, through dedicated social network sites, is less prevalent but still involves around 18 million people and nearly 40 per cent of the adult population. These figures, collected in 2009, undoubtedly understate the volume of social networking as of today, given its rapid growth rate. The current market leader and one of the 'heroes' of the internet is Facebook. Today it has over 750 million members worldwide, which is a staggering number, given that it launched barely seven years ago in February 2004. It now dwarfs former social networking leaders, MySpace and Bebo, which are experiencing substantial decline at the time of writing. The other recent darling of social networking is Twitter, which has been around only since 2006 but has already built up a following of some 175 million users.

As the market has matured so segmentation has begun and the recent trend in social networking sites has been to cater for more specific interests, enabling comment, exchange of content and discussion forums on the basis of 'communities of interest'. Major sites such as LinkedIn, dedicated to business people, and BlackPlanet, for African Americans, operate successfully on a shared interest basis with many millions of users (80 and 20 million respectively) and there are an ever-growing number of social network sites that cater for everything from the gay community (Gays.com with 100,000 users) to pop music (Buzznet with 10 million users).

The future will see further growth in social media and social networking as it appeals to a deep human need – in the global village people behave just like they do in their local village, just more so with the aid of digital technology. TouchPoints tells us that social media users are currently biased to under-44s and social networks to under-34s. Clearly there is now a generation growing up with social media and other technology developments (particularly the growth of smart phones) that will serve to increase both its penetration and use. Even younger than the search engine market, social networks have collectively grown from almost nothing to overtake search engines as the most visited type of website (in May 2010 in the UK according to Hitwise).

For advertisers it offers some very significant opportunities but also poses a number of challenges. The numbers are now huge and Facebook claims that over half its users go onto its site every day, so frequency of usage is also consistently high. Arguably the main opportunity is in building brand awareness, image and reputation – for example brands can have their own Facebook page or YouTube site with content and forums. However, there are a number of other opportunities, including tracking and trying to influence brand reputation (your own brand and your competitors' brands), recruiting potential advocates and even driving traffic to a brand's online site encouraging discussion and views on the product and services. And of course there is the increasing number of display advertising opportunities sold on social network sites.

The challenge for advertisers is how it is used, because the danger is that a brand can easily be perceived as being an unwelcome guest – a bit like a perceived 'outsider' trying to interrupt a group of friends. Furthermore, if it is possible to start a dialogue and create a 'fan base', brands then have to respond positively to comments, suggestions and most importantly criticisms from that group. The skilled people required to implement a social media strategy on a 24/7 basis means it's a significant financial commitment for a brand which, if it ever tries to skimp on it, will likely end up affecting the brand negatively.

We forecast that increasing numbers of leading brand owners will establish and operate what are effectively 24-hour 'newsrooms'. These hubs will be the nerve centres for monitoring and responding to the online chatter about their business and brands in as near a real-time basis as is possible. The big question for them will be whether they choose to run these hubs in-house or to outsource to a third party. On the one hand, company employees should have the deep knowledge of the company culture necessary to respond appropriately to comments and participate in forums without falling into the 'astroturfing' trap, ie faking a grassroots response. On the other, an external agency is more likely to be right up to date with the latest technologies, have a skill set informed by work for other clients and have the adequacy of human resources to scale up rapidly in the event of a crisis. As ever, it's likely that most companies will have some internal resource, which must be part of the marketing team, linking to an outside company with the necessary expertise. In this way social media can be harnessed properly with the other 'earned' media and deployed in proper coordination with all the other channels to create the optimum flow for the brand.

# Mobile

From the customer's point of view the single most important type of device will be the mobile phone and its descendants. A person's phone is arguably already the most indispensable item they have, perhaps with the exception of a wallet or the keys to their home and car. We are already seeing prototypes which, through near field communication (NFC), a subset of radio frequency identification, incorporate these essential functions into one highly portable pocket-sized device. If you've ever used an Oyster card on the London Underground, you've already benefited from RFID technology and many commuters using the Tokyo Metro credit and swipe their mobile phone rather than a dedicated travel card.

By using voice-recognition software a phone can transcribe voice into text, then send it as an e-mail with a photo attached, and the new iPhone has a FaceTime facility for video calls. So the smart phone of the future will enable customers to search and transact online whenever and wherever they wish, with the assistance of live salespeople if required. It will enable them to take advantage of special offers based on not only their previous behaviour but also on their current physical location, made possible by geostationary satellite tracking. In fact, mobile phones, which already contain software and sensors that gather current location (GPS), the direction faced (compass) and even the angle of elevation (accelerometer), will provide information in spatial and semantic context. This layering of additional sensory input onto the perception of one's surroundings is called 'augmented reality'. Live sports events, tourist sites and even other people will appear with 'enhancements' (extra information and maybe even advertisements). Mobile phones are already dissolving the barriers between online and offline, between cyber-space and meatspace (reality). Posters and other analogue printed media can, without any additional technology, incorporate images that when photo-graphed via a smart phone are recognized as hard links (real-world hyper-links) to additional information, promotional incentives or even outright purchasing facilities. A simple form of this, popular in Japan since the mid-90s, is the QR code which is in effect a two-dimensional barcode.

One aspect of mobile culture and business where Japan has not demon-strated its usual global leadership is 'mobile applications' or 'apps' as popu-larized by Apple and more recently Google Android. These are small computer programs designed for mobile phones that serve one particular purpose effectively and efficiently. An individual can personalize what their mobile phone can do by their own app selection. This provides a whole new avenue to brands and businesses because they can 'earn' their place on someone's mobile by being useful or entertaining – mobile banking, flight check-in, gaming or even a pollen count for hay fever sufferers!

The result of all this will be that the life and media flows for the majority of people will converge. Whereas in the early part of the 21st century we talk about individuals stepping in and out of the media flow, for younger people it's more accurate to describe them as actually living in and through the media flow. For them, large parts of their interpersonal relationships are established and then conducted through social media with contacts, conver-sations and arrangements all being made online, and then gossiped about in the same places later. Fixed-line telephony is truly a thing of the past.

And of course the smart phone is an advertising medium in its own right and brands will be able to present themselves in an appropriate and timely manner in the palm of their prospect's hand. The data flow that will be derived from the future smart phone, with the user's permission of course, will give a comprehensive picture of that individual's travels through the life and media flows. This past behaviour will also allow inferences to be drawn in relation to that of the peer group and thus enable predictive advertising and marketing communications strategies to be deployed in response to the customer's anticipated desires and needs.

There are some loud voices in the privacy lobby who see all this as a gross invasion of people's private lives and the ultimate in the 'Big Brother' nightmare scenario. Clearly there is a risk that unscrupulous and unethical companies will undermine public confidence in these new technologies, but we are confident that the vast majority of blue-chip organizations, which represent well over 80 per cent of the business, will comply with the high standards imposed by the regulatory, co-regulatory and self-regulatory regimes which operate to varying degrees throughout the world. However, the advertising and marketing communications industry in particular cannot be complacent about this and needs to make sure that their commitment to the protection of customer privacy is sincere. In particular, their websites need to display their 'opt out' facility prominently as part of their strategy to avoid the mandatory 'opt in' that is being argued for in some quarters.

To date, mobile advertising has been a tiny market. But the future power of the mobile is as a media channel, not an individual medium, and it will act to accelerate convergence and provide a gateway into a whole range of other channels and the advertising opportunities those channels will bring with them.

# Media owners in future

So what will media ownership look like in five years' time? To quote Kevin Keegan, a famous footballer, ex-England team manager, and commentator: '… it's much the same as today, except that it's completely different'.

Yes, much of the media will be the same and in many instances consumed in the same way. But, as we have seen, it will also be completely different because the individual media will be distributed across a number of different platforms and channels, which will be available on an increasing number of devices. This will give consumers genuine choice and control over what, how and when they consume the media of their choice – so the same world of media, but expanded and available at the push of a button and the advertising will never be much further than a few clicks away from a potential purchase. It is not only an exciting but also a scary prospect and it will have some major implications on the structure of media ownership.

With the convergence of channels and platforms will come the inevitable consolidation. This will be partly in response to funding pressures but partly because the media owners will need the scale to produce or buy content and then monetize it through advertising, subscriptions and other potential revenue streams, including selling customer data. Though News Corporation withdrew its bid to secure complete control of BSkyB in July 2011 as a result of the phone-hacking scandal, we suspect Murdoch will be back after a decent interval. There will still be concern amongst competitor media companies, who have opposed the purchase, claiming that it will reduce its plurality. Some media buyers will also oppose the deal because it will make News Corporation significantly more powerful in advertising sales. However, we believe the deal will be approved eventually with safeguards, because we don't think that News Corporation will change its stance on programming and editorial across its broadcast channels and newspapers, nor its approach on advertising sales. The objective of securing overall ownership is to ensure that it is able to leverage its overall scale to develop its offline and online channels and to secure and leverage content across all of its channels. Currently BSkyB is the star performer because it has developed a successful subscription and pay-per-view funding model (along with

**FIGURE 26.1**   Sky headquarters in West London

Photograph by Hamish Pringle

advertising revenue), while News Corporation's newspapers and online services are still overly reliant on advertising revenues. Consolidating the overall business will generate operating economies and, more importantly, it will be able to subsidize its developments in print and online products. In this regard it will assist in its objective to develop a profitable 'pay wall' business for its online content.

We predict confidently that, though the News Corporation/BSkyB deal has been shelved for the time being there will be a number of other major consolidations across media. To date, the UK has witnessed mainly mergers and acquisitions within media sectors (ITV, Global Radio etc) but, as the market moves further towards integrated media channels and integrated offline and online content, it is inevitable that a number of major cross-media owners will emerge. It is interesting to speculate who these might be and of course it's impossible to predict, but the obvious contenders are the large international players like Disney, News Corporation, Time Warner, Viacom Bertelsmann AG, and also possibly the successful operators in the new media – what about Google, Microsoft or even Facebook? Obviously we can't know or accurately predict who will be the next media owner 'power houses' in the UK, but we are confident that the next 5/10 years will see some very significant ownership deals which will redefine the UK media owner hierarchy.

The other area of necessary major restructuring will be in advertising sales. There are a number of reasons for this. We have already identified that advertising revenues are unlikely to rise significantly in the next few years in spite of the ever-increasing volume of advertising inventory – a market where supply now far exceeds demand. Furthermore, the sheer volume of advertising inventory requires very different trading systems to manage the process. But there is an additional consideration that reflects the new media market. Historically, and still mainly today, advertising is sold into specific content – a slot in *Coronation Street*, a page in the *Daily Mail*, a 48-sheet poster on the Cromwell Road. This is unlikely to change in the foreseeable future or indeed ever for the major channels and their best content, both offline and online. But another advertising market has already been developed for online media, which is a market where 'the buy' is not for specific content but for a volume of communication, and where its placement is determined by the audience delivery. And very significantly, the advertiser/agency can dictate the audience definition, for example it may be for a particular audience demographic but it can also be for specific consumer sectors such as credit card purchasers or holidaymakers. These campaigns are operated by the ad networks such as Specific Media, Adconion and Tribal Fusion who are primarily involved in selling space across a range of online sites, including the major portals, publishers, price comparison sites and a host of other online properties, including social sites, blogs and even e-mails. Sophisticated technology allows the ads to be served to the various appropriate site pages and also calculates the audience delivery. The cheapest are through 'blind networks', where the advertiser relinquishes virtually all control over which individual sites the ads appear within, but there are also 'vertical networks', which serve ads to specific channels (for example financial or travel content) and 'targeted networks', where technologies are applied, such as behavioural targeting to reach specific types of people as signified by their search and browsing activities. More recent forms of targeting involve combinations of the above, so, for example, a 'financial buy' could be made up of inventory served in financial editorial environments and/or inventory served to an audience showing an interest in finance while browsing elsewhere.

Now all the major online players, including Google, Yahoo!, Microsoft and AOL, operate their own ad networks which include their own inventory and partner publishers. There are also a number of independent ad networks which have secured deals for unsold inventory across a range of online sites. It is a fast-growing sector with most online publishers selling somewhere between 10 and 100 per cent of advertising through networks depending on their size. Though it is currently confined to online it is an approach which could easily be applied to other media channels and undoubtedly will be, in some form, in the future. There are now 'ad exchanges' such as the Double-Click Exchange, a subsidiary of Google which facilitates direct bidding for online inventory from advertisers or media agencies. These have been joined by an ever-growing list of complementary technologies, including 'data exchanges', 'demand side platforms' and 'publisher optimization tools'. All these interoperate and can handle vast volumes of trading in real time. Again we see this trading method swiftly developing for online media but there is similar potential for other media owners and channels as they transition to digital.

So, we are predicting some of the same for the future but many fundamental differences. Differences in how the various media are distributed and accessed by consumers, differences in the number of media available, differences in the hierarchy of media, differences in the ownership structure, differences in their funding and revenue streams, differences in how they transact their advertising sales and differences in the use of technologies – the 'third wave' in the development of the UK's commercial media sector and the move to a fully integrated 'media flow'.

Before we move on to the future of media agencies, we shouldn't leave our assessment of the UK media landscape without mention of the BBC – still arguably the UK's most revered brand and most progressive and commercially astute UK media business, while still being entirely publicly owned.

**FIGURE 26.2**    BBC Television Centre in West London

Photograph by Hamish Pringle

Rather surprisingly, given the stated intentions of the new coalition government with regard to the public sector, the BBC has secured both a continuation of the licence fee funding structure and a pretty generous annual award which maintains its licence fee at the current level until 2017. Though this is the equivalent to a 16 per cent reduction over the period, it will still generate an annual income of around £3.6 billion and of course it is guaranteed, which, in the uncertain world of media, is arguably the most valuable asset it could have. So its next five years or so will involve some cutbacks and economies but the BBC will be largely unaffected by many of the commercial pressures on the other broadcasters and will undoubtedly maintain its core TV, radio and now online services while continuing to experiment with new media formats – so no real change there. However, come the next review in around 2016, it is highly possible that there will be comprehensive review of the BBC and a substantial overhaul of its funding, structure and remit and even the possibility that parts of it will be commercialized. In spite of much of the continued excellence of the BBC's output, a review/overhaul is now overdue because it is allocating too much of its energy, resource and the public's money into services which should be covered by the commercial sector while often paying too little regard to its public service remit. Whether or not the Department for Culture, Media and Sport (DCMS) and the government overall will have the appetite for the fight with the BBC in five years' time is another question!

# 27 Media agencies in future

**F**inally we are going to examine the future for media agencies, the organizations that are going to be spending the client's advertising money in the digital age. The future structure, approach and skill set of media agencies will be based around the requirement to deliver integrated solutions. As we discussed earlier in the book, media has moved on from a set of clearly delineated channels to become a 'media flow' of overlapping channels and content, some of which are bought, but others are either owned by the brand or earned by it. What this in turn means is that 'starting with an ad' is not necessarily the best solution and it could very often be the worst. This is because beginning with a particular creative execution, which entails the use of a specific medium, can lead to a pre-judgement which militates against a better-balanced media schedule. As we have seen, critical to communication effectiveness is the ability to utilize and mix the various channels to their best effect, whether it's the client's own packaging, website, magazine or marketing event (owned media); whether it's a Facebook page, YouTube coverage or a word-of-mouth campaign (earned); or whether it's TV, radio, press, outdoor, internet or search (bought); or most probably a combination of all of these.

We conceive of these media mixes as being designed to bring together what customers need from a brand in terms of fame, advocacy, information, price and availability (FAIPA) and put that content into an individual's life flow in the most appropriate way. We have seen how over the past couple of centuries there has been a steady increase in the availability of media, from a few isolated oases in a dry landscape to a situation where now there is a continuous media flow running parallel to and increasingly intertwined with the life flow. And within the media flow we can see a continuation of the process whereby the 'traditional' media have migrated onto the new digital platforms to provide their readers, viewers and listeners with their content wherever they please through whatever device. Coca-Cola is driven by the mission to make sure that people are never more than an arm's length away from a Coke, and nowadays the goal of a media owner (and indeed any brand) is never to be more than one click away from a customer.

We see the same thing happening in other industries such as music and book publishing which have moved away from single channels focused on physical products to multi-channels including digital formats, live performances and merchandise. Brands too have appreciated the potential to extend themselves into live experience events which create powerful new touch points between them and their customers. Many have created branded merchandise and others have produced programme content as additional ways to create engagement. Social media brands like Facebook have gone even further and created an environment in which their users can immerse themselves for some of the most valuable parts of their day.

The role for media agencies will be to understand and make sense of this new media flow, to design and structure communication plans that leverage all of the various available channels on a combined basis, and then to execute those plans to best effect and most cost-efficiently. The implications of all this for media agencies are profound.

**FIGURE 27.1**   Navigating the flow

Photograph by Hamish Pringle

We have already said that we think it unlikely that there will be a re-combination of creative or content agencies, despite the obvious attractions for clients in delivering more effectively integrated advertising and marketing communications. So how will media agencies of the future be structured? Clearly there will continue to be specialist media agencies that will provide primarily executional services (eg planning and buying based on a set strategy and channel mix) and agencies which will specialize in vertical markets (eg property, financial, entertainment etc). However, the major media agencies will need to broaden and deepen their relationships with their clients and other communication agency partners in order to provide a complete strategic service. This will go beyond planning and buying to include commissioning and managing media.

Clients will look to their media agency to take a grip of their overall business and communication requirements in all three types of channel. Clearly bought media will be the financial mainstay of the activity and given the proliferation of channels agencies will have their work cut out just staying on top of that. But we see media agencies extending their reach into commissioning other paid-for media such as brand experience, branded content and sponsored programming, especially in the UK and Europe following the relaxation of the regulations on product placement. In fact media agencies will also look at the opportunity to become sponsors or owners of content. This they will then sell on to media owners, but in return for advertising inventory as opposed to cash. Clearly this starts to move into the area of broking, but it has the potential to deliver significant benefits for the media owner, who would not otherwise be able to afford the content, clients, who will get access to discounted media inventory, and the media agency, through an additional revenue stream.

Agencies will also take a much bigger role in coordinating and even managing the brand's owned media, whether it be a poster holding, a customer magazine, its employee communications or a website. These media assets can be of considerable value and clients will want to make the most of them, both for their brands and for non-competing ones which can provide a revenue stream. For example, the UK government has recently woken up to the fact that it has massively underutilized holdings in many different media and will need the expertise of a media agency working with media owners to monetize them. These latent assets include poster sites outside and within government properties, a myriad of public service mailings, and of course the BBC which it is in the process of pressurizing to re-start public information communications which could appear on television, radio, magazines and websites. There are currently 400 BBC websites and even though there's a stated intention to reduce the number there will still be 200 at the end of the process.

We also expect agencies to build on their growing expertise in earned media and, as a result, make significant inroads into the public relations arena as social media become increasingly important to managing a brand's reputation. As Gerry Farrell has said of The Leith Agency's approach to marketing iconic Scottish soft drink Irn Bru: 'We use word of mouth to get share of throat.' It may well be the media agency of the future to whom the client will outsource its 24/7 newsroom. So this new world will still require media agencies to maintain their existing areas of expertise, in planning, negotiating and buying the various media, but they will need to develop greater levels of expertise in both data analysis and the use of technologies.

## Data analysis

For many decades the power of customer data has been used by brands to improve their understanding of their target audience, not only to develop their product or service offer, but to improve the accuracy of their advertising and marketing communications. For example, the agency dunnhumby, now wholly owned by Tesco, has made a significant contribution to the growth of the retailer through its management of the Tesco Clubcard. This is a massive repository of customer transactions which can be data-mined to produce the cross-selling scenarios which are proving so effective in building the business. Other agencies such as SapientNitro and LBi, which have great strengths in web design and build and in e-commerce technologies, are building additional capabilities in advertising and marketing communications which are underpinned by highly sophisticated data planning.

Companies such as Occam and Acxiom are leaders in interactive marketing services and their data integration services enable marketers to align their brand communications using consumer information and analytics for every channel to market including digital, internet, e-mail, mobile and direct mail.

So what we're seeing is the evolution of the 'data flow' which comprises the billions of bits of information about customer transactions that new technologies make increasingly visible to, and accessible by, marketers. We envisage a future in which the media and data flows become ever more closely interrelated, thus allowing a far greater appreciation of the detailed nature of the flow of people's lives, and their myriad of journeys from 'not buying' to 'buying', and all points in between.

**FIGURE 27.2**   The future evolution of the media flow

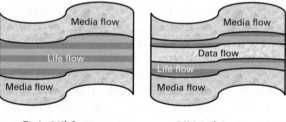

Early 21$^{st}$ Century          Mid 21$^{st}$ Century

As more and more of these data are tracked in real time, and as the algorithms applied to them become more accurate, it will become far easier to serve up advertising and marketing communications addressed to specific individuals. Customers will benefit from the utility of being able to access information, pricing and availability of the brands they're considering with perfect timing as they approach a purchasing decision. Meanwhile, the same sort of analytical processes will be used to anticipate a customer's future behaviour with greater precision, thus directing the display advertising that creates fame and advocacy more cost-effectively.

# Technologies

Both media owners and media agencies share a mutual challenge presented by the avalanche of real-time information about customers' use of media, especially online search, their self-publishing disclosure via social websites and their purchasing data. There will be increasing pressure from clients for their brands to respond to this real-time data and of course the resultant advertising and marketing communications in themselves will precipitate more customer data. It seems inevitable that a significant proportion of this activity will have to be automated – it's simply beyond human processing capability, even if it's massive and located in the lowest-cost nations of the world.

Additionally, as we have already discussed, the media trading environment is evolving into two different distinct markets: the traditional one that will continue to sell advertising in specified content, albeit across a number of channels, and the emerging market which will not sell content but a volume of viewers, readers or listeners (or a combination of all of these) in unspecified content. To date, this approach has been confined to the online channel and has been applied by media owners or sales operations, through 'ad networks' and 'ad exchanges'. At the moment each of the big agency groups is developing its own electronic trading platform and this will become a standard method of trading alongside the traditional negotiating and buying. But it will deliver significant operating and cost efficiencies for both media agencies and the media. In fact, given the volume of advertising inventory now available, it is arguable whether the future market will be able to exist without these new trading technologies.

But there is also a problem here. It is possible to develop and sustain a trading platform with individual media owners (for example, Double Click with Google) but, if the financial markets are anything to go by, it seems highly unlikely that this approach is sustainable across a wider range of media owners and channels owing to the huge costs involved both on the agency and on the media owner sides. Somehow or other a single dominant platform per country or economic bloc will evolve as it has done in markets such as oil, metals, foodstuffs, meat products, and stocks and shares. It's likely that such a platform will be owned by a core group of agencies, and ideally with the participation of media owners too, so that it is as near to a low-cost cooperative venture as possible. In the UK it's conceivable that it could even be run by a Joint Industry Committee, or JIC, much as the various media research currencies are.

In conclusion we can see that the media landscape has evolved through three waves, each of which has been dominated largely by one medium: firstly newspapers, secondly television and thirdly online. Media agencies, which are the interface between these media and advertisers, have evolved accordingly, and are still very much in the process of coming to terms with the digital media environment. We believe that media agencies will continue to operate as a separate sector, even though the majority are now owned by the major global advertising groups, with the notable exception of Aegis. They are unlikely to be reintegrated into creative agencies, in spite of their shared ownership in many instances. If anything, they could be more closely aligned with those agencies that have specialized in direct marketing and in web design and build. There is already a cultural affinity between these sorts of companies with their strong numerical and data skills. Such a combination would also lead to a greater focus on outcomes as opposed to inputs, and generate improved remuneration terms with clients.

We believe that the vast majority of the 'old skills' will be retained by the future media agencies. They will operate with a 'hub' of client account managers and strategy/channel planners, while also operating with specialist expertise in all the old and new media channels – from TV to mobile and from sponsorship to social media. However, they will have to expand their content commissioning capability and their analytical skills and systems in customer data analysis systems. They will also have to introduce technologies to manage the interface with media owners to access the most effective and cost-efficient media inventory while incorporating significant operating efficiencies into their processes.

Though we have talked about the much-increased role and importance of data and systems, we're convinced that the human element should not be underestimated. In the future scenario one can envisage the danger that marketers and agencies may fall too much in love with the brilliance of the technology and become over-preoccupied with the scientific perfection of the media channels at their disposal at the expense of the content they carry. We have no doubt that people will continue to respond far better to emotional as opposed to purely rational communications, and that the clever juxtaposition between message and medium for their mutual enhancement will always deliver a more cost-effective result. This is especially true for those challenger brands which lack the financial muscle to exploit the 'law' of share of voice versus share of market and instead must rely on the combination of award-winning creativity and astute channel planning to gain competitive advantage.

As part of this evolving process, we believe that media agencies will have to overhaul their commercial and charging models. The current system, designed when the media landscape and the business of planning and buying media were comparatively simple, is no longer viable if these new areas of expertise and integrated communications planning are developed and resourced effectively. Clearly this is one of the more fundamental challenges for the sector. However, it is not an insurmountable problem, particularly if the media agencies can combine improved operating efficiencies with incremental incomes for new services and additional revenues from media owners, through ad exchanges, content deals and data sales.

Finally, we believe that media planners and buyers will remain the ultimate matchmakers between brands and their customers, between media owners and advertisers, and between creative content and the channels it runs in. In the future the life, media and data flows will converge and it's essential for an effective agency to be sitting at the confluence, navigating for their client on behalf of the brand.

**FIGURE 27.3**    The life, media and data flows converge

Photograph by Hamish Pringle

# Multi-media strategies in future

**A**s Dr Johnson said in January 1759: 'Advertisements are now so numerous that they are very negligently perused.'

This problem is still with us today and likely to get worse in future. So the media planner (and the creative strategist) needs to allow for it in constructing the brand's multi-communications strategy. They must create the best possible combination of content and channel to position the brand within the life and media flows, and then analyse the data flow to understand if the campaign is succeeding in engaging people.

It is estimated that approximately one-third of the population would consider themselves to be 'ad avoiders', and while this number may be overstated owing to a research effect, it's not a bad mindset for the professional media planner to be fully aware of. Even the majority of the population who see a utility in advertising have an extraordinary ability to screen out those commercial messages which are irrelevant, dull or downright annoying – though there are of course those rare beasts which are 'so bad they're good', such as Ferrero Rocher's commercial set in an embassy with its immortal line 'Ooh Ambassador, you are spoiling us!'

In 2007 Microsoft Digital Advertising Solutions and agency Starcom commissioned Millward Brown and Greenfield Consulting Group to carry out research to explore the attitudes and media behaviour of consumers who claim to dislike advertising and therefore avoid their exposure to marketers' messages. In their report they produced a useful model – their 'Advertising Evaluation Framework' – which helps media planners put themselves in the shoes of an 'Ad Avoider', and probably everybody else in the market at some time or another!

The report concluded that by recognizing our place as advertisers in the world of consumers, rather than naively thinking that consumers live in an advertiser created world, and by respecting consumers' space and time, any brand can transform itself from a nuisance to a welcomed and even helpful presence. They listed four tenets to help ensure that all marketing is relevant, respected and welcomed by Ad Avoiders, and more generally, the non-avoiding population at large:

**FIGURE 28.1**    Advertising Evaluation Framework

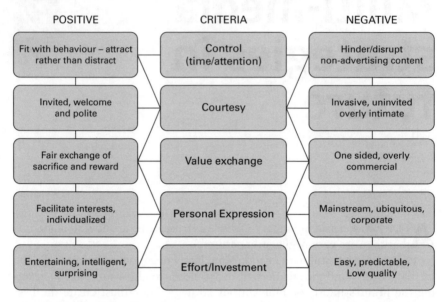

| POSITIVE | CRITERIA | NEGATIVE |
| --- | --- | --- |
| Fit with behaviour – attract rather than distract | Control (time/attention) | Hinder/disrupt non-advertising content |
| Invited, welcome and polite | Courtesy | Invasive, uninvited overly intimate |
| Fair exchange of sacrifice and reward | Value exchange | One sided, overly commercial |
| Facilitate interests, individualized | Personal Expression | Mainstream, ubiquitous, corporate |
| Entertaining, intelligent, surprising | Effort/Investment | Easy, predictable, Low quality |

Reproduced by permission of Starcom

1 Respect Ad Avoiders' barter-based mindset by providing them with a tangible reward, conversational currency or content that fuels their passions.

2 Give Ad Avoiders a 'choose your own AD-venture', either through providing them the means through which to become ad editors and personally select advertising they want to engage in, or by providing them the ability to become advertising content creators.

3 Rotate media formats, not just creative or copy as, not surprisingly, ad wear-out occurs more quickly with Ad Rejecters.

4 Be a good guest, not a gatecrasher, by creating both pull- and pass-along tactics that afford rejecters the ability to invite marketers into their personal space and that of their network.

These good media manners are perennial in their relevance but are being taken to another level by the whole new area of multi-media strategy which has been opened up by new thinking encouraged by the IPA Excellence Diploma and in particular the winning essays published as part of the programme. Faris Yakob won the President's Prize in the IPA Excellence Diploma 2006/7. He based his essay on the idea of 'transmedia planning'. In this model, there's an evolving non-linear brand narrative with different channels used to communicate different, self-contained elements that build to create a larger brand story. As they dip in and out of the media flow consumers can pick up these different elements and piece the narrative together for themselves. Given that there are a variety of interest groups within the brand's customer base which will be accessing the communications from different media entry points, there's the potential for the formation of communities centred around Facebook, Twitter or TV. So transmedia planning seeks to generate these brand communities, and to encourage them to come together to share elements of the narrative. Thus it has a word-of-mouth driver built in.

**FIGURE 28.2**   The new world of 'transmedia' planning

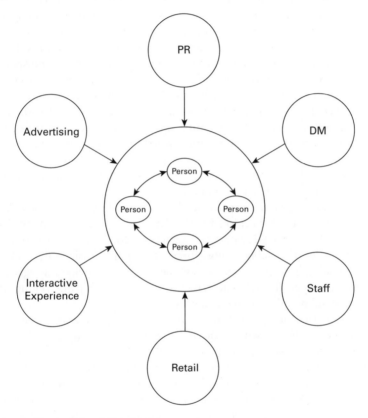

Reproduced with permission of Faris Yakob.

**SOURCE:** Future of Brands by Faris Yakob, President's Prize, IPA Excellence Diploma 2006/7

Yakob suggests that alternative reality games, such as Audi's Art of Heist by US agency McKinney+Silver, are early examples of this form of communication. It may be that some brands appear to lack the depth that this model requires, but given the consumer preparedness to engage with branded content that provides genuine entertainment value, the barriers lie only in the imagination and the creativity of the brand team. Clearly the burgeoning availability and user-friendliness of interactive media channels provide great opportunities for brands to engage with their consumers.

The President's Prize winner in the IPA Excellence Diploma 2009/10 was Tim Jones with his essay on 'Gaming Brands'. This puts forward an interesting approach to brand planning that applies the principles of gaming to brand-building and represents a fundamental shift from building brands as message transmission devices to building brands as behaviour change systems. Jones gives Lynx/Axe as a prime example of a brand which employs this innovative media planning strategy. In his view, gaming brands represents a fundamental shift in brand planning, providing brands with interaction at their core. The brand 'win condition' is at the heart of this approach. Defining brands in this way focuses the marketing mix around developing brand activities that help consumers 'win' at a behaviour they either have to do, or want to do. This positions the brand and its products as tools that help consumers to 'win at life', making the brand both attractive and indispensable. The key question for marketers shifts from 'how will my brand activity communicate my message?' to 'how will brand activity help my consumers win?'

The concept of 'Gaming Brands' clearly has implications for those who see consumers as active participants and wish to build truly interactive brands to suit their needs by putting overtly rewarding bits of 'bait' into their life flow.

Meanwhile, the relatively recent application of behavioural economics thinking to media planning is making a big impact. An early example of how this works in practice is provided by the 2010 IPA Effectiveness Awards paper by agency DDB London for the Training and Development Agency for Schools (TDA), the UK's national agency responsible for the training and development of the school workforce. The paper, titled 'Best in class: how influencing behaviour with a new media strategy helped nudge teacher recruitment to record levels', describes a radical switch from 'selling' teaching to 'helping' people become teachers.

The media thinking got off on the right foot with a classic piece of work on the target audience which showed that prior campaigns had not been focusing on the most important people. Previously the audience had been treated as a single entity but close inspection of the data revealed there were actually two distinct groups. Firstly, there were final year university undergraduates who were about to enter the job market and represented a continuously renewing target audience confident when making decisions about a career. As a result, these students were more likely to leapfrog the TDA's service and apply direct to teacher training providers. Secondly, there were 'career switchers', mainly graduates aged 25–45, who were looking for a change in their career and who were much more cautious in their decision-making.

The DDB analysis revealed that the root of the decline in applicants was with career switchers who made up 77 per cent of the potential target audience and so were the best volume opportunity to meet enquiry and application targets. The research amongst this key group demonstrated that the TDA faced not an attitude problem but a behavioural one: people were thinking the right things about being a teacher, but they just weren't taking all the steps necessary to become one. This wasn't surprising given that switching career to be a teacher is not a relatively simple and unimportant behaviour change like swapping one washing-powder brand for another. On the contrary, the decision to switch careers held massive risks for people who had more responsibilities such as mortgages to pay and a family to look after. They had more to lose because the career switcher becoming a teacher meant accepting a lower salary and starting out all over again. They also had more fear of failure: would they enjoy the job, or be good at it? Would they be appreciated by pupils, parents or even schools? These barriers created a formidable 'decision spiral' which left switchers in permanent limbo and the long application process allowed these real worries to prey on the mind. It was little wonder that many career switchers procrastinated and dropped out along the way in greater numbers than students.

This reframing of the teacher recruitment problem as a behavioural one led to a radically different media strategy, but unusually with little change to the creative content approach from previous years. The new model of communications entailed helping a new target audience of career switchers to take one of the biggest decisions of their lives... via a small series of steps. People's progress towards becoming a teacher wasn't linear or mechanical, as if moving along a funnel. Their behaviour was human – stops and starts, emotional not logical, decisive then uncertain – so the media thinking was too. DDB pictured their campaign as a *pinball machine* perpetually keeping people 'in play' towards another positive TDA experience and ultimately to making an application.

Media were planned and used like a 'pinball machine', stimulating a response and keeping people 'in play' for longer. Research amongst career switchers showed that such people don't make life-changing decisions in neat and tidy campaign cycles, so there was a move away from big bursts of media exclusively in key periods to a spread of activity to create a more continuous backdrop of TV, press and online. This involved using a wider range of media, doubling the number of channels used from 7 to 15 to build a campaign more in tune with people's lives, working with, rather than against, the grain of their natural inclinations. It also entailed finding new ways to meet people's needs through media where they were already looking, such as search engines and online jobsites, and putting more information in new places to inspire further consideration. Media most likely to get people to *do something* were prioritized and media were selected to work together, nudging potential career switchers from one point to another. Media were also deployed at times and places where people would feel least satisfied with their current careers and likely to be experiencing the 'working blues' – for example, advertisements on Monday mornings in newspapers popular with commuters, poster sites on the underground and rail platforms, where people stand in the same place every day, and at 'dark' moments like January, or October once the clocks went back for daylight saving. Ads were also taken out on social networking sites, where people time-waste in working hours.

**FIGURE** 28.3    Media planning as 'pinball'

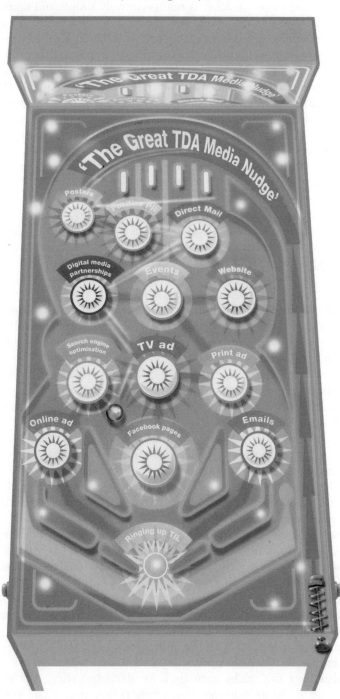

Reproduced by permission of DDB and MEC

**FIGURE 28.4** Increased media channels

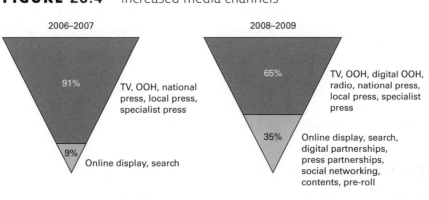

2006–2007

91%

9%

TV, OOH, national press, local press, specialist press

Online display, search

2008–2009

65%

35%

TV, OOH, digital OOH, radio, national press, local press, specialist press

Online display, search, digital partnerships, press partnerships, social networking, contents, pre-roll

Reproduced by permission of DDB and MEC

From this case study it can be seen that incorporating behavioural economics thinking into media planning requires the consideration of how audiences experience and navigate a campaign, not just the messages within it. It involves understanding that small levers are as important to campaign success as the 'big idea', if not more so, and that a single big creative idea can comprise smaller, interconnected media ideas that influence and shape behaviour. It also entails the recognition that shifting behaviours can lead to changes in attitudes, rather than the other way around. Indeed, DDB's media 'pinball' approach, designed to nudge behaviour persistently, was strongly rooted in behavioural economics best practices as can be seen in the table below.

**FIGURE 28.5** Applying behavioural economics to media planning

| Behavioural economic principles | | |
| --- | --- | --- |
| **Barrier** | **Our approach** | **What behavioural economics call this** |
| Scared of the unknown, worried they wouldn't be a good teacher | Help them visualize authentic positive classroom experiences | Anchoring |
| The easiest thing to do is to leave the decision until another day | Communicate frequently across the year | Immediacy value |
| Scared about starting out all over again – emotionally and financially | Showcase experiences offsetting fear of losing current status | Loss aversion |
| That it's too big a leap to make in one go | Break the application process into small steps | Chunking |

Reproduced by permission of DDB and MEC

The paper highlights how, contrary to conventional marketing models, humans aren't 'rational' beings that respond at once to messages – they're impulsive, unstructured creatures that respond intuitively to sets of behavioural stimuli. The TDA campaign used a series of behavioural triggers to 'nudge' people through their career-switching journey, turning a big decision into a series of small steps. It achieved a minimum payback of £101 for every £1 spent, increasing teacher enquiries and applications to record-breaking levels on a smaller spend, thus putting itself at the top of the IPA Effectiveness Awards 'ROMI Hall of Fame'.

**FIGURE 28.6**    The IPA Effectiveness Awards ROMI hall of fame

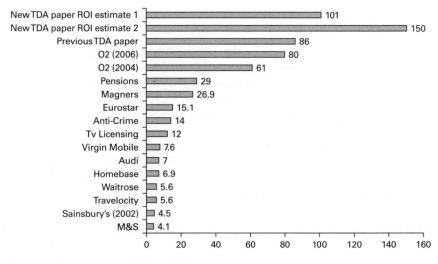

Reproduced by permission of DDB and MEC

The application of behavioural economics and the ideas of 'transmedia planning' and 'gaming brands' show how vibrant and innovative media planning is, and taken together we can see how influential this new thinking can be in understanding how brands can be interwoven into people's lives. The key thing is to recognize that people are creatures of habit with a process of brain development in which neural pathways get reinforced every time the same connections are made. Their desire for minimal effort usually leads them to follow the path of least resistance. So the wise media planner understands these biases and heuristics and goes with the flow.

**FIGURE** 28.7    Follow the path of least resistance

Photograph by Hamish Pringle

# APPENDIX

The following calculations are the basis of Accenture Media Management's estimate of the average UK individual's exposure to ads being 1,009 daily. While some of the research used at the time of their calculations has had new editions since, Accenture advise that this would not materially change their estimate.

## TV

Thinkbox research carried out in 2008 ascertained that in 2008 there were 2.4 billion ads a day seen in the UK. Thinkbox calculated this to represent 42 ads being seen per person every day. This is based on an average day's viewing being 2 hours, 21 minutes of commercial TV.

## Radio

Data for RAJAR for September 2009 recorded that the average listening time per week on commercial radio was 8.3 hours per week, which breaks down to 71 minutes per day. There is no restriction on the number of radio ads per hour but the assumption is that it is roughly 8 minutes. Average time length for an ad is 30 seconds – so we assume 17 ads per day.

## Newspapers

Readership figures for daily newspapers = 56.8 per cent of adults (inc. nationals, locals and frees) – National Readership Survey. 'The trend is for publishers to create more news pages and to enhance their products through value-added supplements and colour magazines. The current (2007) average pagination for a British newspaper is 64 pages' (British Library; **http://liber.library.uu.nl/publish/articles/000259/article.pdf**). We then work on the assumption that there are 0.8 ads per page: $0.8 \times 64 = 51.2$.

If the average is 51.2, multiply the percentage of readership times the average number of insertions to get $51.2 \times 56.8\% = 29.08$ ads per day. This is assuming the whole newspaper is read and does not fully account for supplements.

# Magazines

Magazine circulation in the UK is just shy of 1,500,000,000 annually (**http://www.oft.gov.uk/shared_oft/reports/comp_policy/oft1028.pdf**).

The UK adult population of 48,532,000 (BARB) gives 1,500,000,000/48,532,000 = 30.91 magazines read per year per person. Average pagination of a (Scottish) magazine = 69 pages (**http://www.ppa.co.uk/ppa-scotland/ppa-scotland/ppa-scotland-research/~/media/Documents/PPA%20Scotland/PPAScotlandSizeandValueofindustry.ashx**).

Total number of pages viewed annually = 30.91 × 69 = 2,133. Pages viewed daily = 5.8. Number of ads per page unknown. Assumed to be similar to newspapers as above, ie between 0.6 per page and 1. So call it 0.8 ads per page × pages viewed daily = magazine ads viewed per day = 0.8 × 5.8 = 4.64 ads per day.

# Outdoor

Outdoor, more so than the other media, will be affected by location. There will be a huge disparity in the number of exposures from someone living in the countryside compared to a commuter working in central London. Therefore, we have put this figure at anywhere between 40 and 600 ads per day, averaging out to 320. This initially appears high, but with billboards, buses and the Underground this number can rise extremely quickly.

# Digital

The number of pages viewed by a user varies significantly by demography etc but on average 100–150 pages are viewed per person per day, so for this exercise we should use 100 pages as a base.

Google accounts for 6 per cent of internet traffic and there are usually 11 paid search results on each page, with 10 organics. Therefore on average 6 search pages are seen each day with 21 ads on each, which is 126 ads – 66 paid and 60 organic.

On each page (not including search results pages) there can be between 0 and 20+ ads (skyscrapers, banners, classified, Google AdSense etc) but this is highly dependent on the actual page viewed. If we assume that there are 5 ads on each page (e-mail sites and social networks which account for a significant proportion of traffic tend to have fewer ads than newspapers), then on the 94 pages that are not search results there are approximately 470 exposures to online display advertising.

Therefore on a daily basis we can assume that there are:

66 paid search

60 organic search

470 display ads – 30% of these will be the traditional banners etc and the rest text ads such as Google AdSense

Total 596 ads per day

**Overall total – 1,009 exposures per day.**

With permission of Accenture Media Management:
**http://www.accenture.com/Global/Consulting/
Accenture-Interactive/Media-Management/default.htm**

# BIBLIOGRAPHY

## Reports

Bennett, G, Ross, M, Uyenco, B and Willerer, T (2007) *Lifestyles of the Ad Averse: A proposal for an advertising evaluation framework*, WM3 Conference ESOMAR

*Best Practice in Narrative Reporting: An international perspective* (2009) Brand Finance/IPA

Binet, L and Field, P (2007) *Marketing in the Era of Accountability*, IPA Datamine Warc

Buck, S (2001) *Advertising and the Long-term Success of the Premium Brand*, World Advertising Research Center

*Cadbury's Hidden Brand Gems 'Stolen' through Poor Financial Reporting?* (2010) Brand Finance

Cox, K, Crowther, J, Hubbard, T and Turner, D (2011) *Datamine 3: New Models of Marketing Effectiveness: From Integration to Orchestration*, IPA report

Field, P (2010) *The Link Between Creativity and Effectiveness: New findings from The Gunn Report and the IPA Databank*, Thinkbox/IPA

Field, P (2011) *The Link Between Creativity and Effectiveness: The Growing Imperative to Embrace Creativity*, IPA/Gunn Report

Ford-Hutchinson, S and Rothwell, A (2002) *The Public's Perception of Advertising in Today's Society*, Advertising Standards Authority, The Thinking Shop

'Four inspiring essays on the future of brands and brand communications from the IPA Excellence diploma delegates class of 2009–10', DDS, *Campaign* and IPA

*How Analysts View Marketing* (2005) IPA report

*How Share of Voice Wins Market Share: New findings from Nielsen and the IPA Databank* (2009) IPA report

*KPIs for Marketing Reporting* (2008) IPA report

Langmaid, R and Gordon, W (1986) *A Great Ad – Pity they can't remember the brand – true or false?*, Acacia Avenue

*Price Promotion during the Downturn: Shrewd or crude?* (2009) IPA report

Robinson, L, Beck, J and Wilcox, S (2006) *The IPA TouchPoints Initiative: Creating the Missing Link*, WM3 Conference ESOMAR

'Six inspiring essays on the future of brands and brand communications from the IPA Excellence diploma delegates class of 2007–8', DDS, *Campaign* and IPA

*Social Media Futures* (2009) Future Foundation and IPA

*The Future of Advertising and Agencies – A 10 year perspective* (2007) Future Foundation and IPA

*The Media Research Landscape in the UK 2010* (2011) IPA report

## Books

Ambler, T and Tellis, G, eds (2007) *The Sage Handbook of Advertising*, Sage, Thousand Oaks, CA

Bird, D (1982) *Commonsense Direct and Digital Marketing*, Kogan Page, London and Philadelphia

Broadbent, S (1999) *When to Advertise*, Admap Publications, London

Broadbent, S and Jacobs, B (1984) *Spending Advertising Money*, Business Books, London

Bullmore, J (2003) *Behind the Scenes in Advertising*, Warc, Henley-on-Thames

Burkitt, H and Zeally, J (2006) *Marketing Excellence*, John Wiley & Sons, Chichester

Chippindale, P and Franks, S (1992) *Dished! Rise and Fall of British Satellite Broadcasting*, Simon & Schuster, London

Cook, C and Stevenson, J (2005) *The Routledge Companion to European History since 1763*, Routledge, London

Dawson, N (2008) *Advertising Works 16 – proving the payback on marketing investment*, Warc, Henley-on-Thames

Dawson, N (2009) *Advertising Works 17 – proving the payback on marketing investment*, Warc, Henley-on-Thames

Dawson, N (2010) *Advertising Works 18 – proving the payback on marketing investment*, Warc, Henley-on-Thames

Dawson, N (2010) *Advertising Works 19 – proving the payback on marketing investment*, Warc, Henley-on-Thames

du Plessis, E (2005) *The Advertised Mind*, Millward Brown and Kogan Page, London

Earls, M (2007) *Herd: How to change mass behaviour by harnessing our true nature*, John Wiley & Sons, Chichester

Fletcher, W (2008) *Powers of Persuasion: The inside story of British advertising1951–2000*, Oxford University Press, Oxford

Franzen, G (1994) *Advertising Effectiveness*, NTC Publications, Henley-on-Thames

Franzen, G and Bouwman, M (2001) *The Mental World of Brands*, World Advertising Research Centre, Henley-on-Thames

Green, A (2010) *From Prime Time to My Time: Audience measurement in the digital age*, Warc, Henley-on-Thames

Heath, C and Heath, D (2007) *Made to Stick: Why some ideas survive and others die*, Random House, New York

Heath, R (2001) *The Hidden Power of Advertising: How low involvement processing influences the way we choose brands*, NTC Publications, London

Ingram, A and Barber, M (2005) *Advertiser's Guide to Better Radio Advertising*, John Wiley & Sons, Chichester

Jones, J P (1995) *When Ads Work*, Lexington Books, Lanham, MD

Larreche, J C (2008) *The Momentum Effect: How to ignite exceptional growth*, Wharton School Publishing, Upper Saddle River, NJ

Levitt, S and Dubner, S (2006) *Freakonomics*, Penguin, Harmondsworth

Negropronte, N (1995) *Being Digital*, Hodder and Stoughton, London

Pringle, H and Field, P (2008) *Brand Immortality: How brands can live long and prosper*, Kogan Page, London

Quelch, J and Jocz, K (2007) *Greater Good*, Harvard Business School Publishing, Boston, MA

Sharp, B and the researchers of the Ehrenberg-Bass Institute (2010) *How Brands Grow*, Oxford University Press, Oxford

Sims, M (2005) *Working with Agencies: An insider's guide*, John Wiley & Sons, Chichester

Swinfen-Green, J, ed (2000) *E-media: How to use electronic media for effective marketing communications*, Admap Publications, London

Thaler, R and Sunstein, C (2008) *Nudge: Improving decisions about health, wealth and happiness*, Yale University Press, New Haven, CT
Whatling, S and Gillis, R (2009) *Defining Sponsorship*, Redmandarin, London
Wiley Roberts, K (2006) *SiSoMo: The future on screen*, powerHouse Books, Brooklyn, NY

# Webography

A Day Without Media
**http://withoutmedia.wordpress.com/**

Acacia Avenue
**http://www.acacia-avenue.com/**

Acxiom
**http://www.acxiom.com/**

Adconion Media Group
**http://www.adconion.com**

Advertising Association (AA)
**http://www.adassoc.org.uk**

Advertising Association: Advertising Industry Statistics
**http://www.adassoc.org.uk/aa/index.cfm/adstats/**

The Advertising Association/Warc Expenditure Report
**http://expenditurereport.warc.com/**

Advertising Research Foundation (ARF)
**http://thearf.org**

Advertising Standards Authority (ASA)
**http://www.asa.org.uk**

Agency People
**http://www.agency-people.co.uk/**

All Our Best Work
**http://www.allourbestwork.com**

American Association of Advertising Agencies (4As)
**http://www.aaaa.org**

ASOS
**http://www.asos.com/**

Association of the British Pharmaceutical Industry (ABPI)
**http://www.abpi.org.uk/**

Association of National Advertisers (ANA)
**http://www.ana.net/**

Association of Online Publishers (AOP)
**http://www.ukaop.org.uk**

Association of Publishing Agencies (APA)
http://www.apa.co.uk/

Audi's 'The Art of the Heist' Campaign Launched with Stolen A3 (2005 article)
http://www.audiworld.com/news/05/060805/content.shtml

Audit Bureau of Circulations (ABC)
http://www.abc.org.uk

BAFTA
http://www.bafta.org/

BBC Trust
http://www.bbc.co.uk/bbctrust/index.shtml/

Blueprint for consumer-centric holistic measurement
http://www.wfablueprint.org/home.php/

Brand Republic
http://www.brandrepublic.com

British Library Advertising Industry Guide http://www.bl.uk/reshelp/
findhelpindustry/advertising/advertising.html

Broadcaster's Advertising Research Board (BARB)
http://www.barb.co.uk

The British Academy of Film and Television Arts (BAFTA)
http://www.bafta.org/

British Broadcasting Corporation (BBC)
http://www.bbc.co.uk

Brand Finance
http://www.brandfinance.com

British Brands Group
http://www.britishbrandsgroup.org.uk

Burnt Store Anglers fishing methods
http://www.burntstoreanglers.com/6.html

Chime
http://www.chime.plc.uk

Chris Ingram
http://www.ingramenterprise.com/index.php/Articles/Business/
Chris-Ingram-Fifty-Years-in-Media-Campaign-March-2010.html

Clearcast
http://www.clearcast.co.uk/

The Client Brief full best practice guide
http://www.ipa.co.uk/Content/The-Client-Brief-full-best-practice-guide

Committee of Advertising Practice (CAP)
http://www.cap.org.uk/

Communication Strategy best practice guide
**http://www.ipa.co.uk/Content/Communication-Strategy-best-practice-guide**

comScore Inc
**http://www.comscore.com/**

Country Living Fairs
**http://www.countrylivingfair.com**

Creative Showcase Awards
**www.creativeshowcase.net**

Department for Business Innovation and Skills (BIS)
**http://www.bis.gov.uk/**

Diagonal Thinking
**http://www.diagonalthinking.co.uk/**

Digital Cinema Media (DCM)
**http://www.dcm.co.uk**

Direct Marketing Association UK (DMA)
**http://www.dma.org.uk**

Direct Marketing Association (DMA)
**http://www.the-dma.org/index.php**

Direct Marketing Association – Participation Media 2007
**http://www.dma.org.uk/docframe/docview.asp?id=4082&sec=-1**

dunnhumby
**http://dunnhumby.com/**

Econometrics Explained
**http://www.ipa.co.uk/Content/Econometrics-Explained**

Email Stat Center
**http://www.emailstatcenter.com/IndustryStats.html**

eMarketing Association
**http://www.emarketingassociation.com**

ESOMAR
**http://www.esomar.org/**

The Essential Fly
**http://www.theessentialfly.com/**

European Association of Communications Agencies (EACA)
**http://www.eaca.be**

Experian
**http://www.experianplc.com/**

Faris Yakov's blog
**http://farisyakob.typepad.com/**

Financial Services Authority (FSA)
**http://www.fsa.gov.uk/**

Foursquare
**http://foursquare.com/**

Groupon
**http://www.groupon.com/**

GSMA
**http://www.gsmworld.com/**

The Gunn Report
**http://www.gunnreport.com/**

Haymarket Media Group
**http://www.haymarket.com/**

Historical Football Kits
**http://www.historicalkits.co.uk/Articles/History.htm**

History of Advertising Trust (HAT)
**http://www.hatads.org.uk/**

History of Radio timeline
**http://www.mediauk.com/article/8/important-dates-for-uk-radio-broadcasting**

Hobbes' Internet Timeline 10
**http://www.zakon.org/robert/internet/timeline/**

Incorporated Society of British Advertisers (ISBA)
**http://www.isba.org.uk**

Institute of Direct Marketing (IDM)
**http://www.theidm.com**

Institute of Practitioners in Advertising (IPA)
**http://www.ipa.co.uk**

Institute of Promotional Marketing (IPM)
**http://www.theipm.org.uk/Home.aspx**

In-Store Marketing Institute
**http://www.instoremarketer.org/glossary**

Intangibles Reporting
**http://www.ipa.co.uk/Content/Intangibles-Reporting**

Integration™-IMC
**http://www.integration-imc.com/**

Intellectual Property Office
**http://www.ipo.gov.uk**

Internet Advising Bureau (IAB)
**http://www.iabuk.net**

IPA Effectiveness Awards
**http://www.ipaeffectivenessawards.co.uk**

IPA Effectiveness Awards case studies
http://www.ipa.co.uk/cases

IPA Effectiveness Awards case – Cutting the cost of crime
http://www.ipa.co.uk/Content/Acquisition-Crime-COI-Home-Office-Crime-Cutting-the-cost-of-crime-IPA-Effectiveness-Awards-Case-Study-2008

IPA links directory
http://www.ipa.co.uk/Content/Links-Introduction

Joint Industry Committee for Regional Media Research (JICREG)
http://www.jicreg.co.uk

Kingston Smith W1
http://www.kingstonsmith.co.uk/

Lifestyles of the Ad Averse 2007
http://www.esomar.org/web/publication/paper.php?page=1&id=1561&keyword=lifestyles%20of%20the%20ad%20averse

Low Attention Processing
http://www.lowattentionprocessing.com

mad.co.uk
http://www.mad.co.uk

Market Leader
http://www.warc.com/ContentAndPartners/MarketLeader.asp

Market Research Society (MRS)
http://www.marketresearch.org.uk

Marketing Society
http://www.marketing-society.org.uk

Media Research Group (MRG)
http://www.mrg.org.uk

The Michael Aldrich Archive
http://www.aldricharchive.com/snowball.html

Mobile Marketing Association (MMA)
http://mmaglobal.com

Moon-Walking Bear Video
http://www.youtube.com/watch?v=Ahg6qcgoay4

NABS
http://www.nabs.org.uk/

National Advertising Benevolent Society (NABS)
http://www.nabs.org.uk

News International
http://www.newsinternational.co.uk/

Newspaper Death Watch
http://www.newspaperdeathwatch.com/

Newspaper Marketing Agency (NMA)
http://www.nmauk.co.uk

Newspaper Society (NS)
http://www.newspapersoc.org.uk

Nielsen's Three Screen Report for May 2009
http://blog.nielsen.com/nielsenwire/online_mobile/
americans-watching-more-tv-than-ever/

Occam
http://www.occamdm.com

Office of Communications (Ofcom)
http://www.ofcom.org.uk/

Outdoor Advertising Association (OAA)
http://www.oaa.org.uk

Periodical Publishers Association (PPA)
http://www.ppa.co.uk/

Point of Purchase Advertising International (POPAI)
http://www.popai.co.uk

POPAI UK Awards
http://www.popai.co.uk/awards/gallery/2009/default.aspx

Postcomm
http://www.psc.gov.uk/

Posterscope
http://www.posterscope.co.uk

Posterscope poster format sizes
http://www.posterscope.co.uk/downloads/
traditional_poster_dimensions.ppt

Proprietary Association of Great Britain (PAGB)
http://www.pagb.co.uk/

PSc photography
http://www.pscphotography.com/

Public Relations Consultants Association (PRCA)
http://www.prca.org.uk

QR Code
http://en.wikipedia.org/wiki/QR_Code/

Radio Advertising Bureau (RAB)
http://www.rab.co.uk

Radio Advertising Clearance Centre (RACC)
http://www.racc.co.uk/

Radio case studies
http://www.rab.co.uk/rab2009/caseStudiesSearch.aspx

RadioCentre
http://www.radiocentre.org

RadioGauge
http://www.rab.co.uk/rab2009/showContent.aspx?id=1592

Radio Joint Audience Research (RAJAR)
http://www.rajar.co.uk

Royal Academy, RA Magazine
http://www.royalacademy.org.uk/ra-magazine/summer-2010

Royal Mail
http://www.royalmail.com/portal/rm

Royal Mail Marketing Services
http://www2.royalmail.com/marketing-services

Royal Television Society
http://www.rts.org.uk

Salon.com
http://dir.salon.com/story/special/10th/2005/11/14/salon_history/index.html

SiSoMo: The Future on Screen
http://www.sisomo.com/

Specific Media
http://www.specificmedia.com

Spectator
http://www.spectator.co.uk/shop/events

Synergy
http://www.synergy-sponsorship.com

The Technophobe & The Madman
http://www.academy.rpi.edu/projects/technophobe/

Telegraph Media Group 'news hub'
http://www.telegraph.co.uk/finance/2946710/Telegraph-raises-its-game-at-news-hub.html/

TFL Moonwalking Bear video
http://www.youtube.com/watch?v=xNSgmm9Fx2s

Thinkbox
http://www.thinkbox.tv

Tim Jones – Gaming Brands
http://www.ipa.co.uk/Content/IPA-Excellence-Diploma-essays-published-today

T-Mobile Liverpool Street Dance
http://www.t-mobile.co.uk/dance/

Tribal Fusion
http://www.tribalfusion.com

United States Postal Service
http://search.usps.com

WACL
http://www.wacl.info/

Walt Howe Learning Centre
http://www.walthowe.com

Warc
http://www.warc.com

Wikipedia on Online advertising
http://en.wikipedia.org/wiki/Online_advertising

Wiley
http://eu.wiley.com/WileyCDA/

Winterberry Group Research
http://www.winterberrygroup.com/research/

Women in advertising and communications London
http://www.wacl.info/

Women in Film & TV
http://www.wftv.org.uk/wftv/

Word of Mouth Marketing Association (WOMMA)
http://wommauk.org

Work Research
http://workresearch.co.uk

World Federation of Advertisers (WFA)
http://www.wfanet.org/

Your Online Choices: A Guide to Online Behavioural Advertising
http://www.youronlinechoice.co.uk/jargon-buster

YouView
http://www.youview.com/

# INDEX